volume 1

story & art by
HATO HACHIYA

We Swore to Meet in the Next Life and That's When Things Got Weird!

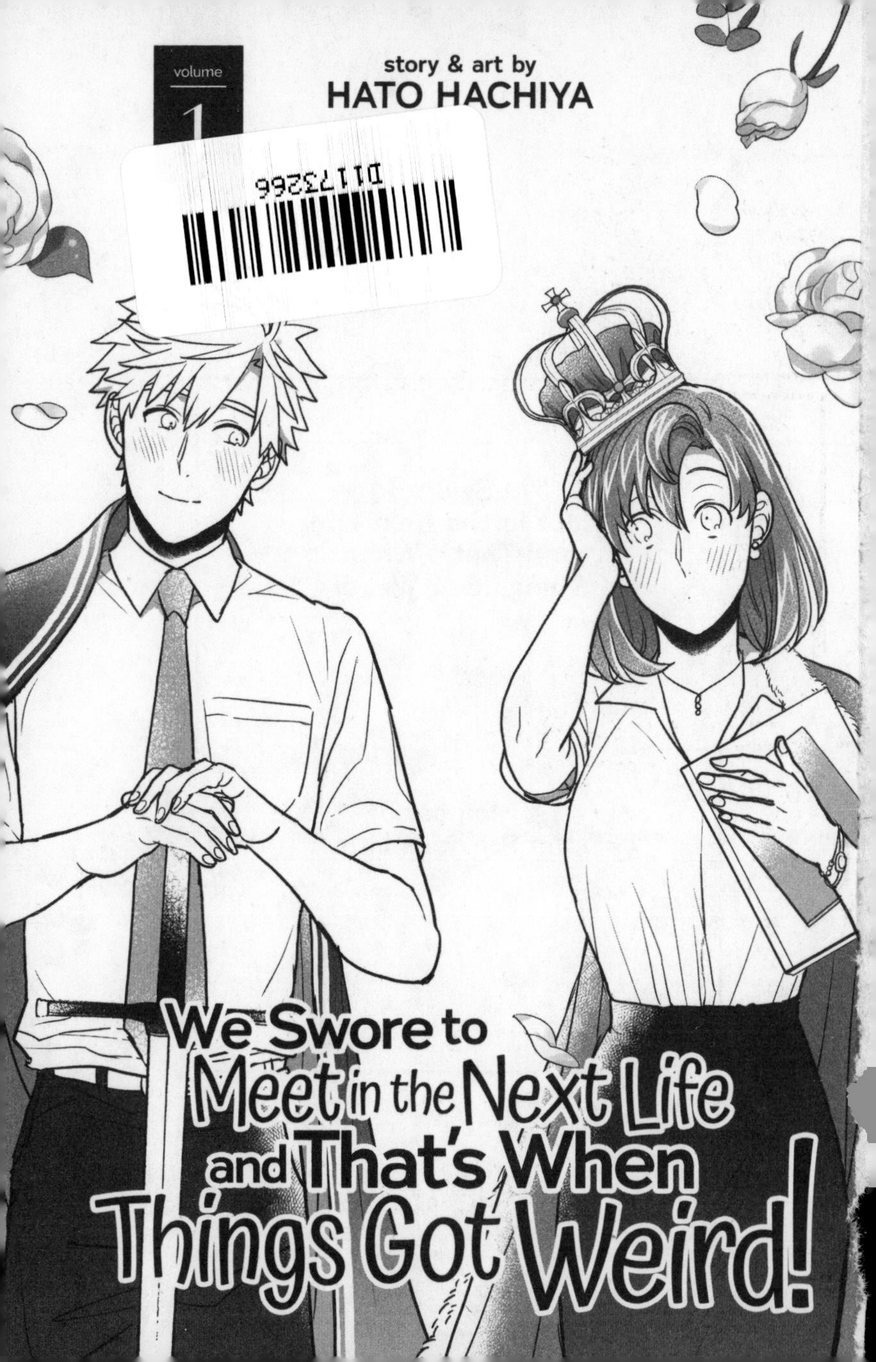

CONTENTS

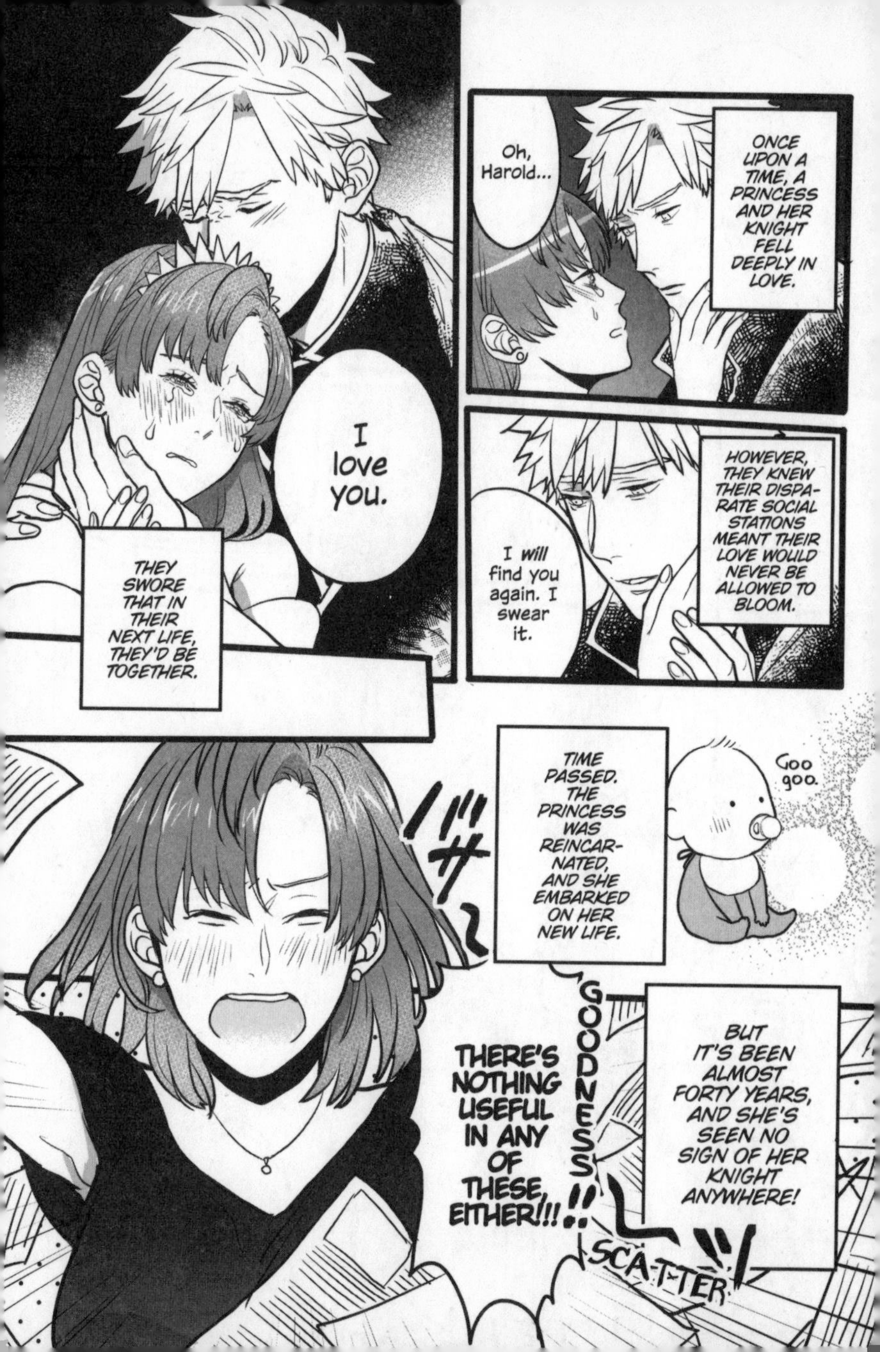
ONCE UPON A TIME, A PRINCESS AND HER KNIGHT FELL DEEPLY IN LOVE.
Oh, Harold...
HOWEVER, THEY KNEW THEIR DISPARATE SOCIAL STATIONS MEANT THEIR LOVE WOULD NEVER BE ALLOWED TO BLOOM.
I will find you again. I swear it.
I love you.
THEY SWORE THAT IN THEIR NEXT LIFE, THEY'D BE TOGETHER.
Goo goo.
TIME PASSED. THE PRINCESS WAS REINCARNATED, AND SHE EMBARKED ON HER NEW LIFE.
BUT IT'S BEEN ALMOST FORTY YEARS, AND SHE'S SEEN NO SIGN OF HER KNIGHT ANYWHERE!
GOODNESS!!
THERE'S NOTHING USEFUL IN ANY OF THESE, EITHER!!!
SCAT-T-TER

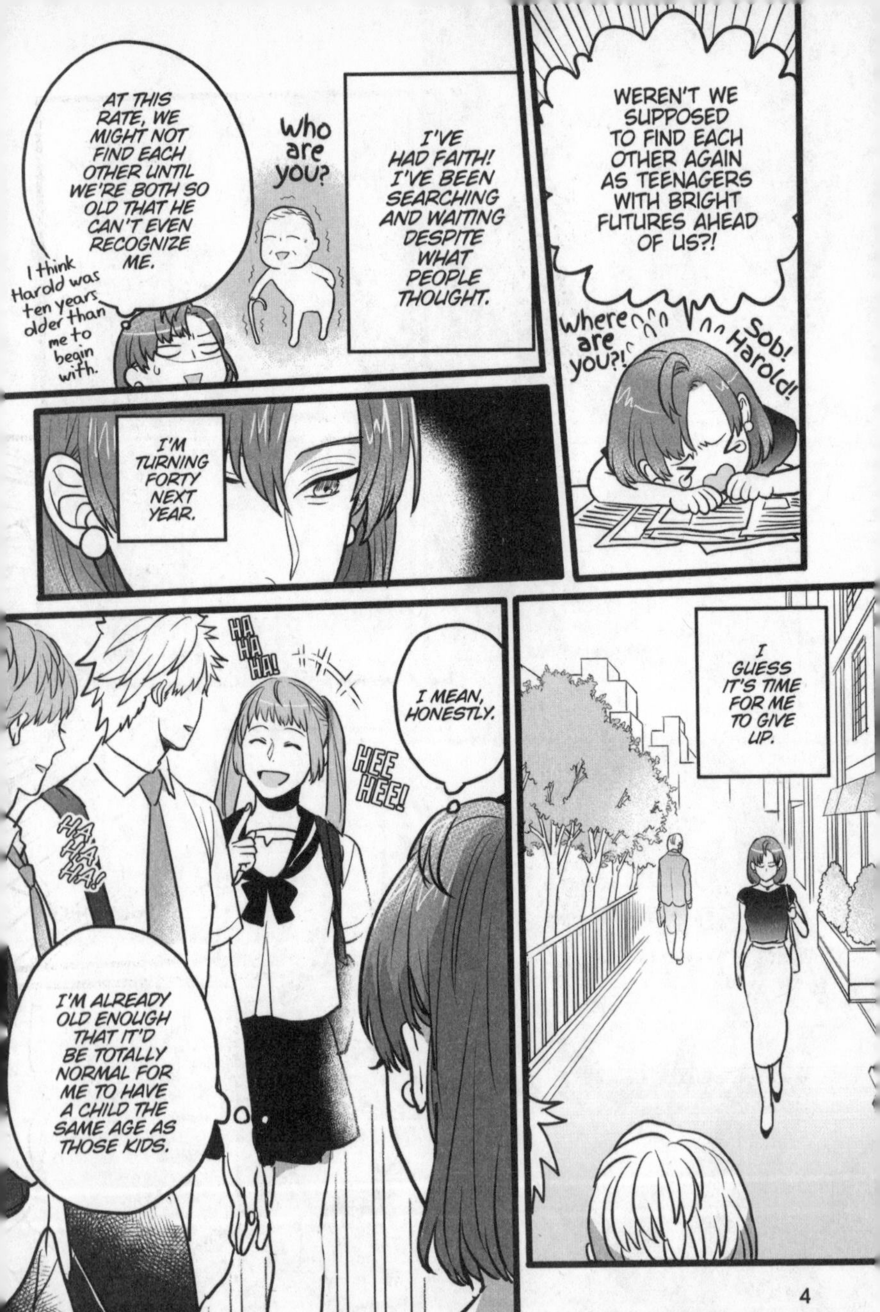
WEREN'T WE SUPPOSED TO FIND EACH OTHER AGAIN AS TEENAGERS WITH BRIGHT FUTURES AHEAD OF US?!
Sob! Harold!
Where are you?!
I'VE HAD FAITH! I'VE BEEN SEARCHING AND WAITING DESPITE WHAT PEOPLE THOUGHT.
Who are you?
AT THIS RATE, WE MIGHT NOT FIND EACH OTHER UNTIL WE'RE BOTH SO OLD THAT HE CAN'T EVEN RECOGNIZE ME.
I think Harold was ten years older than me to begin with.
I'M TURNING FORTY NEXT YEAR.
I GUESS IT'S TIME FOR ME TO GIVE UP.
HA HA HA!
I MEAN, HONESTLY.
HEE HEE!
HA HA HA!
I'M ALREADY OLD ENOUGH THAT IT'D BE TOTALLY NORMAL FOR ME TO HAVE A CHILD THE SAME AGE AS THOSE KIDS.

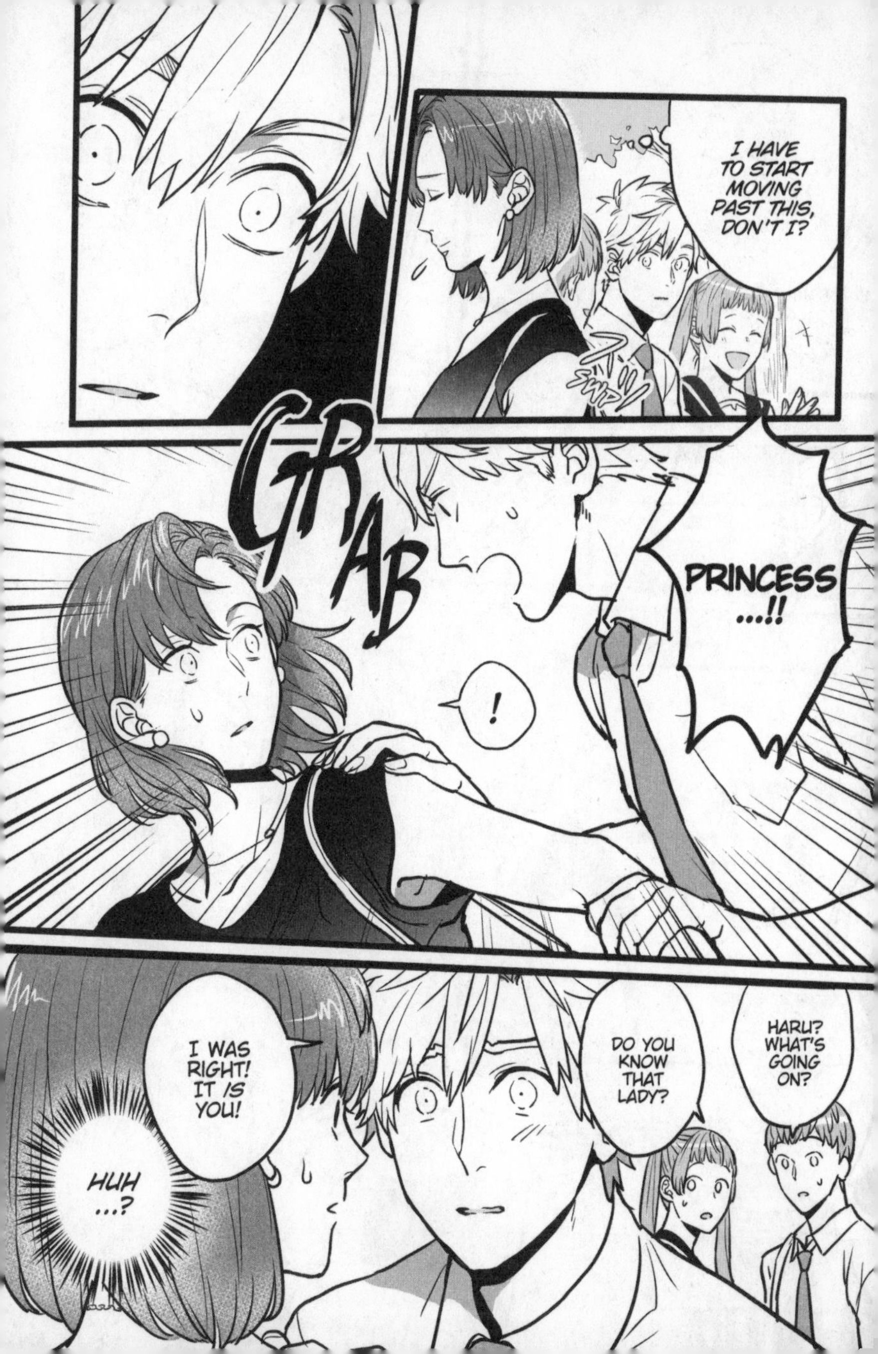
I HAVE TO START MOVING PAST THIS, DON'T I?
SWP
PRINCESS ...!!
GRAB
!
HARU? WHAT'S GOING ON?
DO YOU KNOW THAT LADY?
I WAS RIGHT! IT *IS* YOU!
HUH ...?

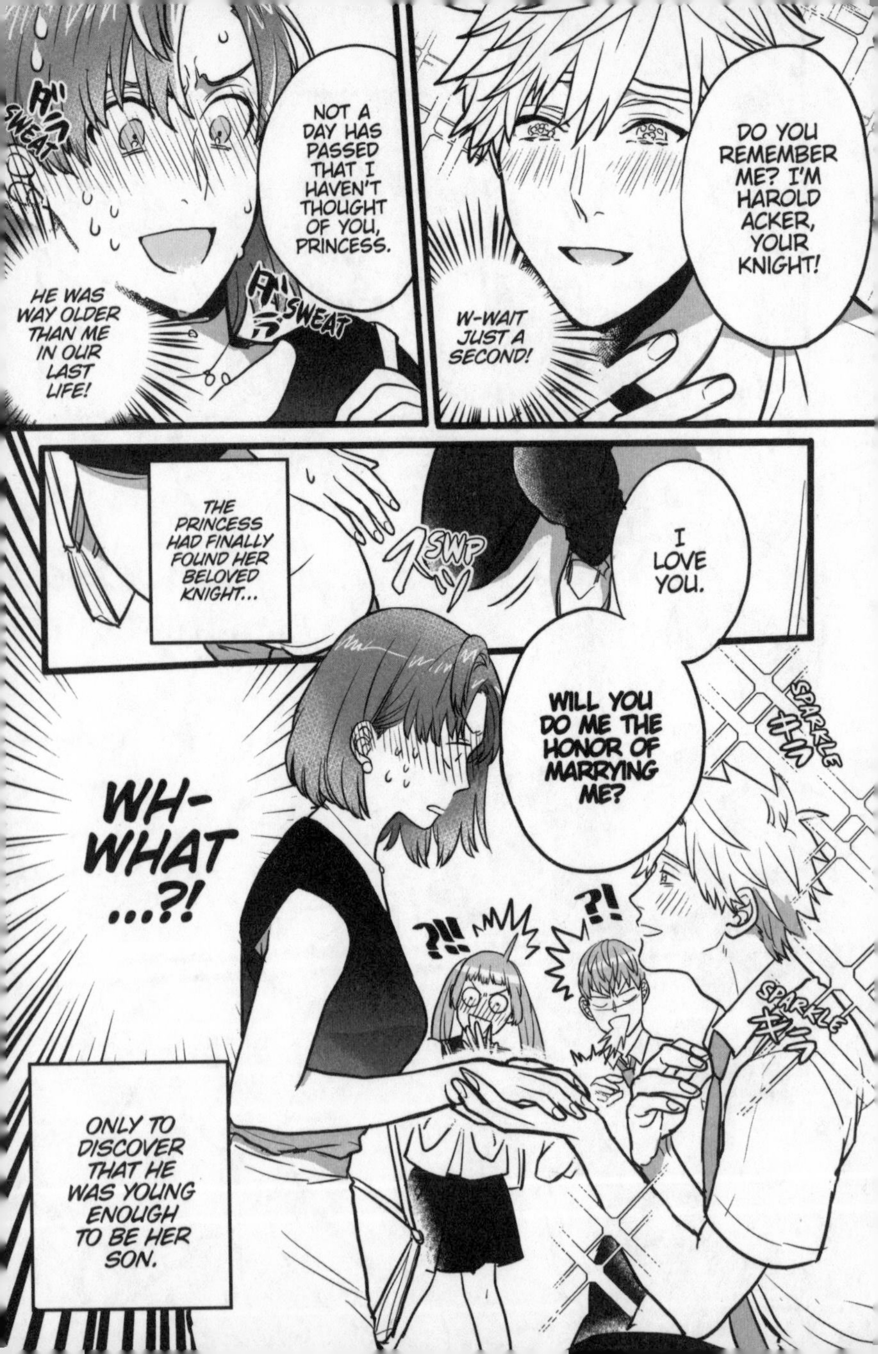
DO YOU REMEMBER ME? I'M HAROLD ACKER, YOUR KNIGHT!
W-WAIT JUST A SECOND!
NOT A DAY HAS PASSED THAT I HAVEN'T THOUGHT OF YOU, PRINCESS.
SWEAT
SWEAT
HE WAS WAY OLDER THAN ME IN OUR LAST LIFE!
I LOVE YOU.
SWP
THE PRINCESS HAD FINALLY FOUND HER BELOVED KNIGHT...
WILL YOU DO ME THE HONOR OF MARRYING ME?
SPARKLE
?!
?!!
WH-WHAT...?!
SPARKLE
ONLY TO DISCOVER THAT HE WAS YOUNG ENOUGH TO BE HER SON.

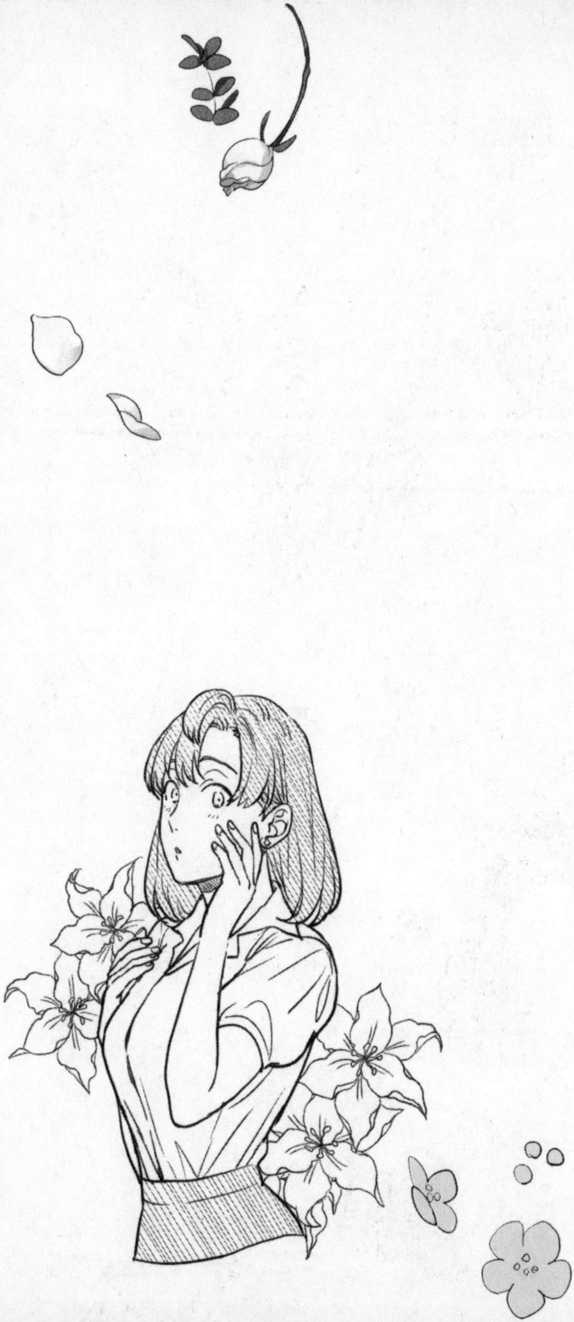

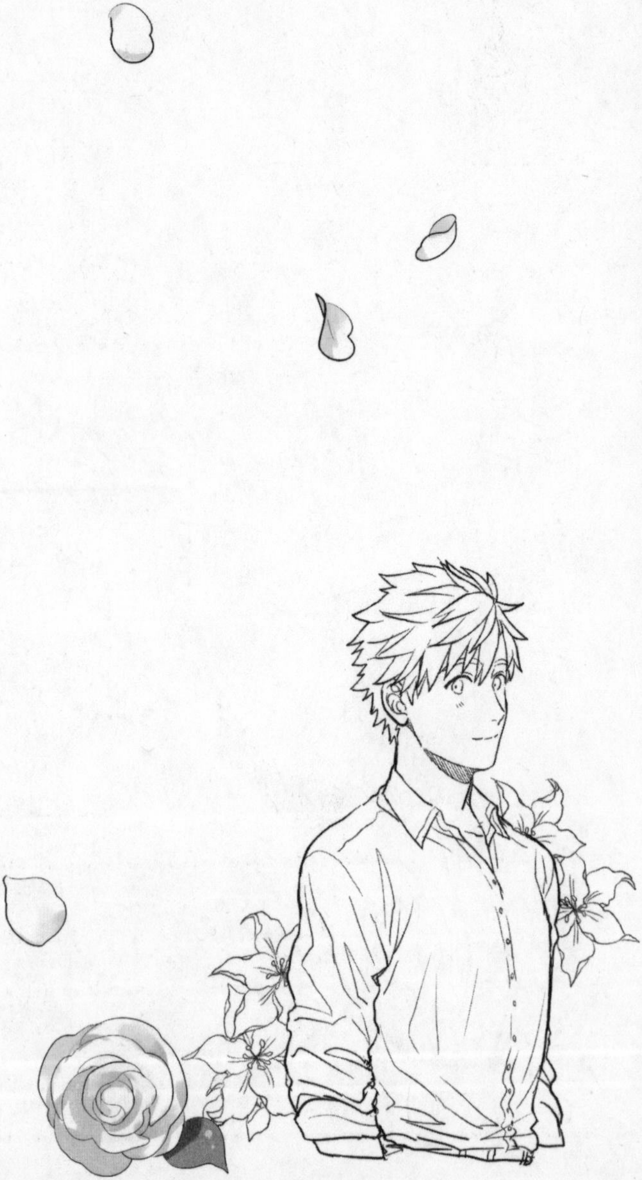

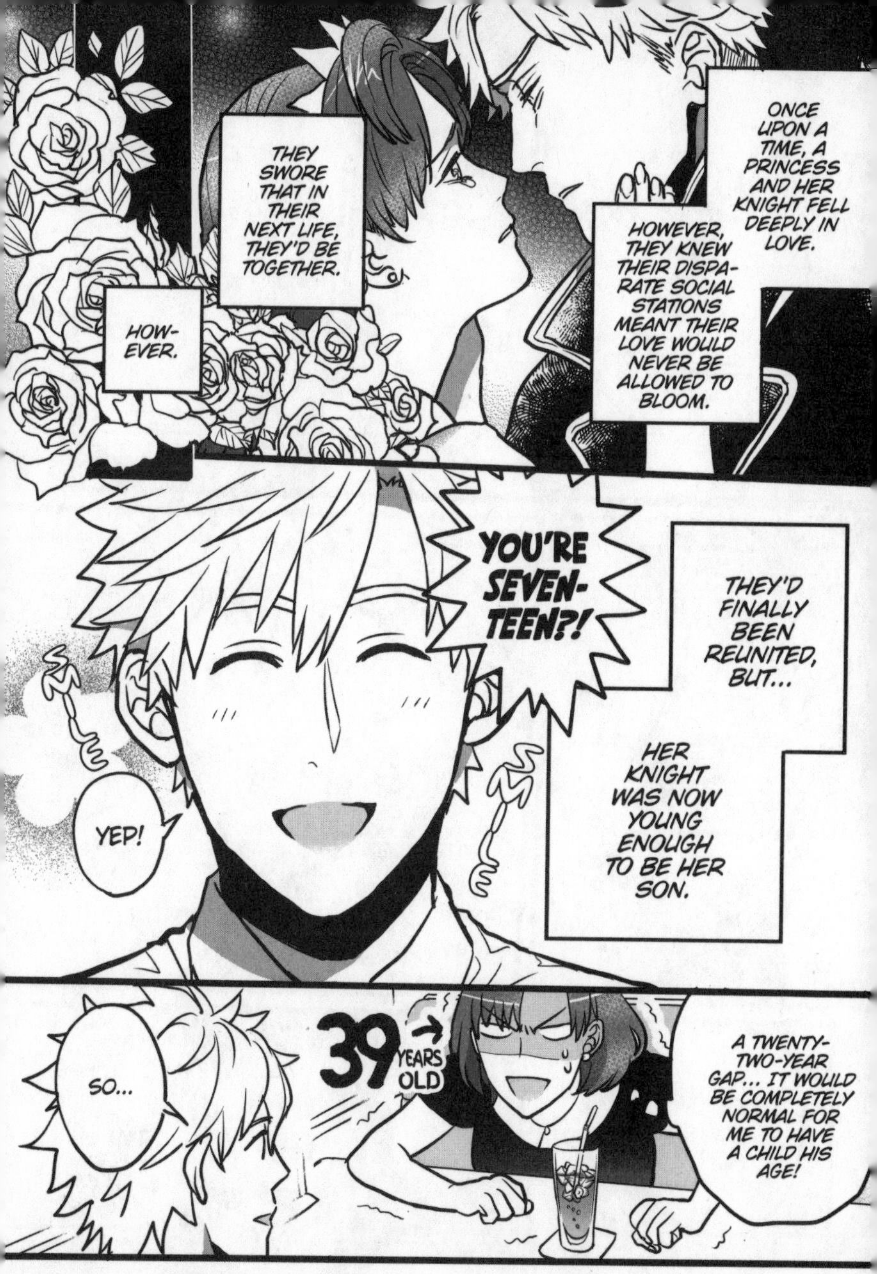
ONCE UPON A TIME, A PRINCESS AND HER KNIGHT FELL DEEPLY IN LOVE.
HOWEVER, THEY KNEW THEIR DISPARATE SOCIAL STATIONS MEANT THEIR LOVE WOULD NEVER BE ALLOWED TO BLOOM.
THEY SWORE THAT IN THEIR NEXT LIFE, THEY'D BE TOGETHER.
HOW-EVER.
THEY'D FINALLY BEEN REUNITED, BUT...
HER KNIGHT WAS NOW YOUNG ENOUGH TO BE HER SON.
YOU'RE SEVEN-TEEN?!
YEP!
A TWENTY-TWO-YEAR GAP... IT WOULD BE COMPLETELY NORMAL FOR ME TO HAVE A CHILD HIS AGE!
39 YEARS OLD
SO...

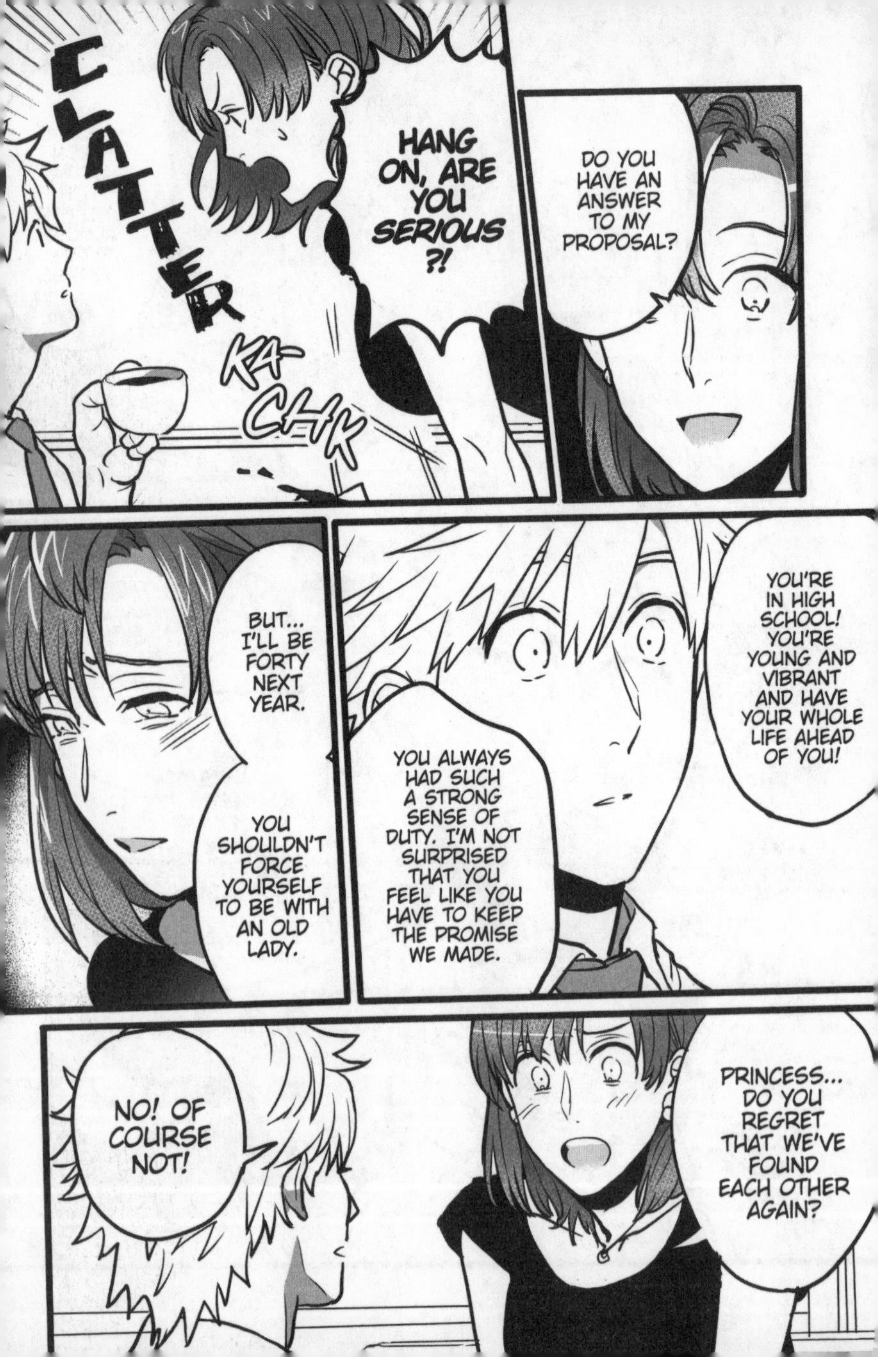
DO YOU HAVE AN ANSWER TO MY PROPOSAL?
HANG ON, ARE YOU SERIOUS ?!
CLATTER
KA-CHK
YOU'RE IN HIGH SCHOOL! YOU'RE YOUNG AND VIBRANT AND HAVE YOUR WHOLE LIFE AHEAD OF YOU!
YOU ALWAYS HAD SUCH A STRONG SENSE OF DUTY. I'M NOT SURPRISED THAT YOU FEEL LIKE YOU HAVE TO KEEP THE PROMISE WE MADE.
BUT... I'LL BE FORTY NEXT YEAR.
YOU SHOULDN'T FORCE YOURSELF TO BE WITH AN OLD LADY.
PRINCESS... DO YOU REGRET THAT WE'VE FOUND EACH OTHER AGAIN?
NO! OF COURSE NOT!

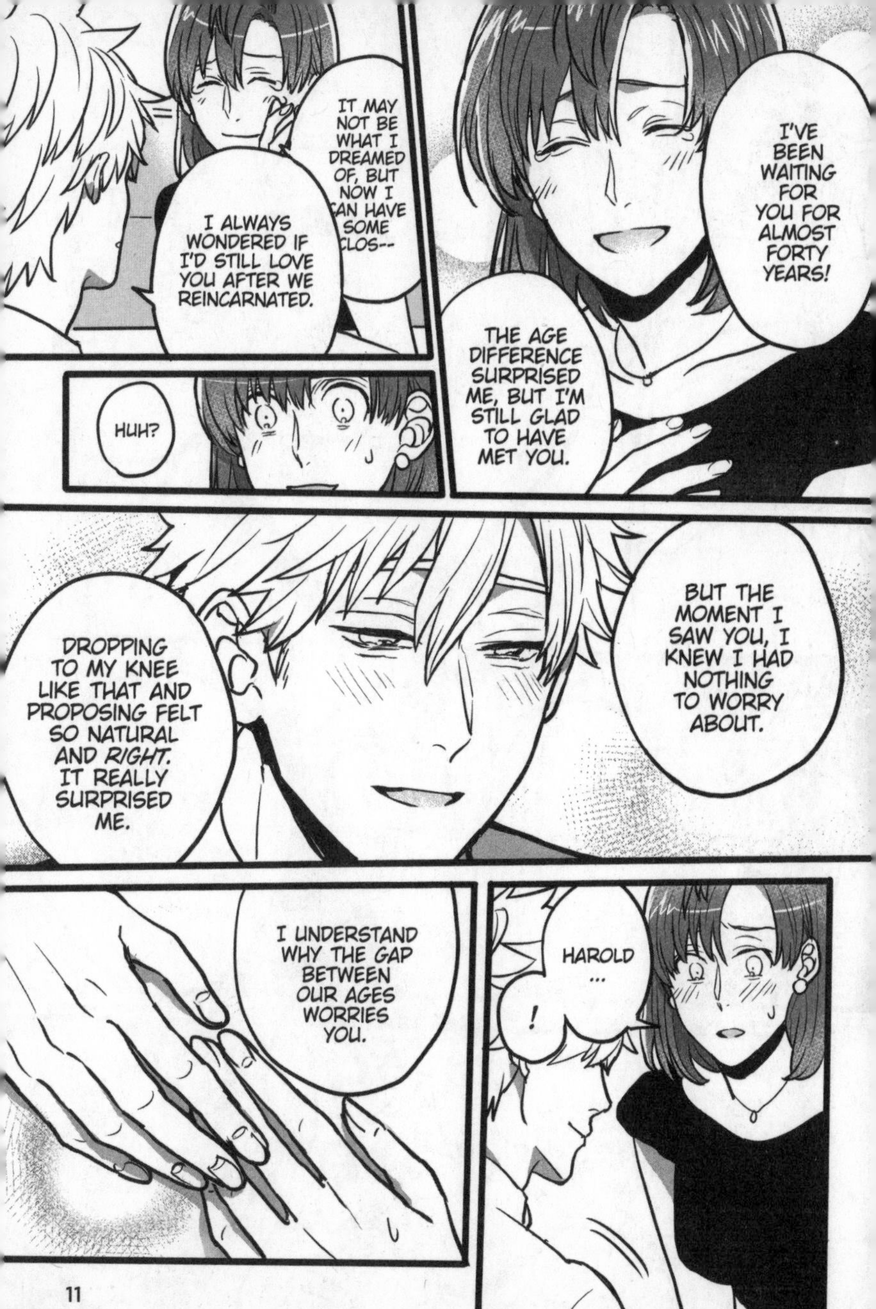
I'VE BEEN WAITING FOR YOU FOR ALMOST FORTY YEARS!
THE AGE DIFFERENCE SURPRISED ME, BUT I'M STILL GLAD TO HAVE MET YOU.
IT MAY NOT BE WHAT I DREAMED OF, BUT NOW I CAN HAVE SOME CLOS--
I ALWAYS WONDERED IF I'D STILL LOVE YOU AFTER WE REINCARNATED.
HUH?
BUT THE MOMENT I SAW YOU, I KNEW I HAD NOTHING TO WORRY ABOUT.
DROPPING TO MY KNEE LIKE THAT AND PROPOSING FELT SO NATURAL AND *RIGHT*. IT REALLY SURPRISED ME.
HAROLD ...
!
I UNDERSTAND WHY THE GAP BETWEEN OUR AGES WORRIES YOU.

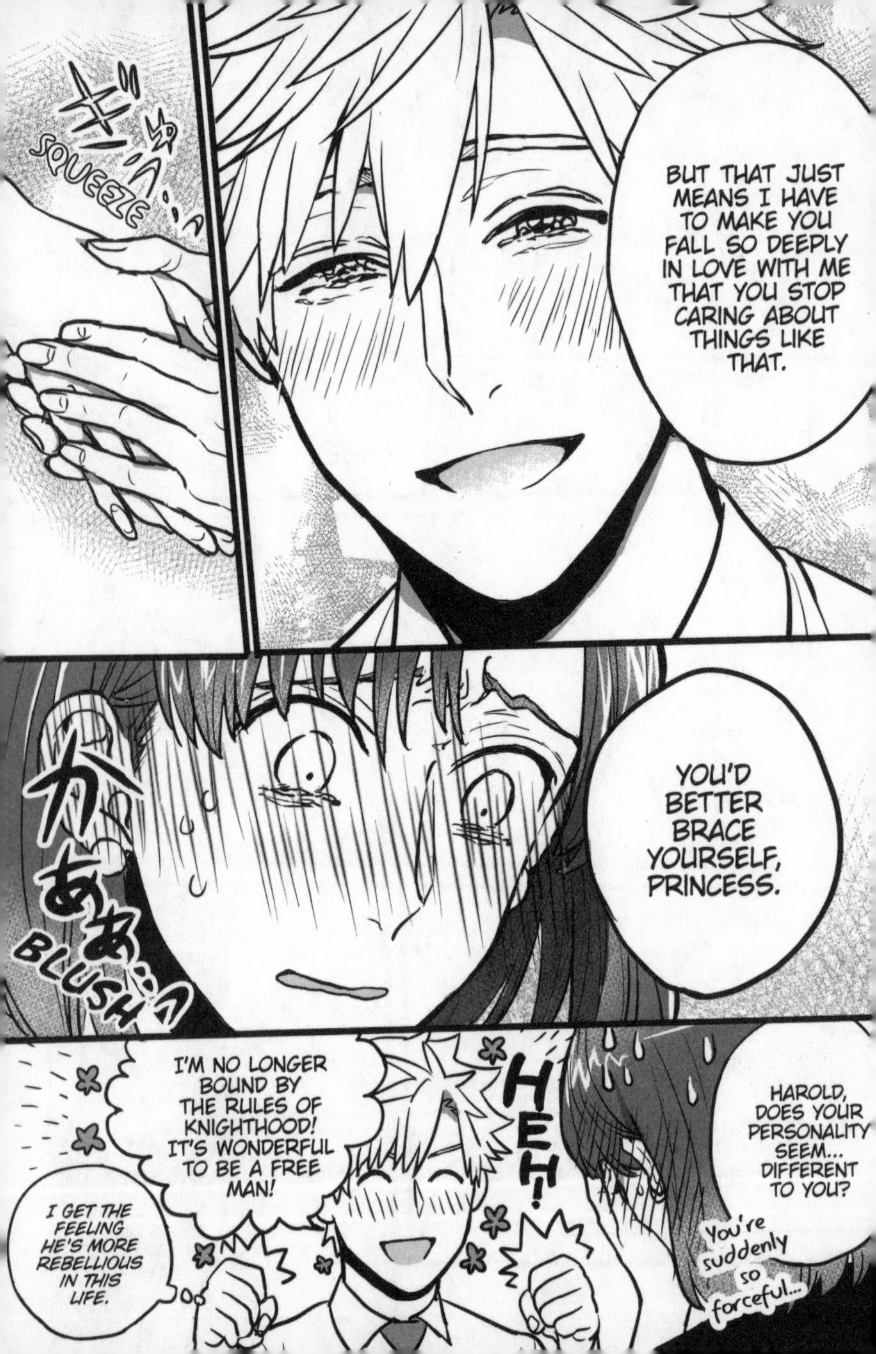
BUT THAT JUST MEANS I HAVE TO MAKE YOU FALL SO DEEPLY IN LOVE WITH ME THAT YOU STOP CARING ABOUT THINGS LIKE THAT.
SQUEEZE
YOU'D BETTER BRACE YOURSELF, PRINCESS.
BLUSH
HAROLD, DOES YOUR PERSONALITY SEEM... DIFFERENT TO YOU?
You're suddenly so forceful...
HEH!
I'M NO LONGER BOUND BY THE RULES OF KNIGHTHOOD! IT'S WONDERFUL TO BE A FREE MAN!
I GET THE FEELING HE'S MORE REBELLIOUS IN THIS LIFE.

We Swore to
Meet in the Next Life
and That's When
Things Got
Weird!

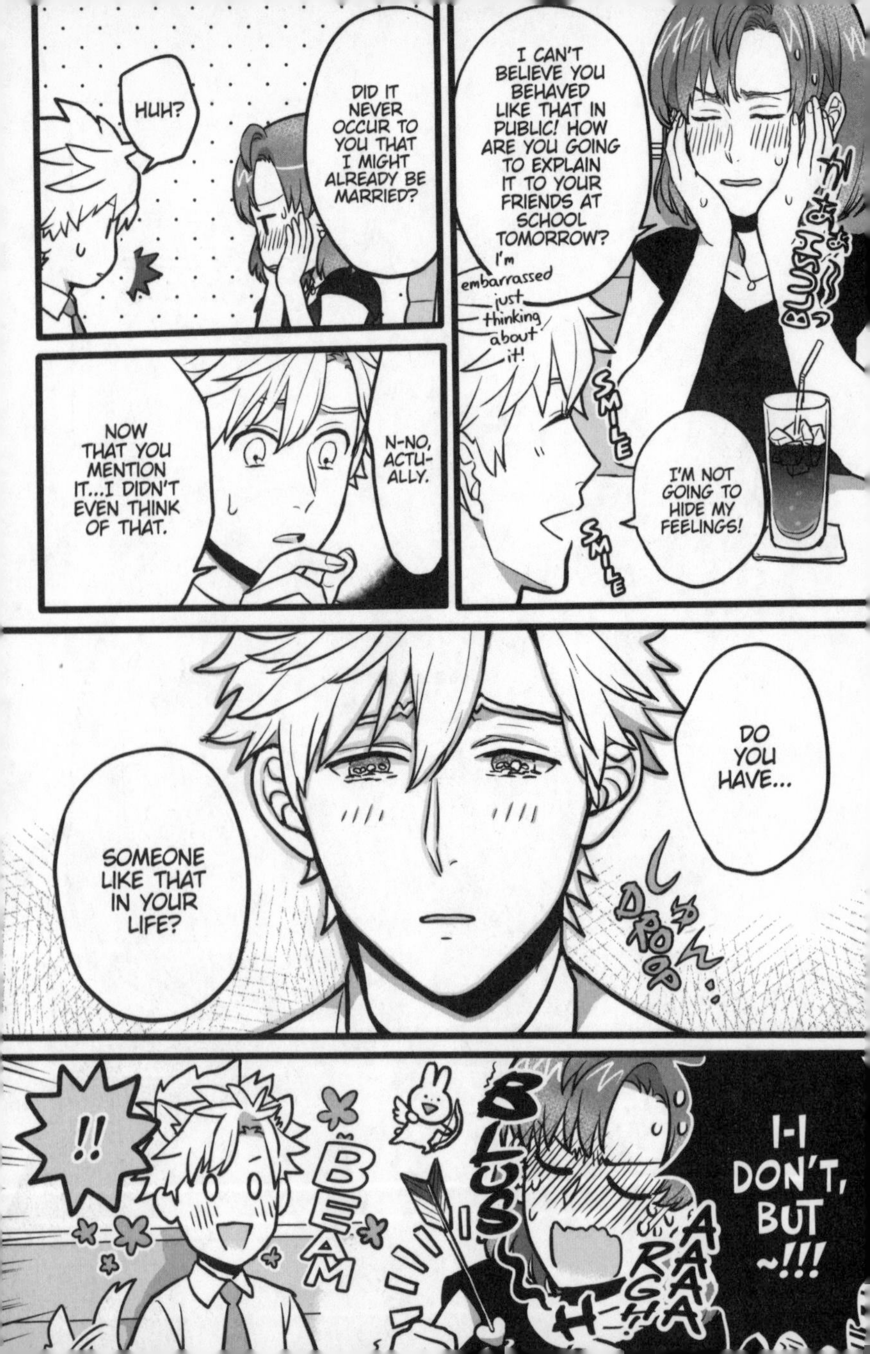
I CAN'T BELIEVE YOU BEHAVED LIKE THAT IN PUBLIC! HOW ARE YOU GOING TO EXPLAIN IT TO YOUR FRIENDS AT SCHOOL TOMORROW?
I'm embarrassed just thinking about it!
BLUSH
SMILE
SMILE
I'M NOT GOING TO HIDE MY FEELINGS!
DID IT NEVER OCCUR TO YOU THAT I MIGHT ALREADY BE MARRIED?
HUH?
N-NO, ACTU-ALLY.
NOW THAT YOU MENTION IT...I DIDN'T EVEN THINK OF THAT.
DO YOU HAVE...
DROOP
SOMEONE LIKE THAT IN YOUR LIFE?
I-I DON'T, BUT ~!!!
BLUSH
BEAM
!!

THE PRINCESS'S VOCABULARY IS DATED.
Huh? You describe young people as "spry," right?! What do you mean, no one says that anymore?!
SHOCK

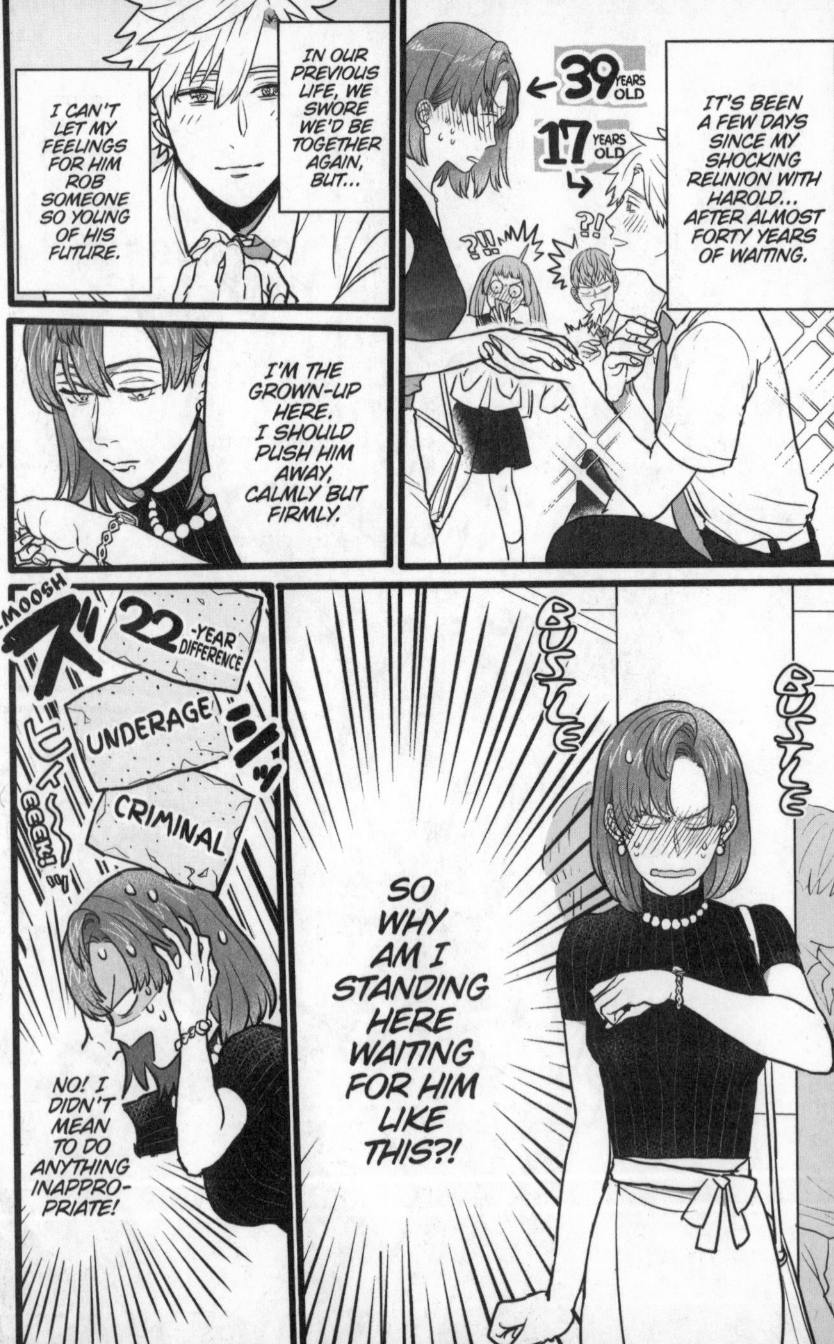

IT'S BEEN A FEW DAYS SINCE MY SHOCKING REUNION WITH HAROLD... AFTER ALMOST FORTY YEARS OF WAITING.
39 YEARS OLD
17 YEARS OLD
?!
?!!
IN OUR PREVIOUS LIFE, WE SWORE WE'D BE TOGETHER AGAIN, BUT...
I CAN'T LET MY FEELINGS FOR HIM ROB SOMEONE SO YOUNG OF HIS FUTURE.
I'M THE GROWN-UP HERE. I SHOULD PUSH HIM AWAY, CALMLY BUT FIRMLY.
BUSTLE
BUSTLE
SO WHY AM I STANDING HERE WAITING FOR HIM LIKE THIS?!
ZMOOSH
22-YEAR DIFFERENCE
UNDERAGE
CRIMINAL
EEEK!
NO! I DIDN'T MEAN TO DO ANYTHING INAPPROPRIATE!

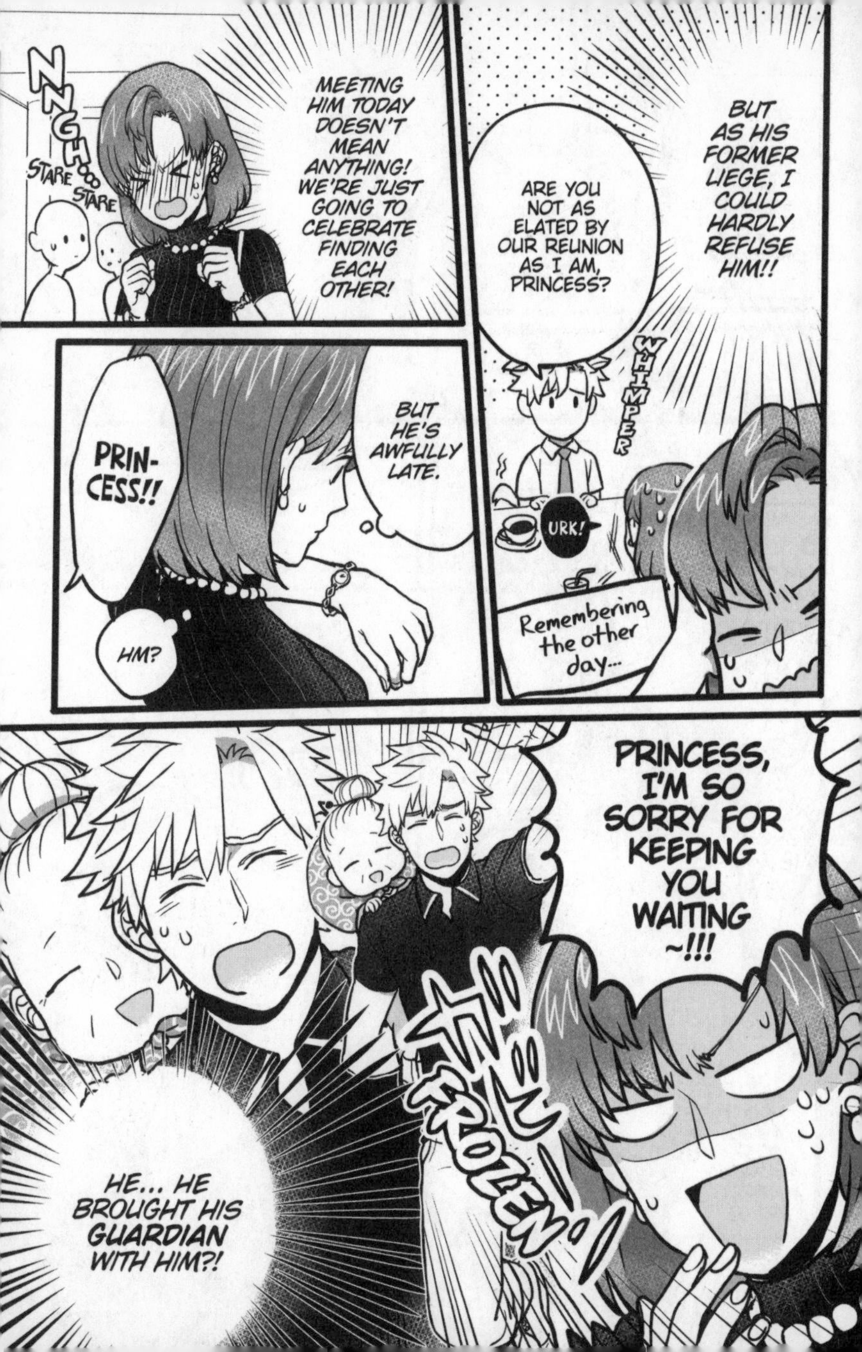
NNGHOOO
STARE
STARE
MEETING HIM TODAY DOESN'T MEAN ANYTHING! WE'RE JUST GOING TO CELEBRATE FINDING EACH OTHER!
BUT AS HIS FORMER LIEGE, I COULD HARDLY REFUSE HIM!!
ARE YOU NOT AS ELATED BY OUR REUNION AS I AM, PRINCESS?
WHIMPER
URK!
Remembering the other day...
BUT HE'S AWFULLY LATE.
PRIN-CESS!!
HM?
PRINCESS, I'M SO SORRY FOR KEEPING YOU WAITING ~!!!
FROZEN
HE... HE BROUGHT HIS GUARDIAN WITH HIM?!

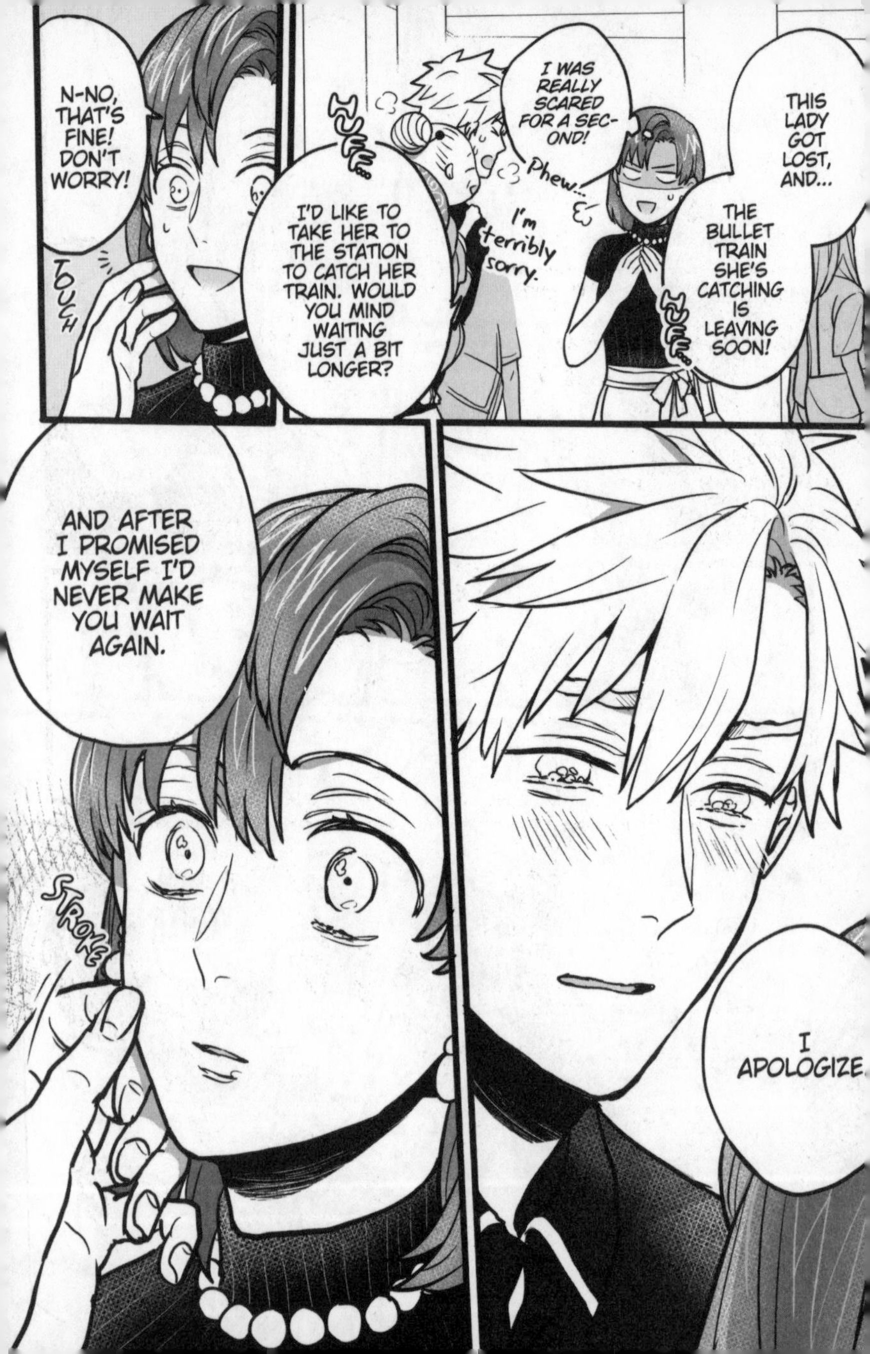
THIS LADY GOT LOST, AND...
THE BULLET TRAIN SHE'S CATCHING IS LEAVING SOON!
HUFF...
I WAS REALLY SCARED FOR A SEC-OND!
Phew...
I'm terribly sorry.
HUFF...
I'D LIKE TO TAKE HER TO THE STATION TO CATCH HER TRAIN. WOULD YOU MIND WAITING JUST A BIT LONGER?
N-NO, THAT'S FINE! DON'T WORRY!
TOUCH
I APOLOGIZE.
AND AFTER I PROMISED MYSELF I'D NEVER MAKE YOU WAIT AGAIN.
STROKE

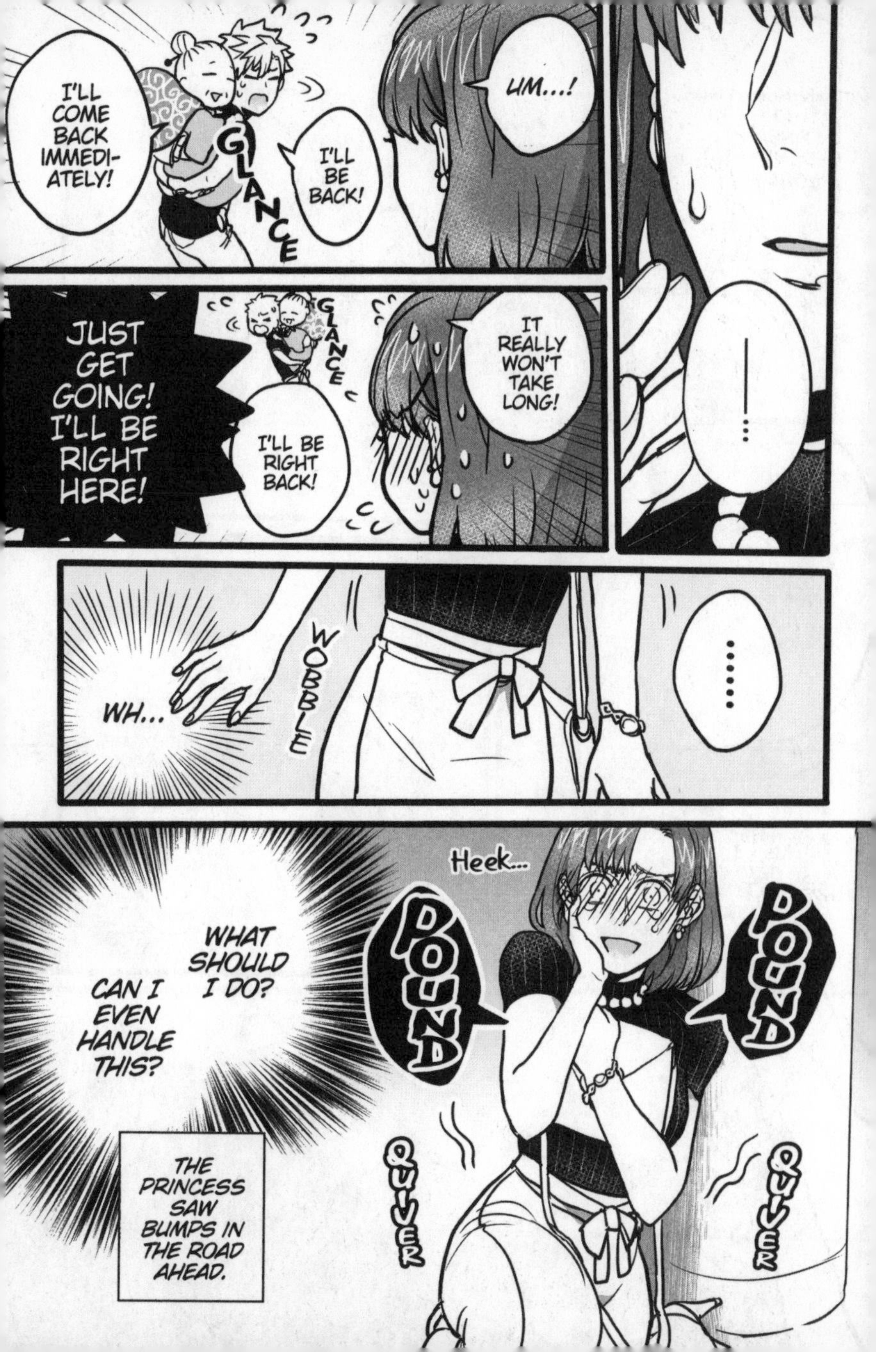
—......
UM...!
I'LL BE BACK!
GLANCE
I'LL COME BACK IMMEDIATELY!
IT REALLY WON'T TAKE LONG!
GLANCE
I'LL BE RIGHT BACK!
JUST GET GOING! I'LL BE RIGHT HERE!
......
WOBBLE
WH...
Heek...
POUND
POUND
WHAT SHOULD I DO?
CAN I EVEN HANDLE THIS?
QUIVER
QUIVER
THE PRINCESS SAW BUMPS IN THE ROAD AHEAD.

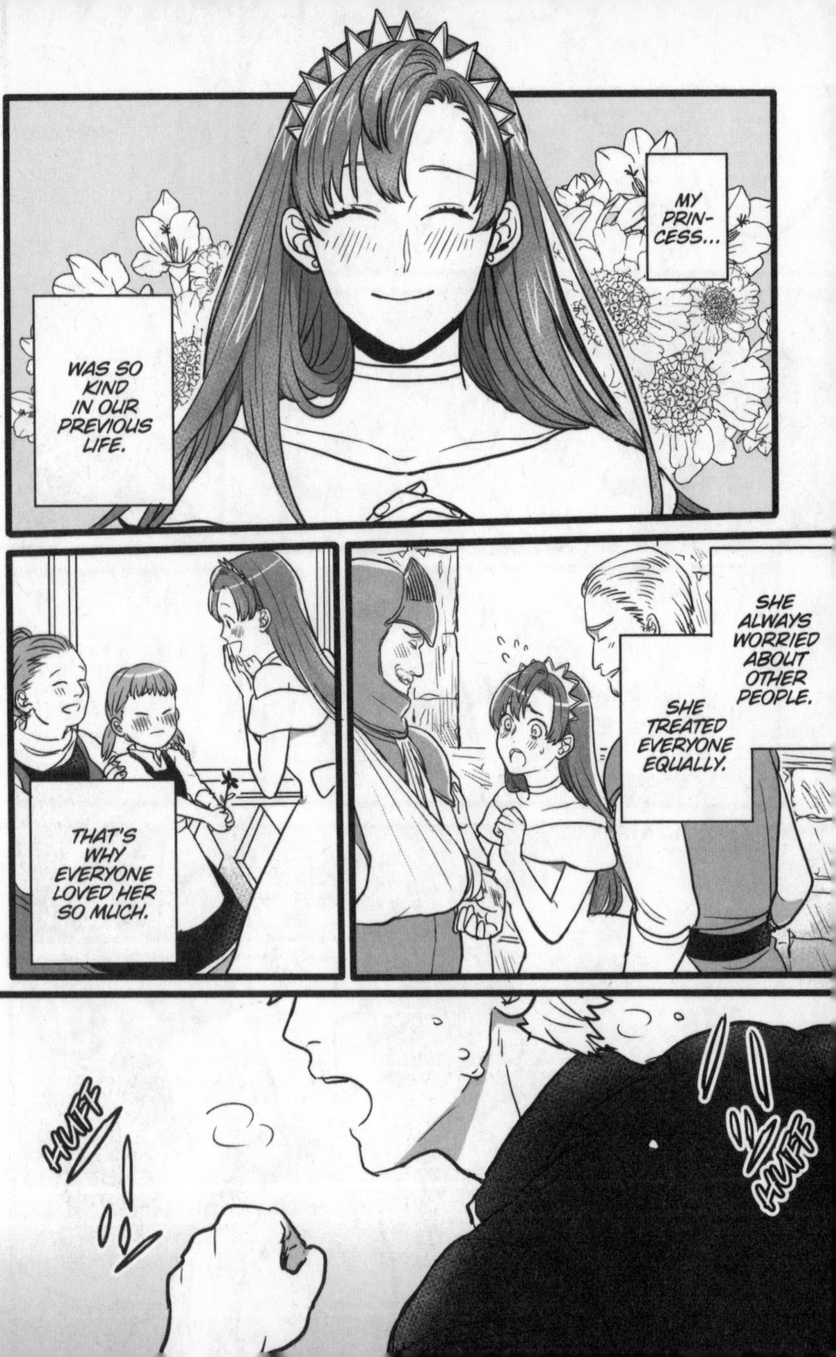
MY PRINCESS...
WAS SO KIND IN OUR PREVIOUS LIFE.
SHE ALWAYS WORRIED ABOUT OTHER PEOPLE.
SHE TREATED EVERYONE EQUALLY.
THAT'S WHY EVERYONE LOVED HER SO MUCH.
HUFF
HUFF

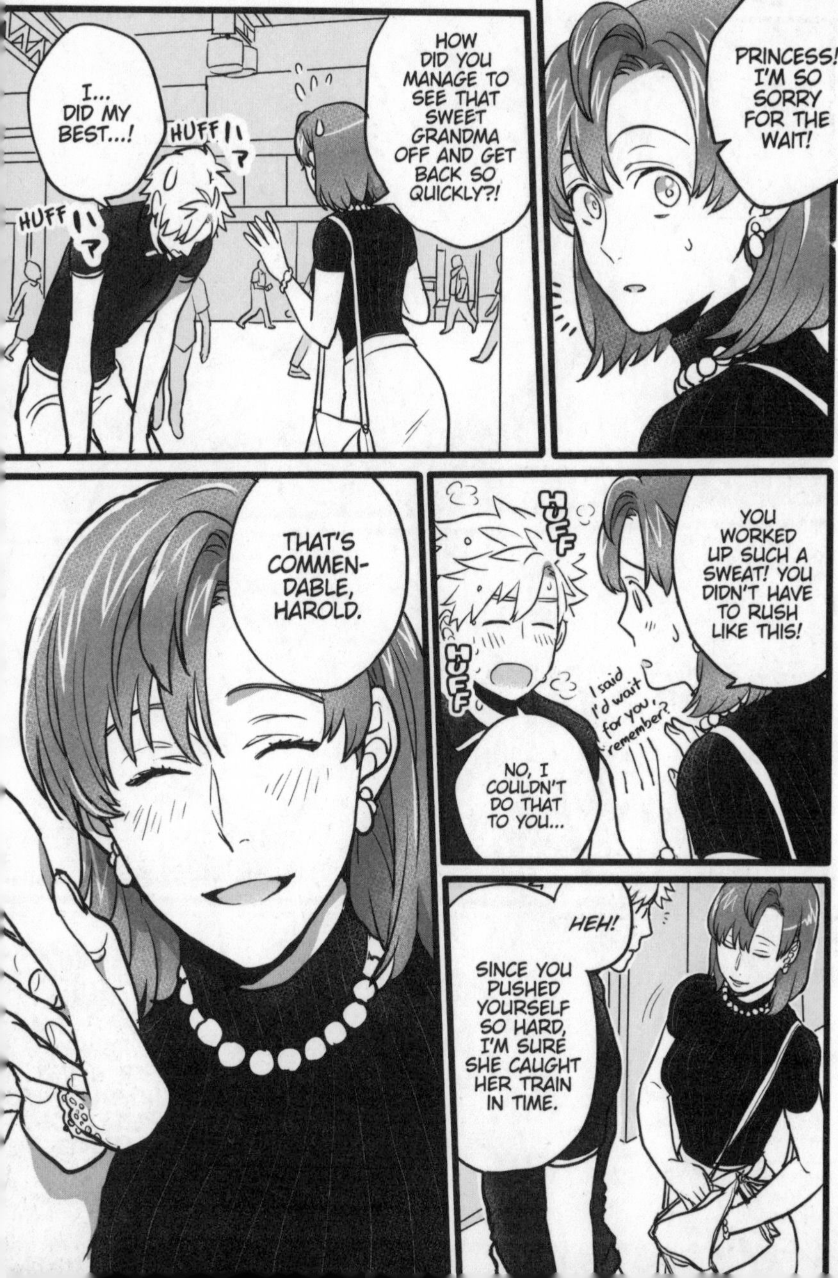
PRINCESS! I'M SO SORRY FOR THE WAIT!
HOW DID YOU MANAGE TO SEE THAT SWEET GRANDMA OFF AND GET BACK SO QUICKLY?!
HUFF
HUFF
I... DID MY BEST...!
YOU WORKED UP SUCH A SWEAT! YOU DIDN'T HAVE TO RUSH LIKE THIS!
HUFF
HUFF
I said I'd wait for you, remember?
NO, I COULDN'T DO THAT TO YOU...
HEH!
SINCE YOU PUSHED YOURSELF SO HARD, I'M SURE SHE CAUGHT HER TRAIN IN TIME.
THAT'S COMMEN-DABLE, HAROLD.

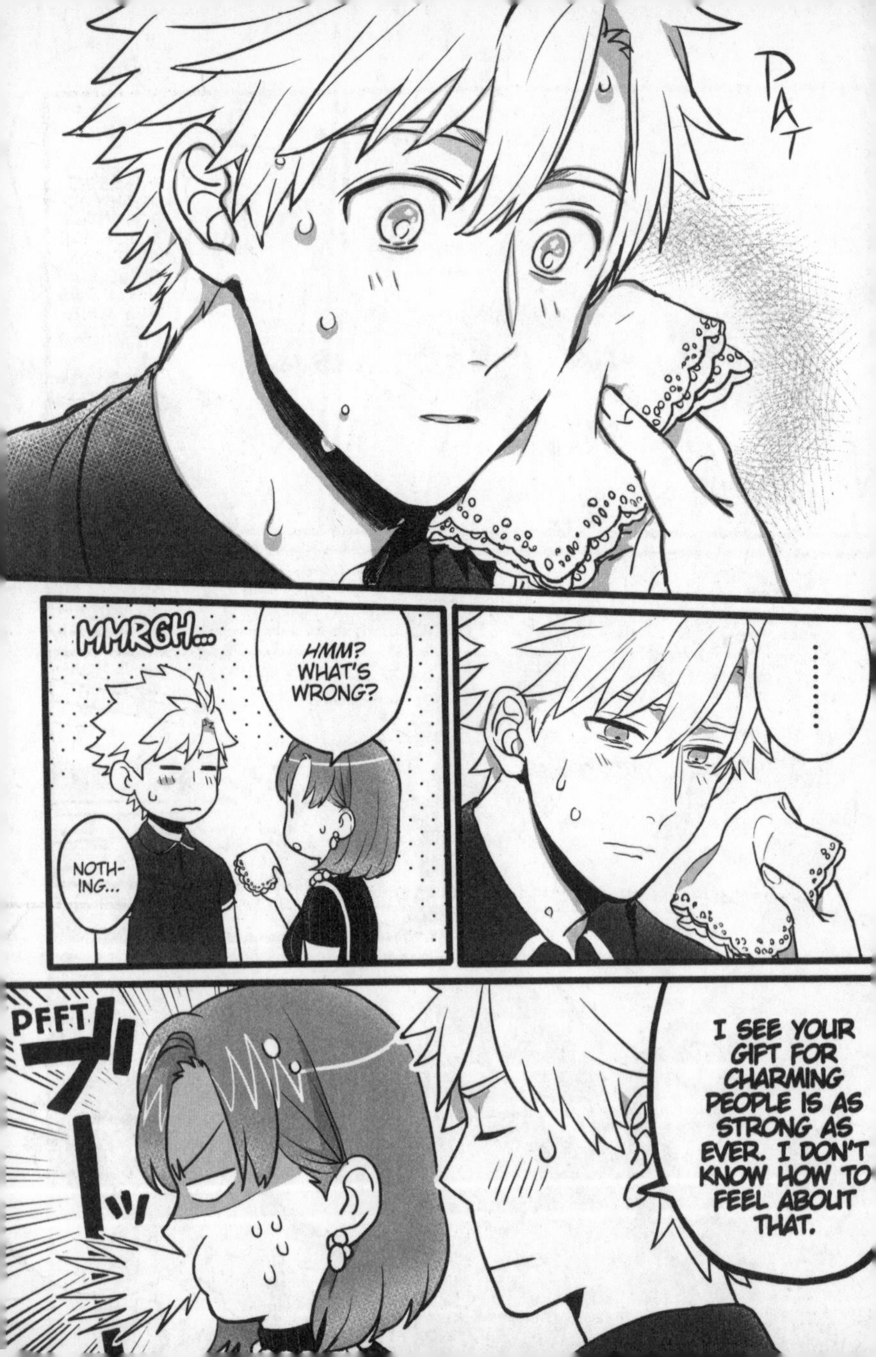
PAT
......
HMM? WHAT'S WRONG?
MMRGH...
NOTH-ING...
I SEE YOUR GIFT FOR CHARMING PEOPLE IS AS STRONG AS EVER. I DON'T KNOW HOW TO FEEL ABOUT THAT.
PFFT

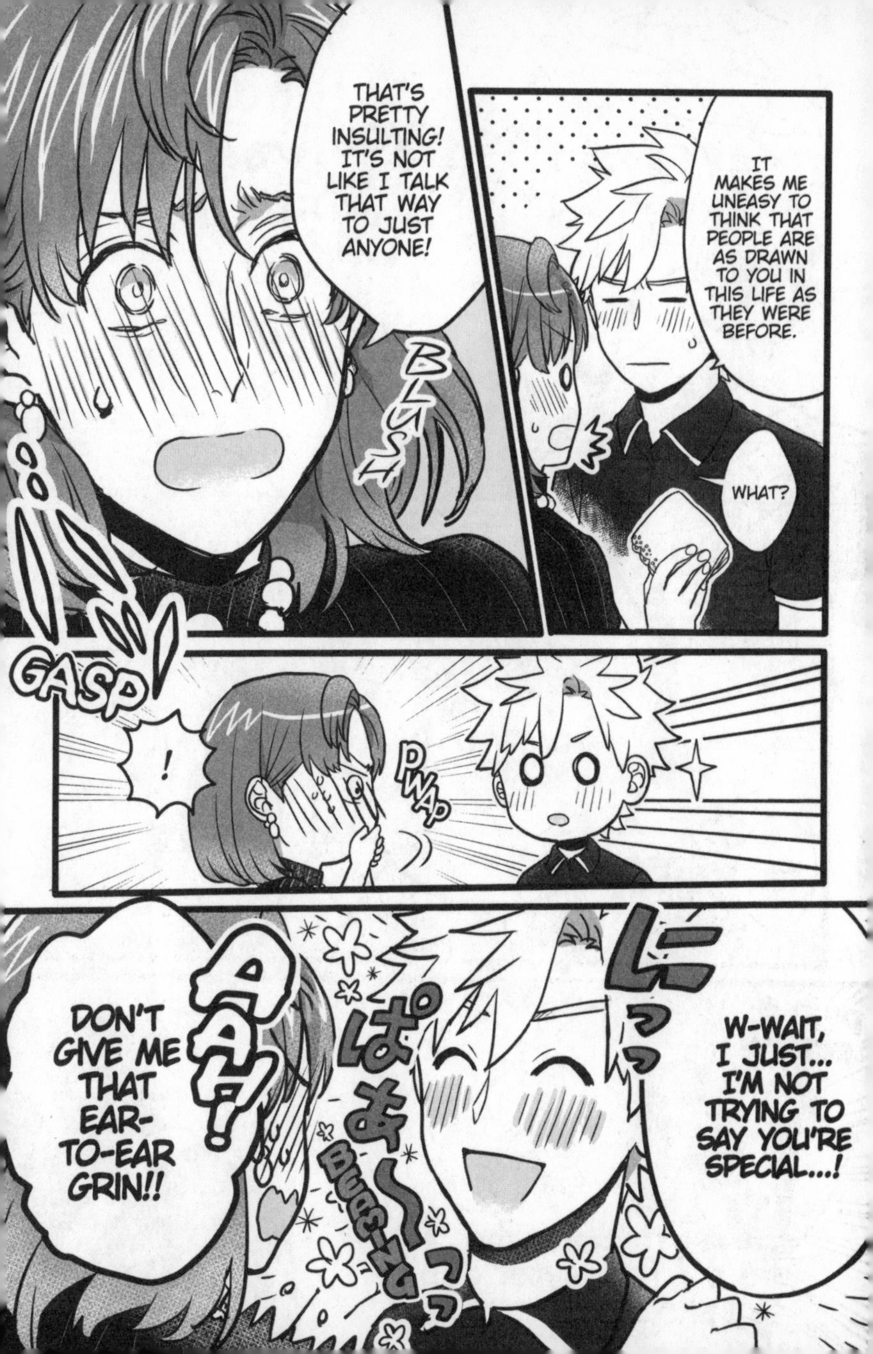
IT MAKES ME UNEASY TO THINK THAT PEOPLE ARE AS DRAWN TO YOU IN THIS LIFE AS THEY WERE BEFORE.
WHAT?
THAT'S PRETTY INSULTING! IT'S NOT LIKE I TALK THAT WAY TO JUST ANYONE!
BLUSH
GASP
!
PWAP
W-WAIT, I JUST... I'M NOT TRYING TO SAY YOU'RE SPECIAL...!
にっ
ぱぁ〜っ
BEAMING
AAH!
DON'T GIVE ME THAT EAR-TO-EAR GRIN!!

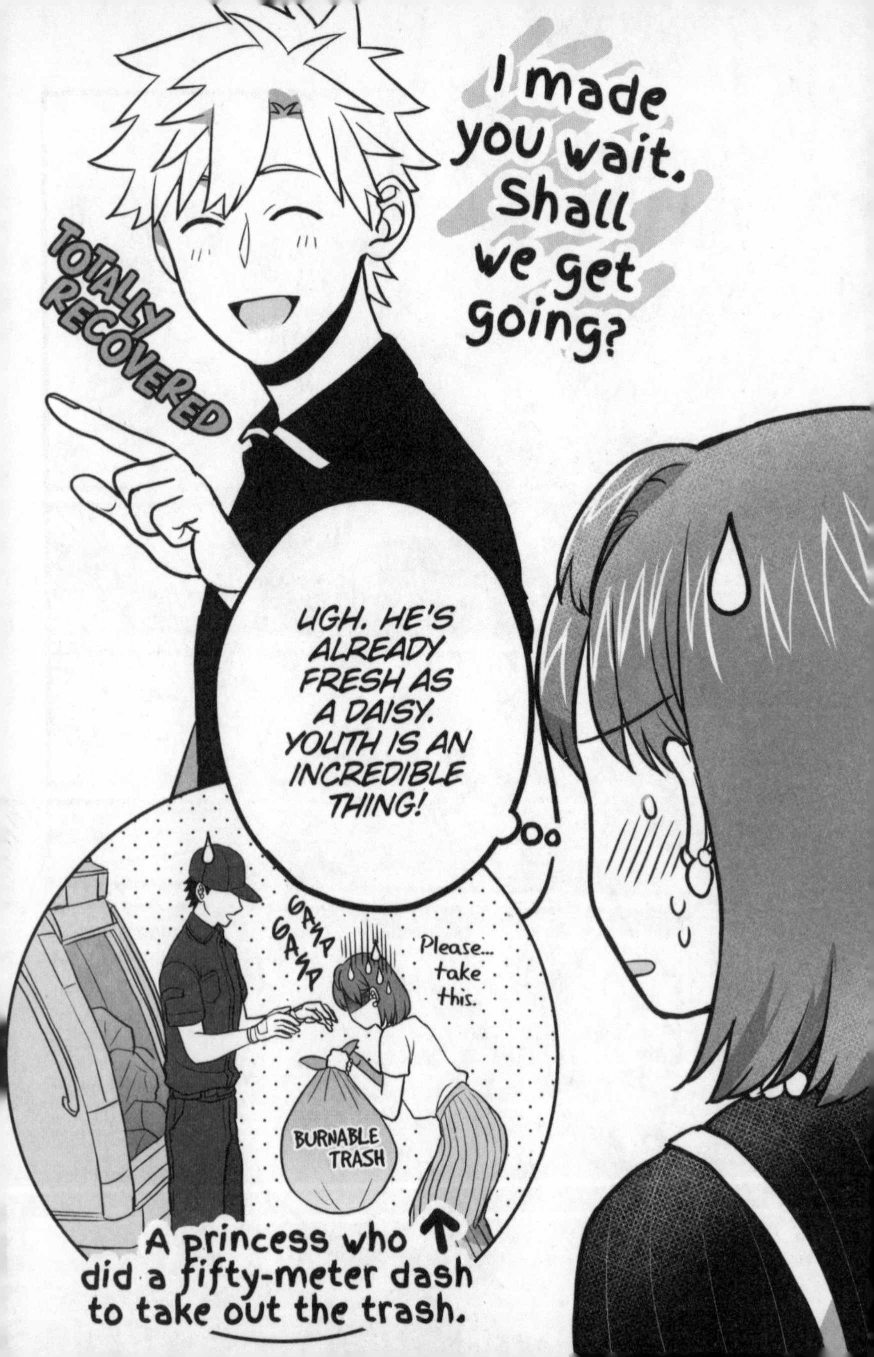
I made you wait. Shall we get going?
TOTALLY RECOVERED
UGH. HE'S ALREADY FRESH AS A DAISY. YOUTH IS AN INCREDIBLE THING!
GASP GASP
Please... take this.
BURNABLE TRASH
A princess who did a fifty-meter dash to take out the trash.

THE THINGS HAROLD SAYS AND THE WAY HE BEHAVES KEEP KNOCKING ME OFF-BALANCE EMOTIONALLY.

I can't wait!

The café we're going to is famous for its cake!

SETTING EVERYTHING ELSE ASIDE...

HAROLD IS STILL A CHILD RIGHT NOW!!

BUT I CAN'T LET THINGS CONTINUE THIS WAY!

GRRGH

KRAKL

HIS NEW, ASSERTIVE ATTITUDE IS PROBABLY DUE TO YOUTHFUL ENTHUSIASM!

I'M THE ADULT HERE! I HAVE TO BE MORE MATURE!

?

KRAKL

25

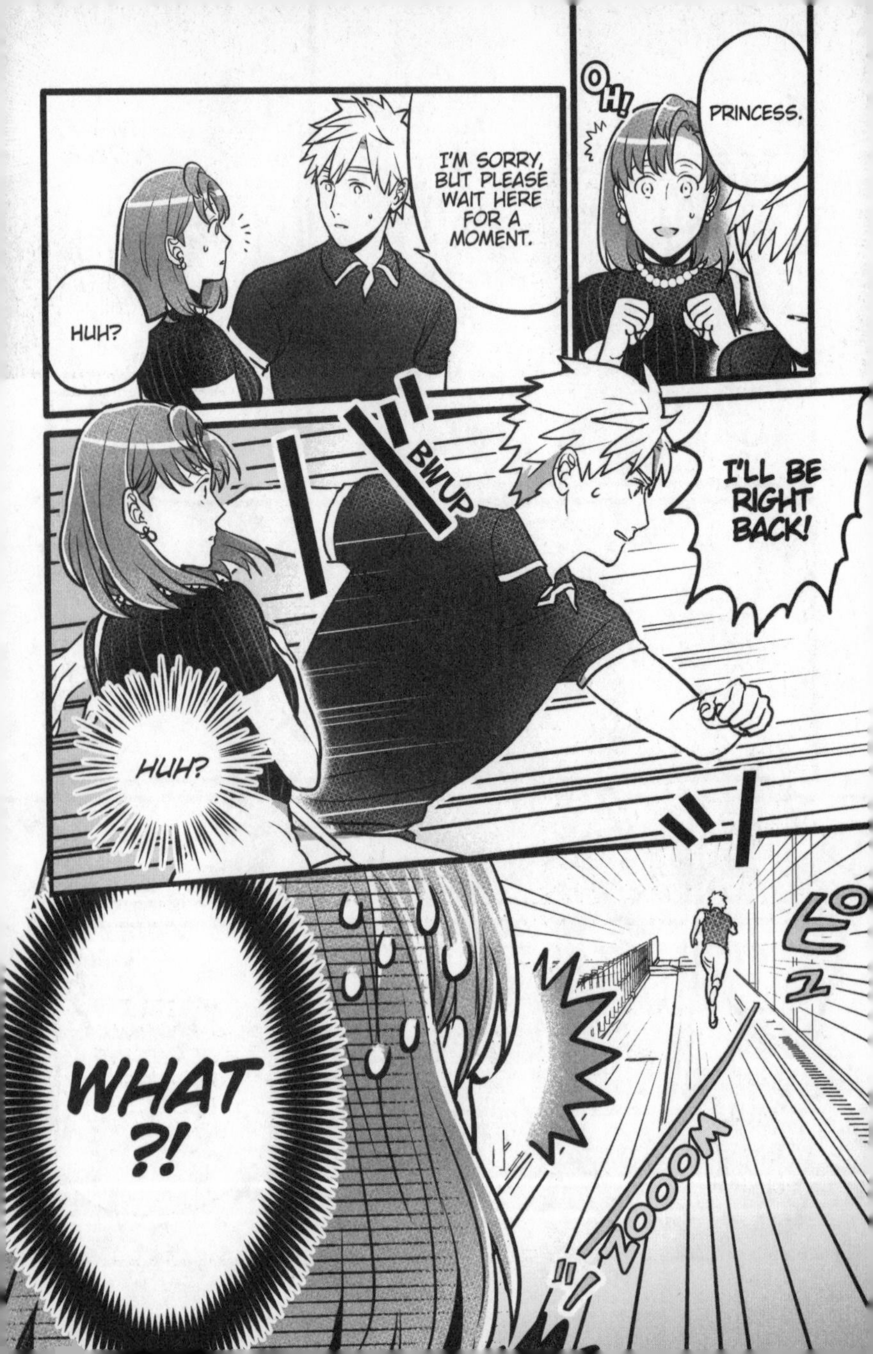
PRINCESS.
OH!
I'M SORRY, BUT PLEASE WAIT HERE FOR A MOMENT.
HUH?
I'LL BE RIGHT BACK!
BWUP
HUH?
ZOOOM
WHAT ?!

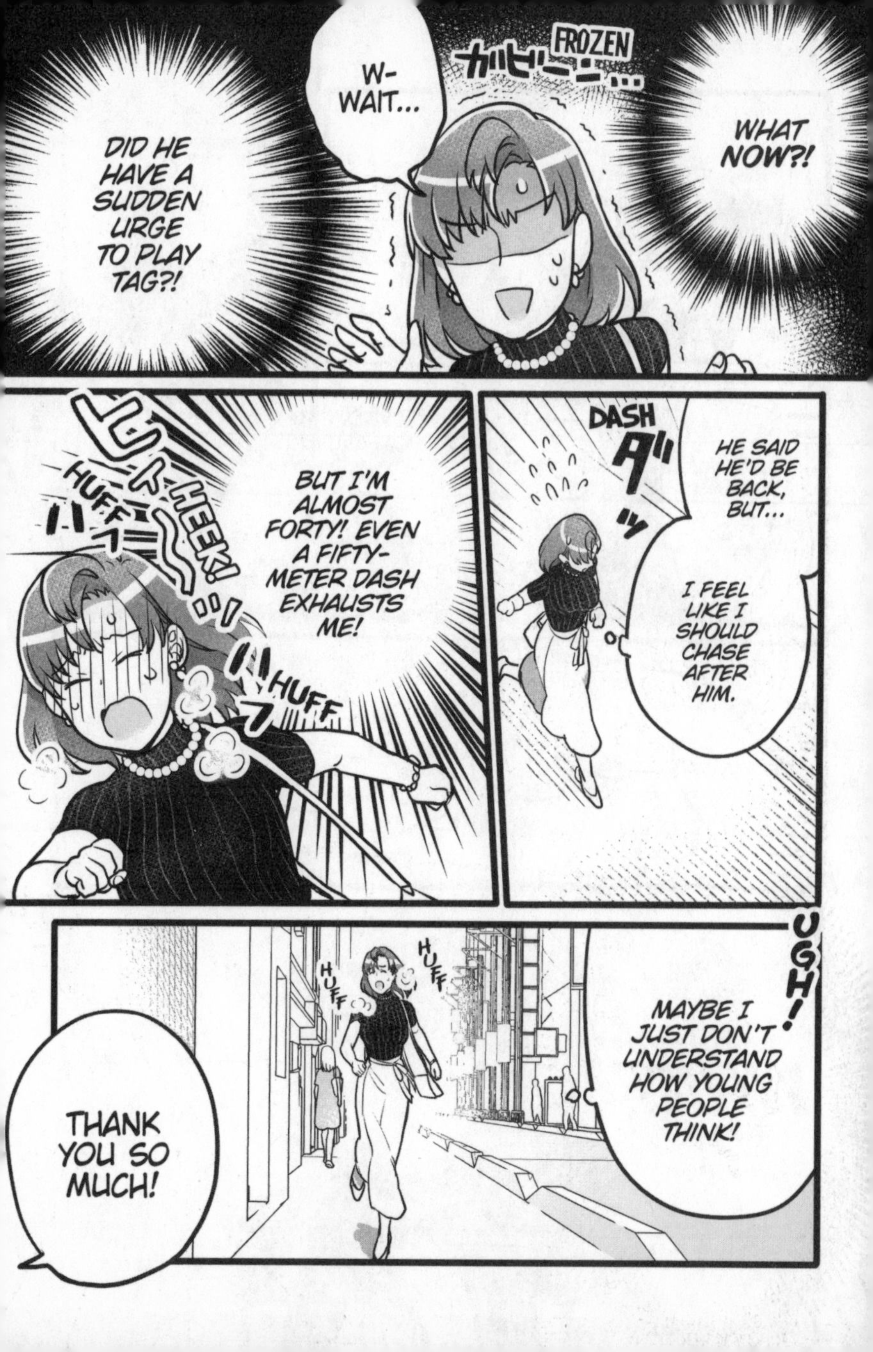
WHAT NOW?!
FROZEN
W-WAIT...
DID HE HAVE A SUDDEN URGE TO PLAY TAG?!
DASH
HE SAID HE'D BE BACK, BUT...
I FEEL LIKE I SHOULD CHASE AFTER HIM.
BUT I'M ALMOST FORTY! EVEN A FIFTY-METER DASH EXHAUSTS ME!
HEEK!
HUFF
HUFF
UGH!
MAYBE I JUST DON'T UNDERSTAND HOW YOUNG PEOPLE THINK!
HUFF
HUFF
THANK YOU SO MUCH!

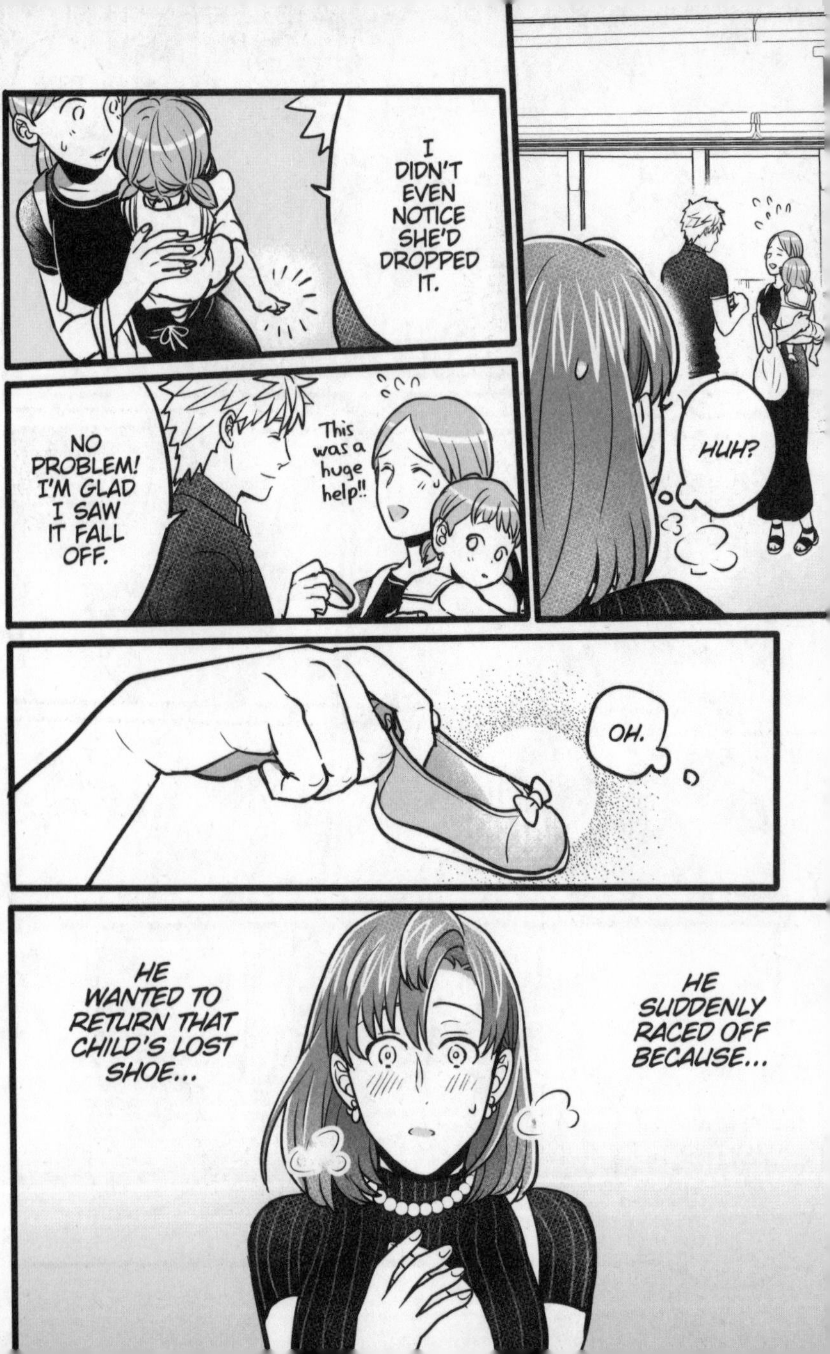
HUH?
I DIDN'T EVEN NOTICE SHE'D DROPPED IT.
This was a huge help!!
NO PROBLEM! I'M GLAD I SAW IT FALL OFF.
OH.
HE SUDDENLY RACED OFF BECAUSE...
HE WANTED TO RETURN THAT CHILD'S LOST SHOE...

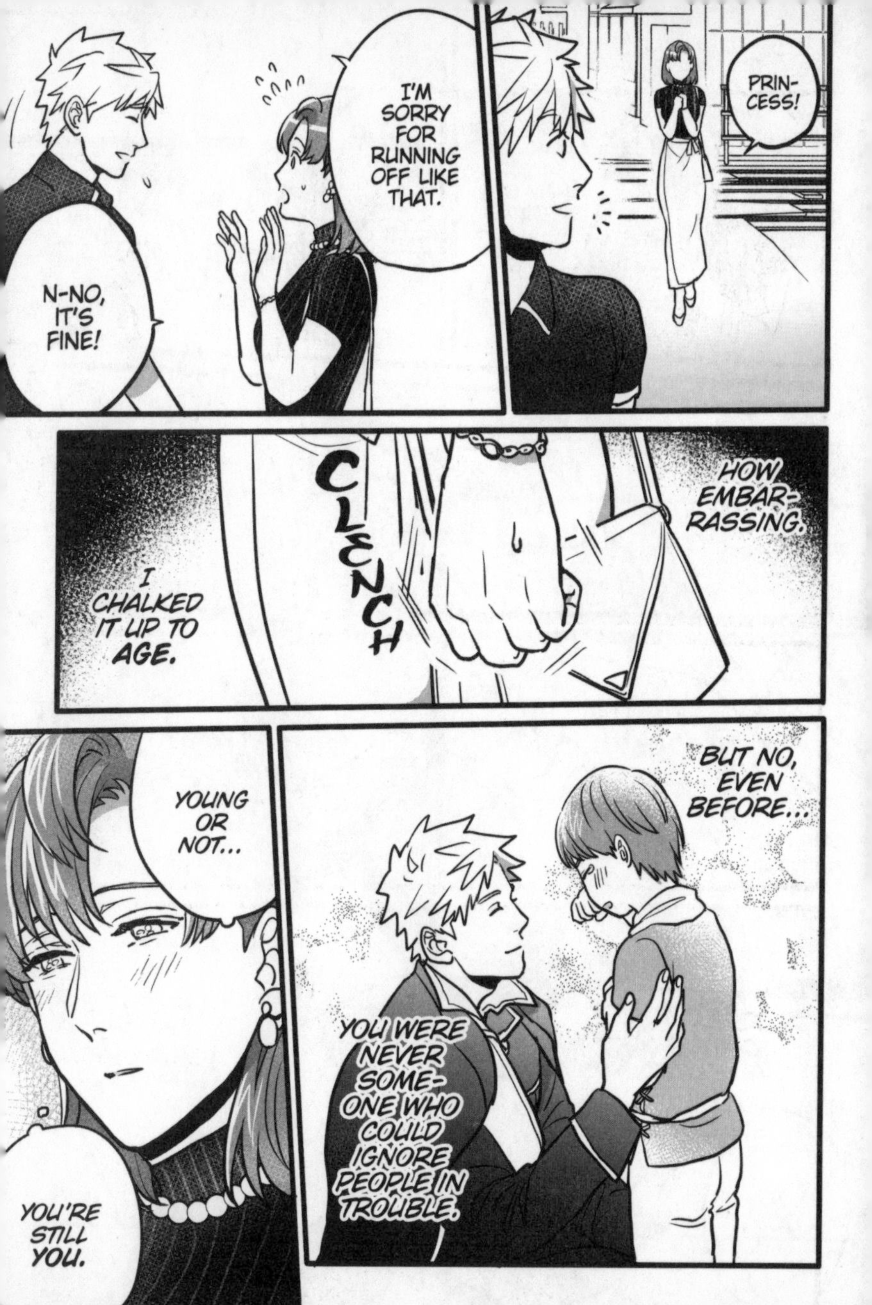
PRIN-CESS!
I'M SORRY FOR RUNNING OFF LIKE THAT.
N-NO, IT'S FINE!
HOW EMBAR-RASSING.
CLENCH
I CHALKED IT UP TO AGE.
BUT NO, EVEN BEFORE...
YOU WERE NEVER SOME-ONE WHO COULD IGNORE PEOPLE IN TROUBLE.
YOUNG OR NOT...
YOU'RE STILL YOU.

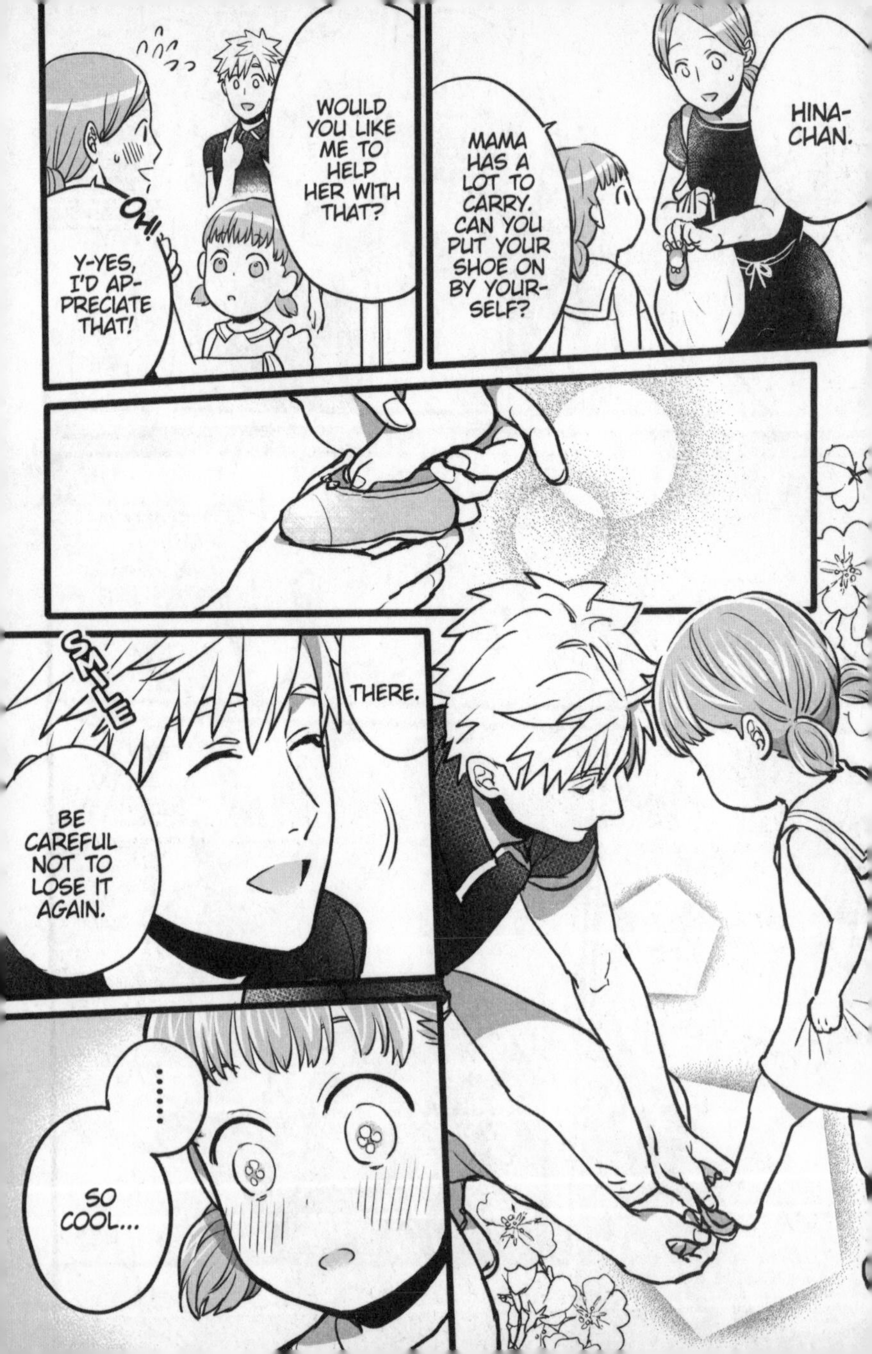
HINA-CHAN.
MAMA HAS A LOT TO CARRY. CAN YOU PUT YOUR SHOE ON BY YOURSELF?
WOULD YOU LIKE ME TO HELP HER WITH THAT?
OH!!
Y-YES, I'D APPRECIATE THAT!
THERE.
SMILE
BE CAREFUL NOT TO LOSE IT AGAIN.
......
SO COOL...

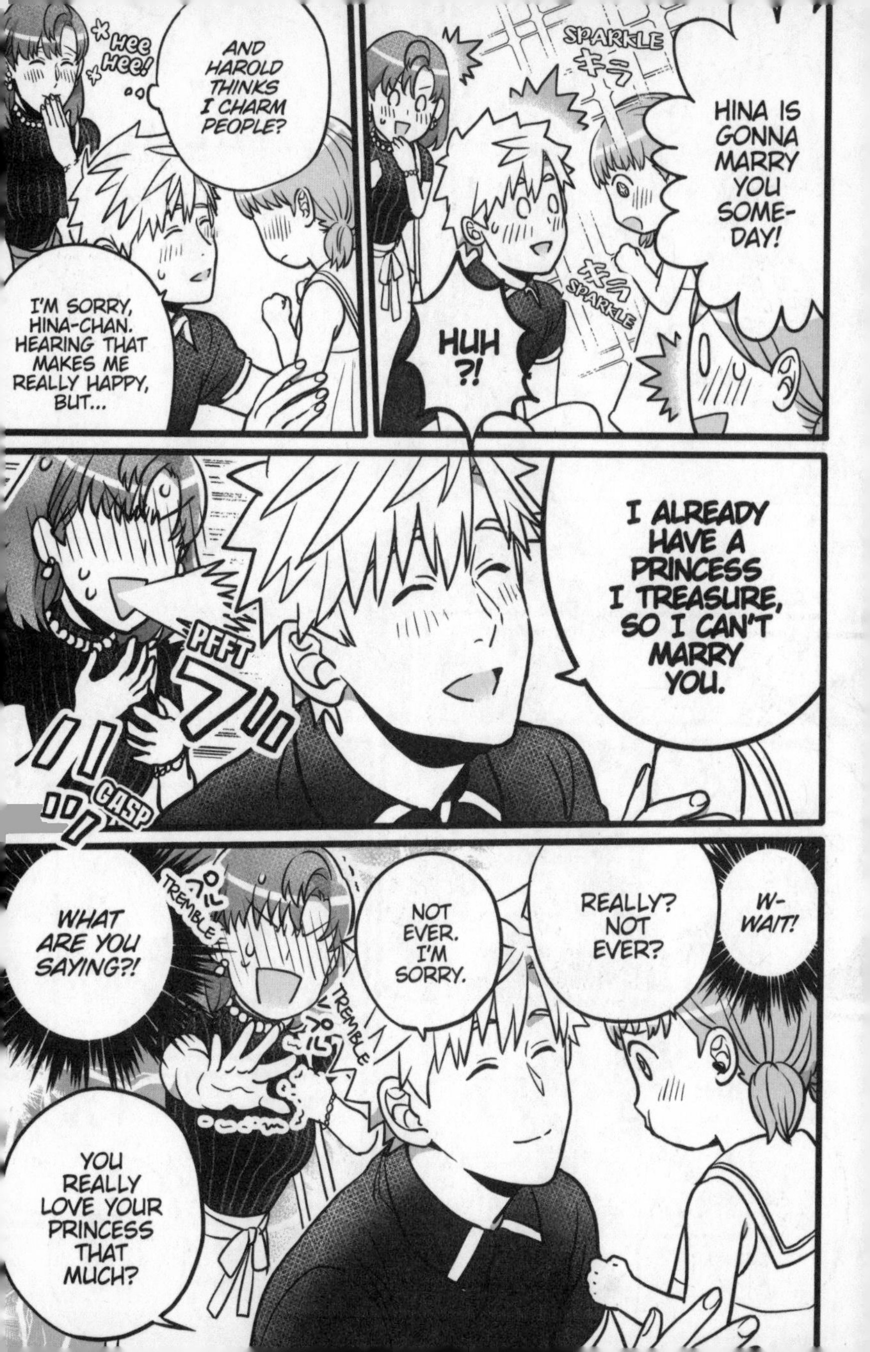
HINA IS GONNA MARRY YOU SOME-DAY!
SPARKLE
キラ
キラ
SPARKLE
HUH ?!
HEE HEE!
AND HAROLD THINKS I CHARM PEOPLE?
I'M SORRY, HINA-CHAN. HEARING THAT MAKES ME REALLY HAPPY, BUT...
I ALREADY HAVE A PRINCESS I TREASURE, SO I CAN'T MARRY YOU.
PFFT
GASP
W-WAIT!
REALLY? NOT EVER?
NOT EVER. I'M SORRY.
TREMBLE
WHAT ARE YOU SAYING?!
TREMBLE
YOU REALLY LOVE YOUR PRINCESS THAT MUCH?

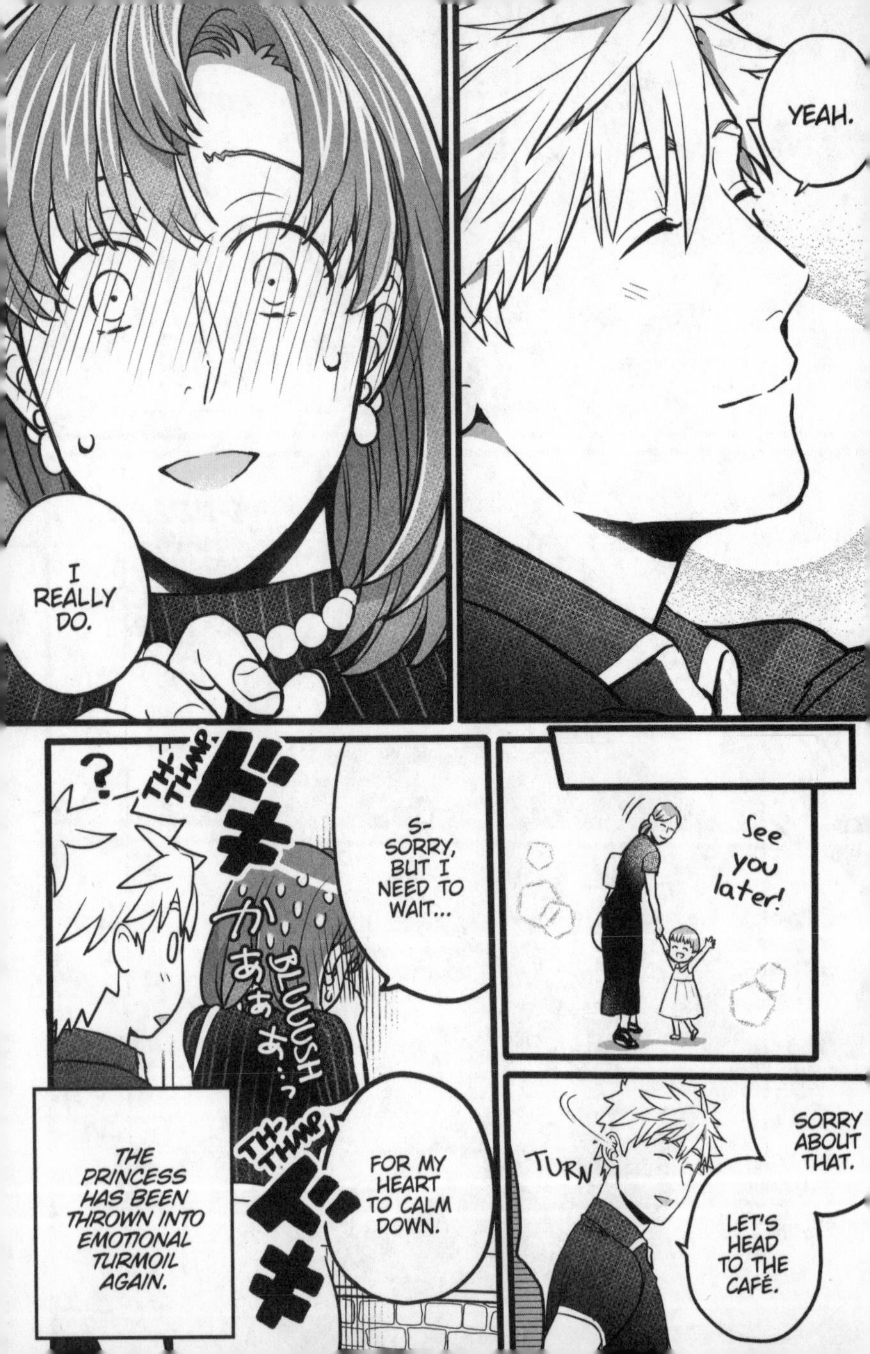
YEAH.
I REALLY DO.
See you later!
TURN
SORRY ABOUT THAT.
LET'S HEAD TO THE CAFÉ.
?
TH-THMP
S- SORRY, BUT I NEED TO WAIT...
BLUUUSH
かぁぁぁ…
TH-THMP
FOR MY HEART TO CALM DOWN.
THE PRINCESS HAS BEEN THROWN INTO EMOTIONAL TURMOIL AGAIN.

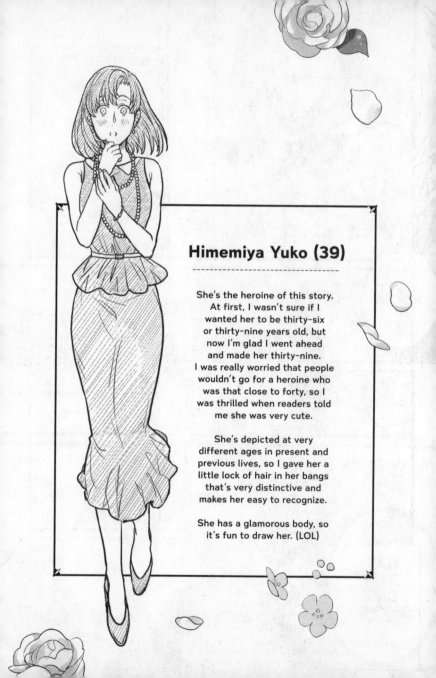

Himemiya Yuko (39)

She's the heroine of this story. At first, I wasn't sure if I wanted her to be thirty-six or thirty-nine years old, but now I'm glad I went ahead and made her thirty-nine. I was really worried that people wouldn't go for a heroine who was that close to forty, so I was thrilled when readers told me she was very cute.

She's depicted at very different ages in present and previous lives, so I gave her a little lock of hair in her bangs that's very distinctive and makes her easy to recognize.

She has a glamorous body, so it's fun to draw her. (LOL)

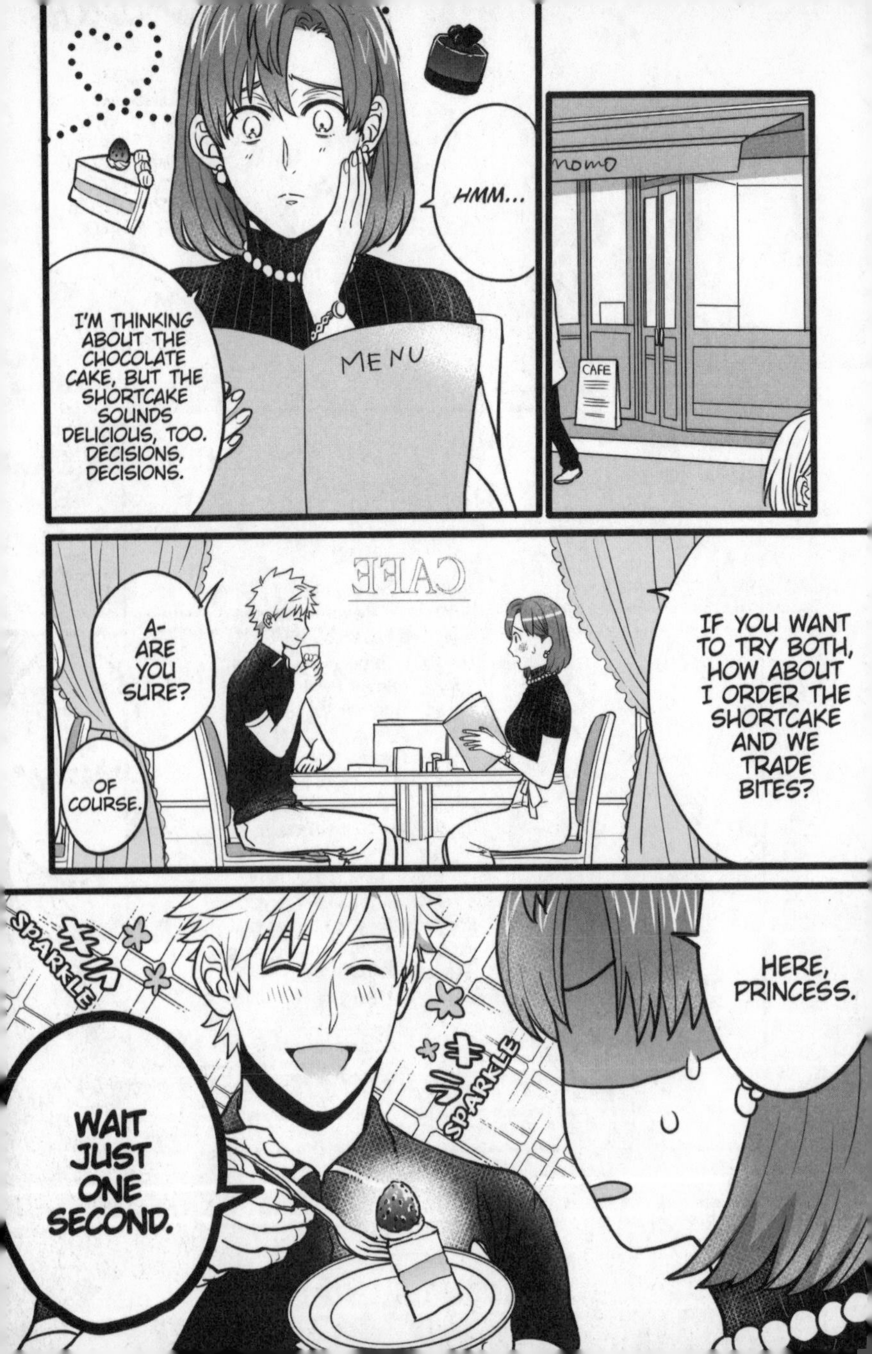
momo
CAFE
HMM...
I'M THINKING ABOUT THE CHOCOLATE CAKE, BUT THE SHORTCAKE SOUNDS DELICIOUS, TOO. DECISIONS, DECISIONS.
MENU
IF YOU WANT TO TRY BOTH, HOW ABOUT I ORDER THE SHORTCAKE AND WE TRADE BITES?
A- ARE YOU SURE?
OF COURSE.
HERE, PRINCESS.
SPARKLE
SPARKLE
WAIT JUST ONE SECOND.

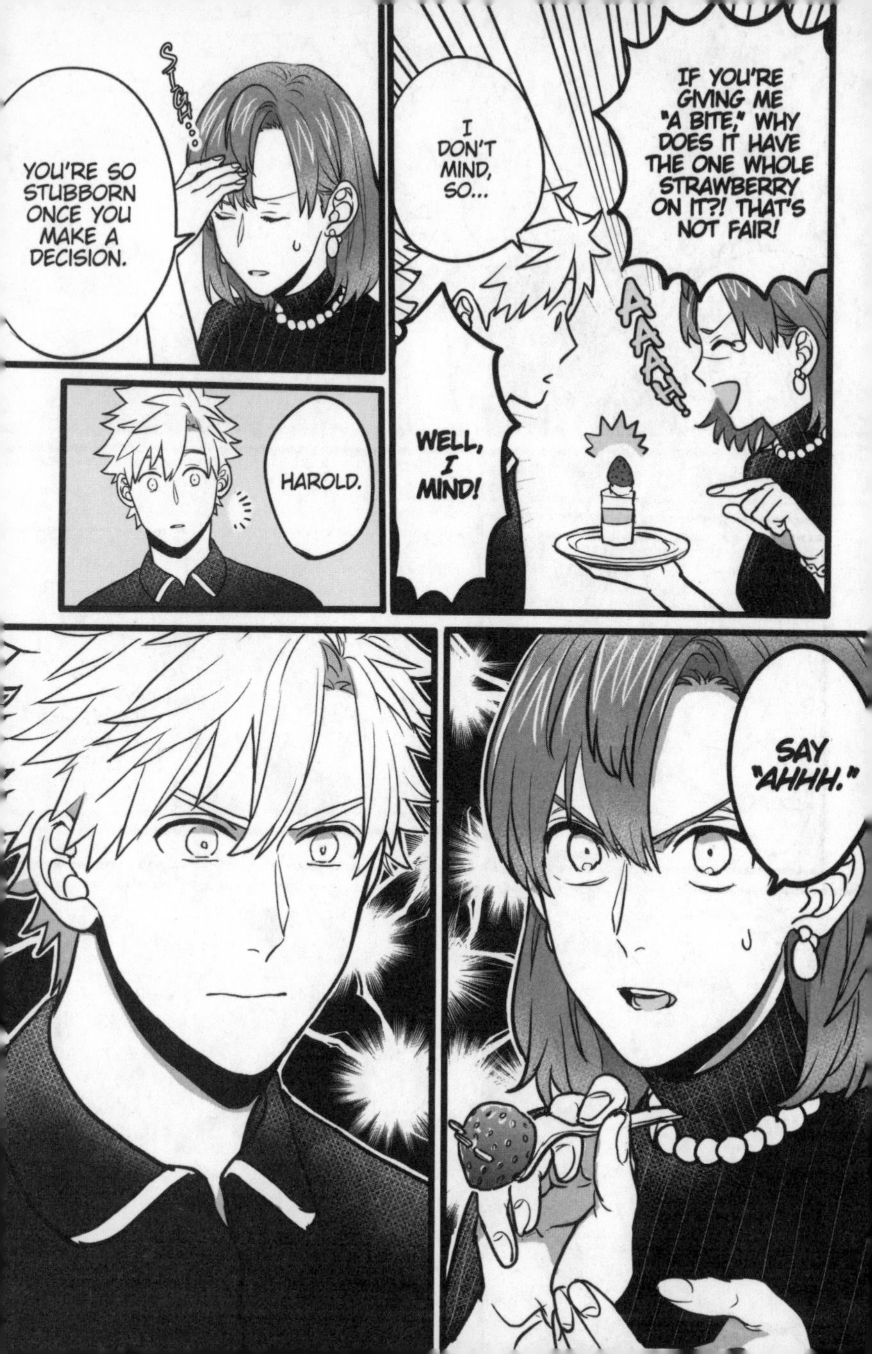
IF YOU'RE GIVING ME "A BITE," WHY DOES IT HAVE THE ONE WHOLE STRAWBERRY ON IT?! THAT'S NOT FAIR!
I DON'T MIND, SO...
AAAH!
WELL, I MIND!
SIGH...
YOU'RE SO STUBBORN ONCE YOU MAKE A DECISION.
HAROLD.
SAY "AHHH."

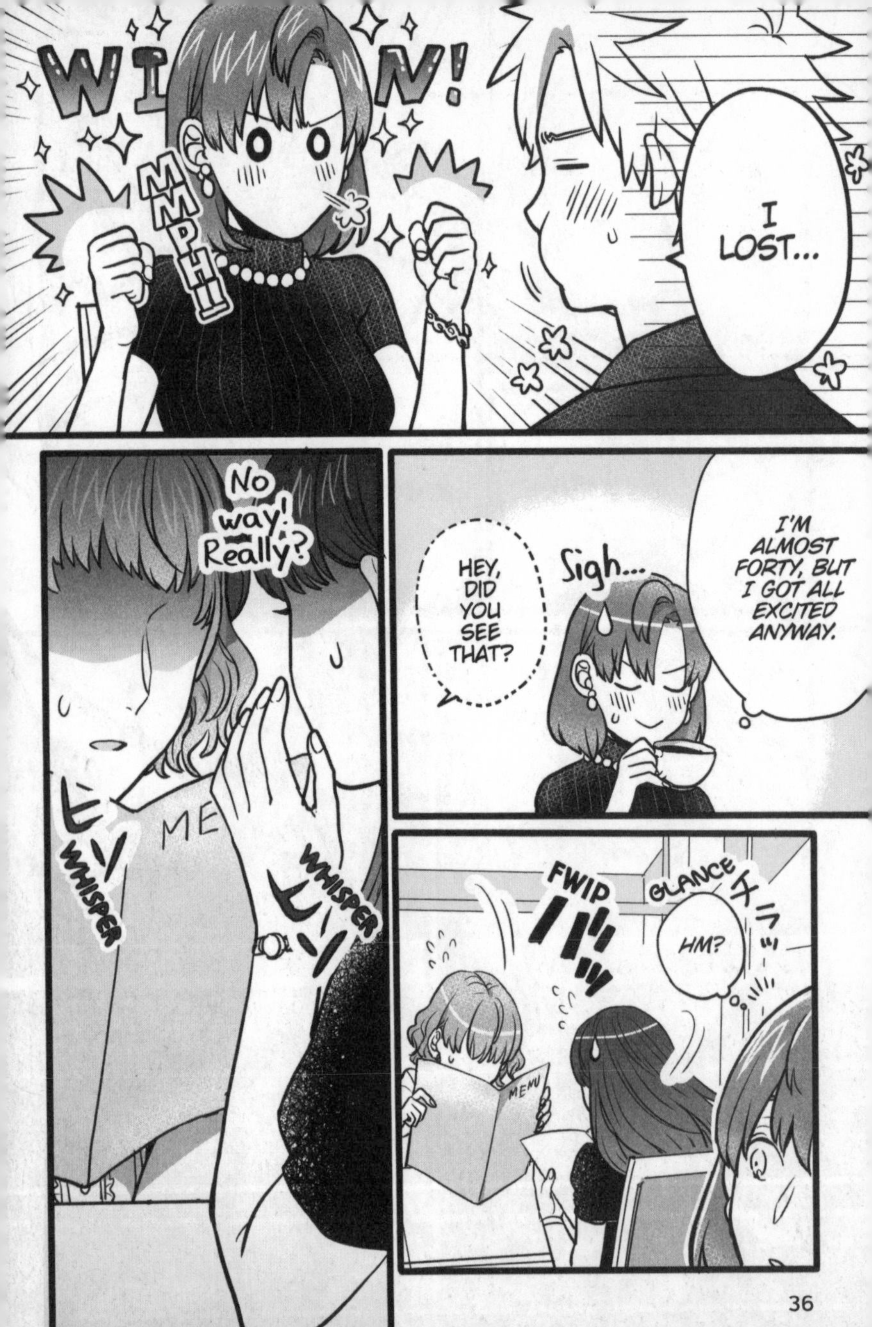
WI N!
MMPH!!
I LOST...
I'M ALMOST FORTY, BUT I GOT ALL EXCITED ANYWAY.
Sigh...
HEY, DID YOU SEE THAT?
GLANCE チラッ
HM?
FWIP バッ
No way! Really?
WHISPER ヒソ
WHISPER ヒソ
MENU

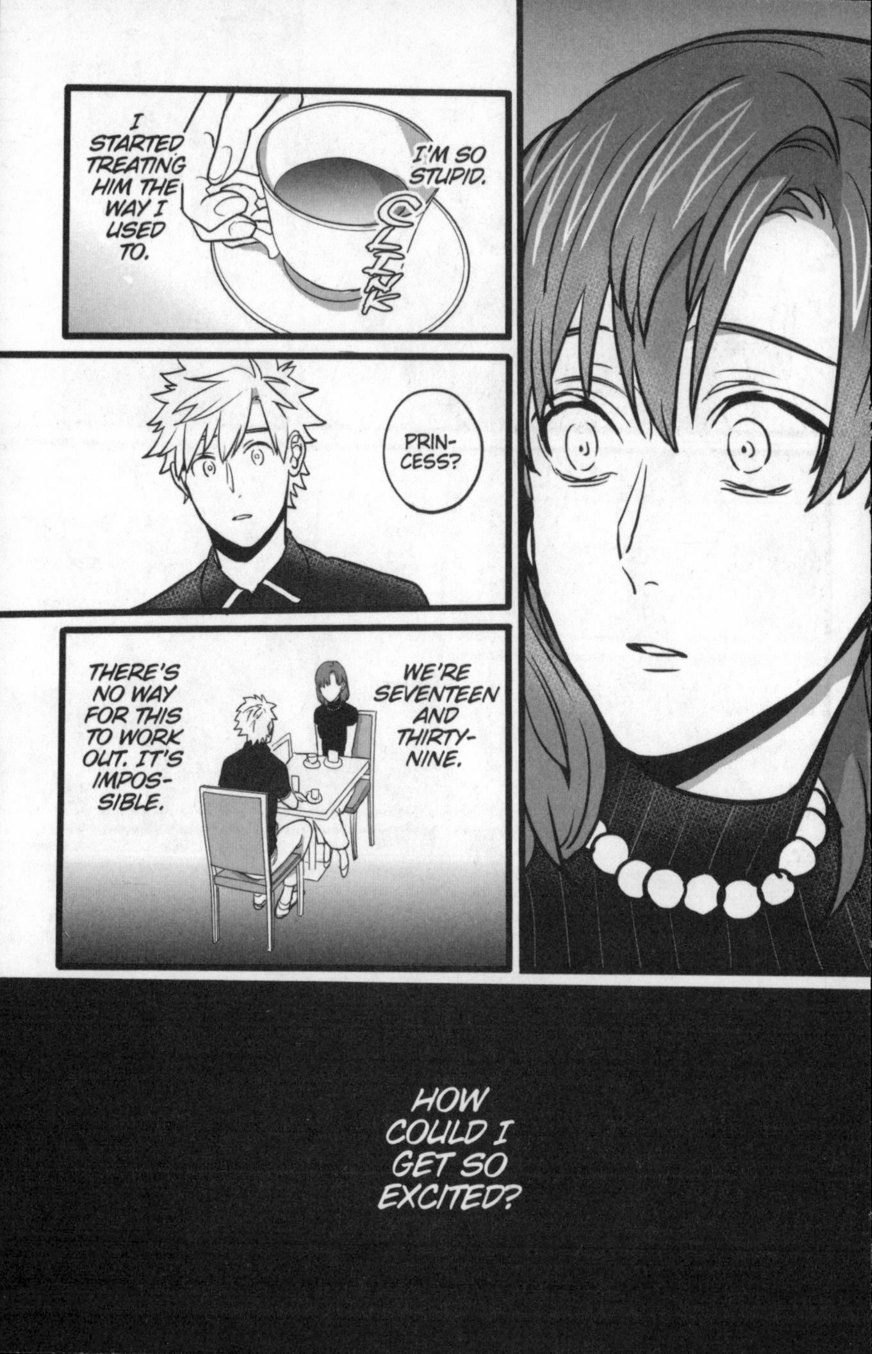
I'M SO STUPID.
CLINK
I STARTED TREATING HIM THE WAY I USED TO.
PRINCESS?
WE'RE SEVENTEEN AND THIRTY-NINE.
THERE'S NO WAY FOR THIS TO WORK OUT. IT'S IMPOSSIBLE.
HOW COULD I GET SO EXCITED?

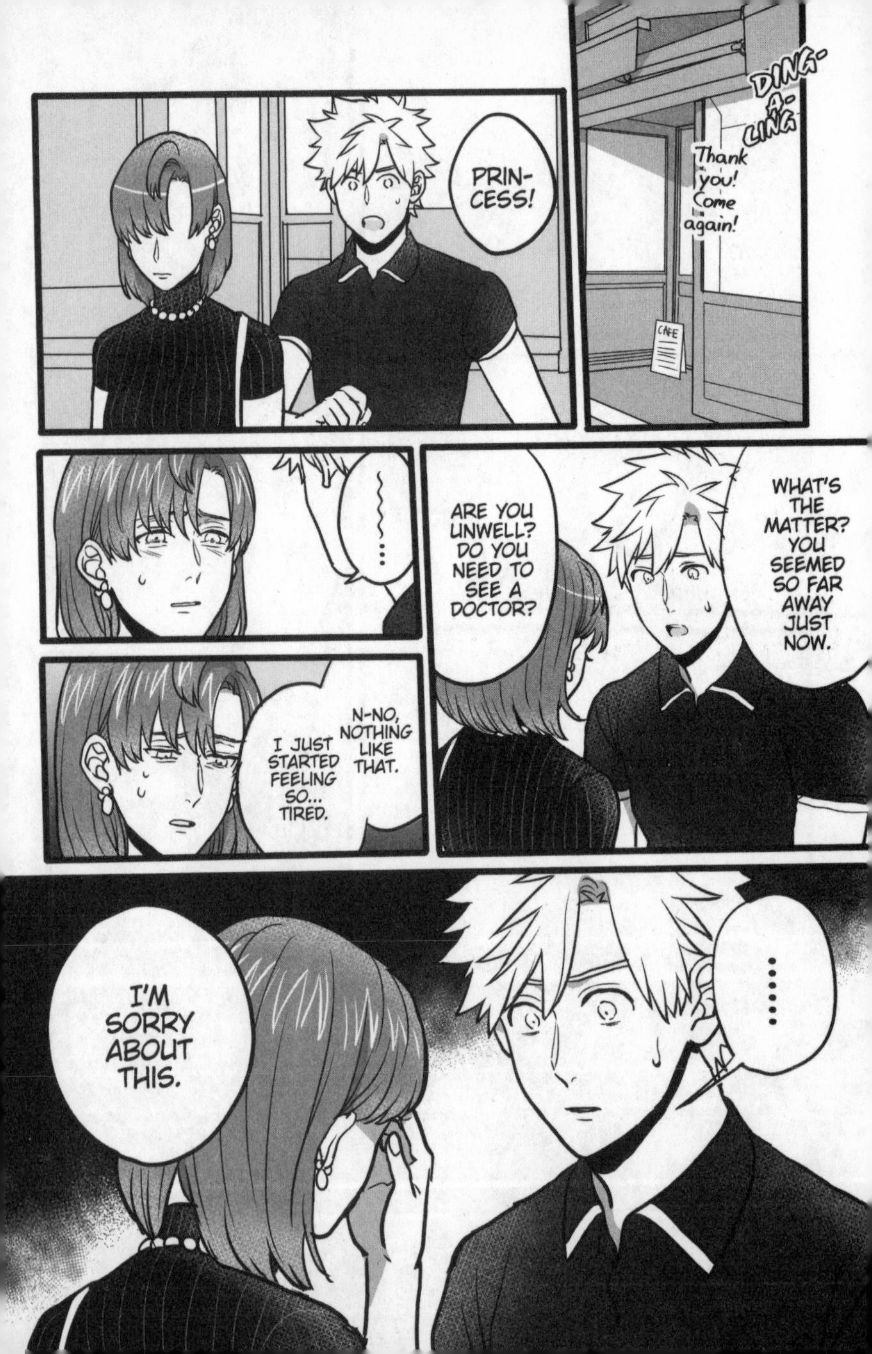
DING-A-LING
Thank you! Come again!
PRIN-CESS!
WHAT'S THE MATTER? YOU SEEMED SO FAR AWAY JUST NOW.
ARE YOU UNWELL? DO YOU NEED TO SEE A DOCTOR?
......
N-NO, NOTHING LIKE THAT.
I JUST STARTED FEELING SO... TIRED.
......
I'M SORRY ABOUT THIS.

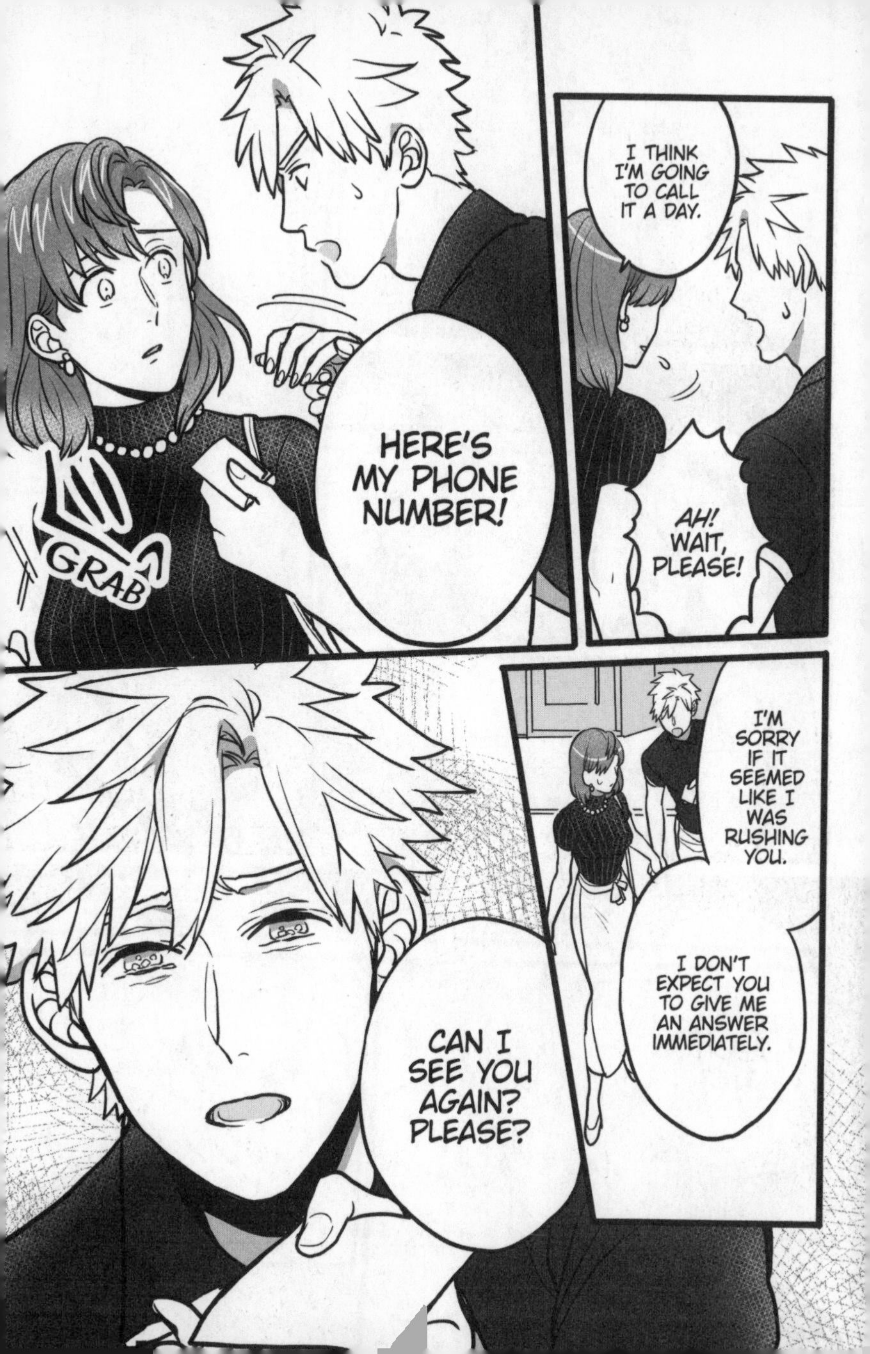
I THINK I'M GOING TO CALL IT A DAY.
AH! WAIT, PLEASE!
HERE'S MY PHONE NUMBER!
GRAB
I'M SORRY IF IT SEEMED LIKE I WAS RUSHING YOU.
I DON'T EXPECT YOU TO GIVE ME AN ANSWER IMMEDIATELY.
CAN I SEE YOU AGAIN? PLEASE?

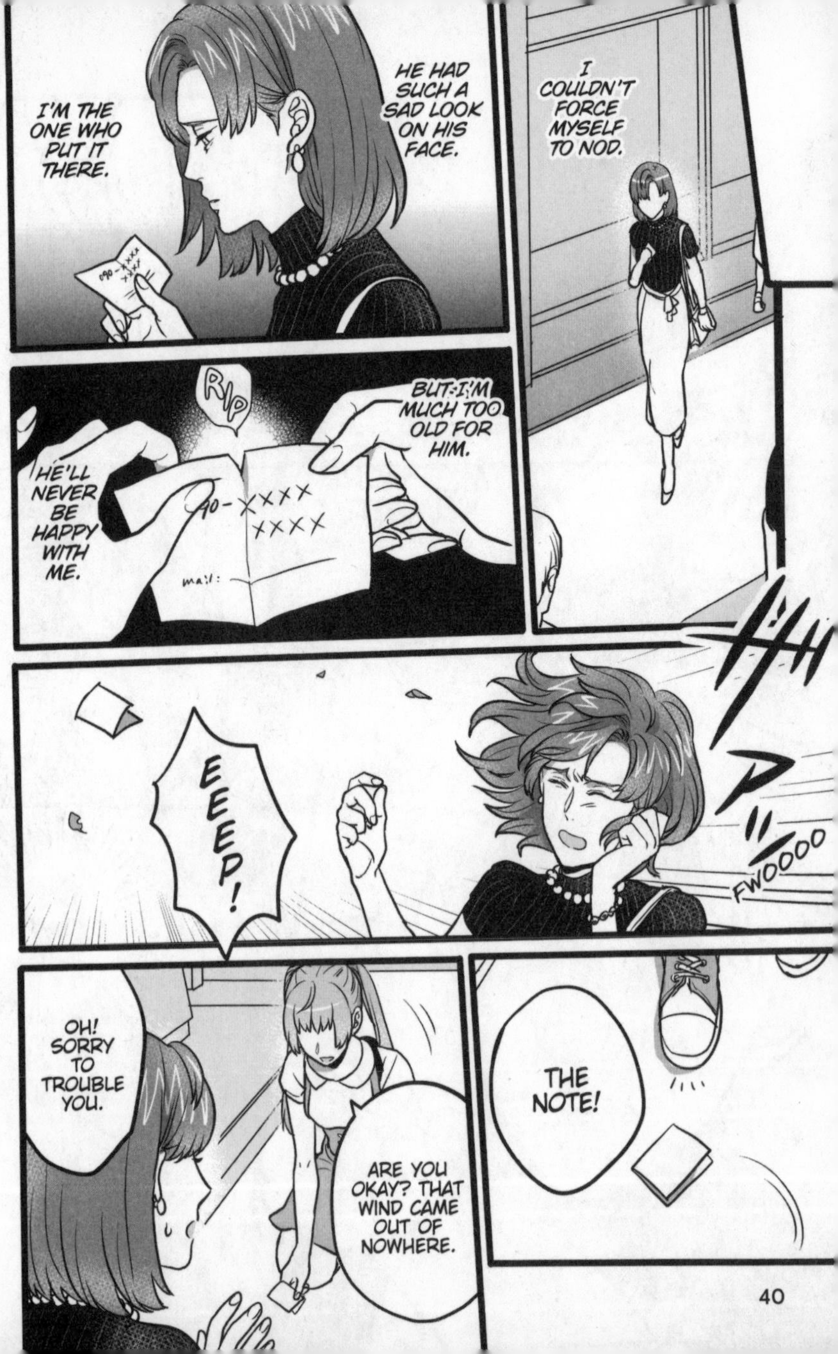
I COULDN'T FORCE MYSELF TO NOD.
HE HAD SUCH A SAD LOOK ON HIS FACE.
I'M THE ONE WHO PUT IT THERE.
RIP
BUT I'M MUCH TOO OLD FOR HIM.
90-XXXX XXXX
mail:
HE'LL NEVER BE HAPPY WITH ME.
FWOOOO
EEEP!
THE NOTE!
ARE YOU OKAY? THAT WIND CAME OUT OF NOWHERE.
OH! SORRY TO TROUBLE YOU.

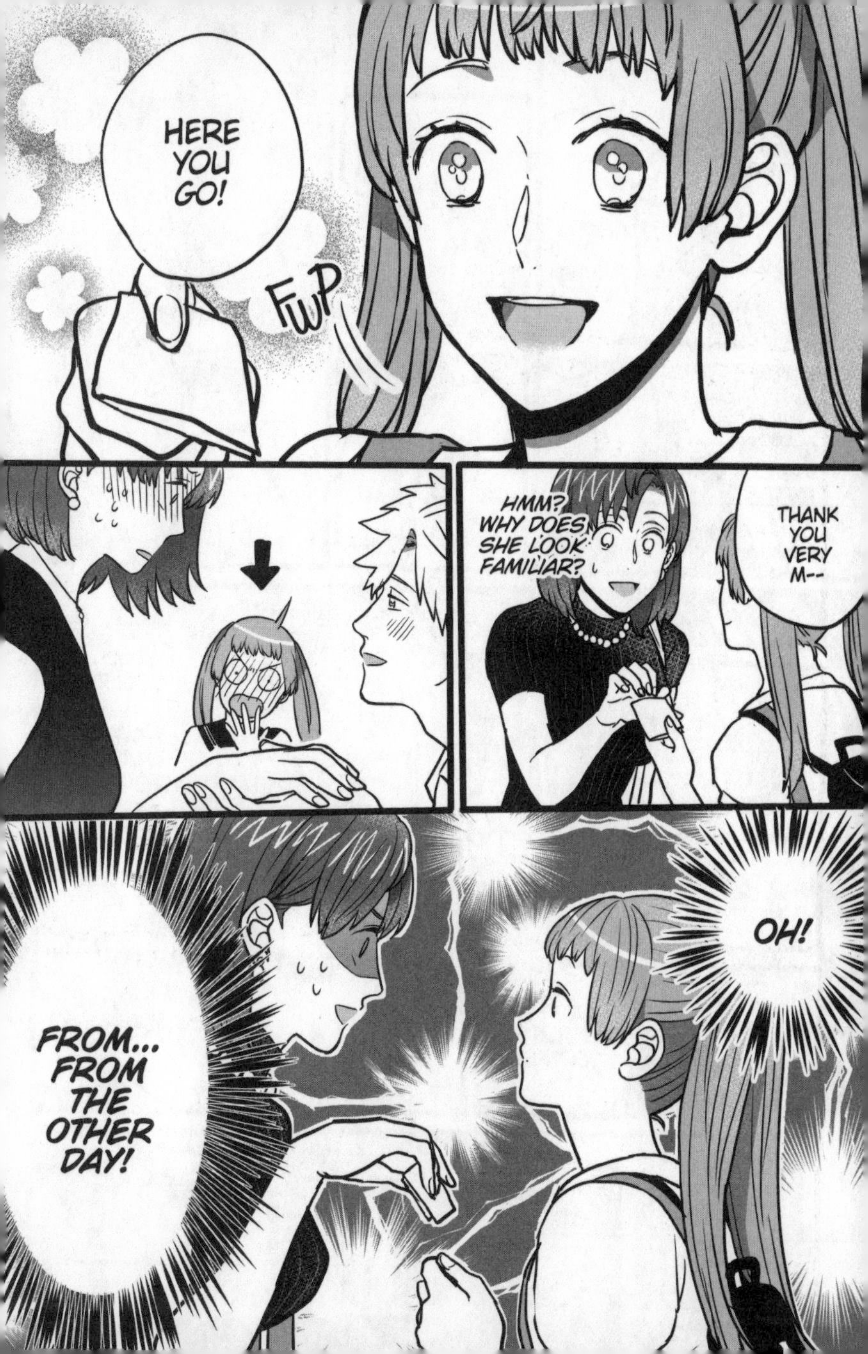
HERE YOU GO!
FWP
THANK YOU VERY M--
HMM? WHY DOES SHE LOOK FAMILIAR?
OH!
FROM... FROM THE OTHER DAY!

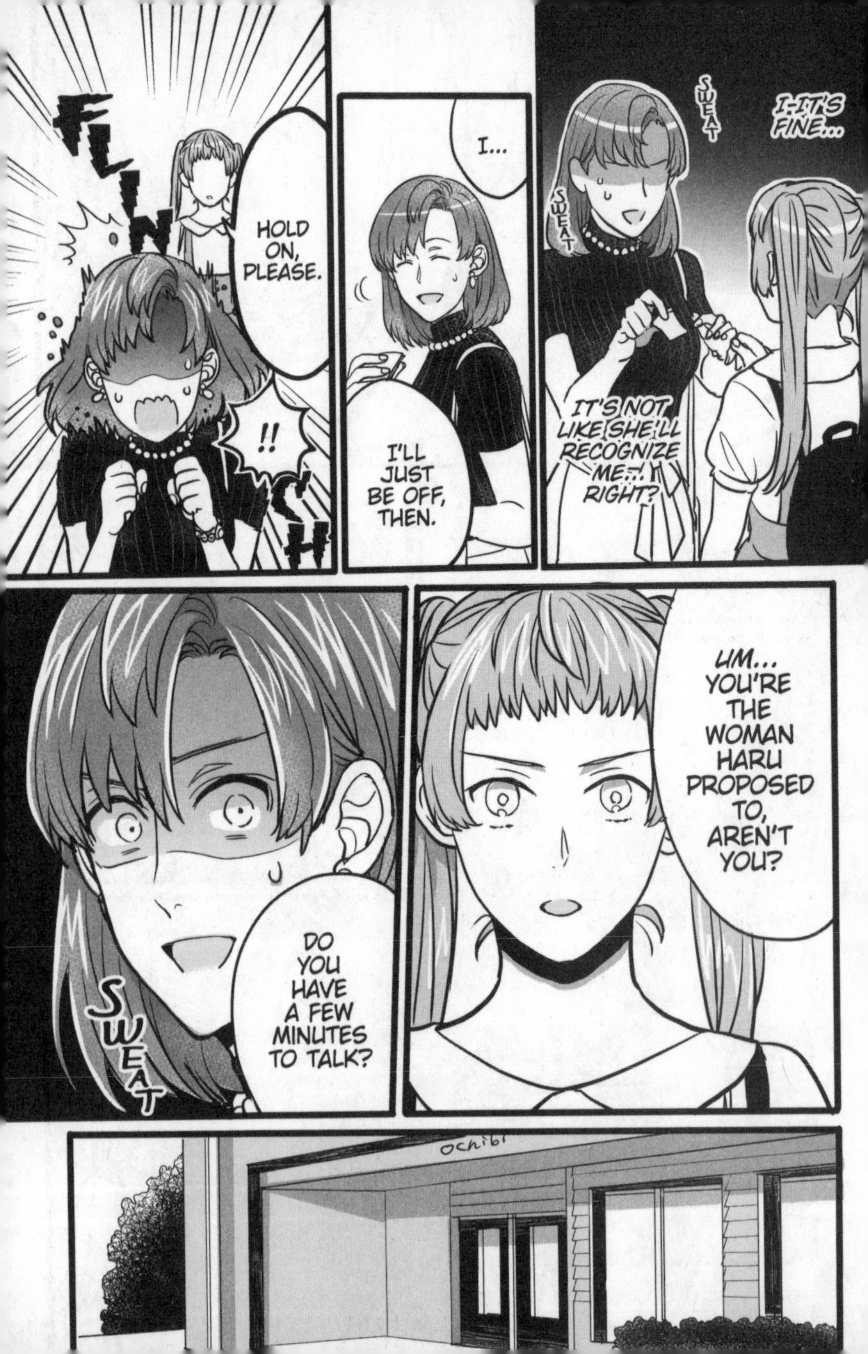
I-IT'S FINE...
SWEAT
SWEAT
IT'S NOT LIKE SHE'LL RECOGNIZE ME...! RIGHT?
I...
I'LL JUST BE OFF, THEN.
HOLD ON, PLEASE.
FLINCH
!!
UM... YOU'RE THE WOMAN HARU PROPOSED TO, AREN'T YOU?
DO YOU HAVE A FEW MINUTES TO TALK?
SWEAT
ochibi

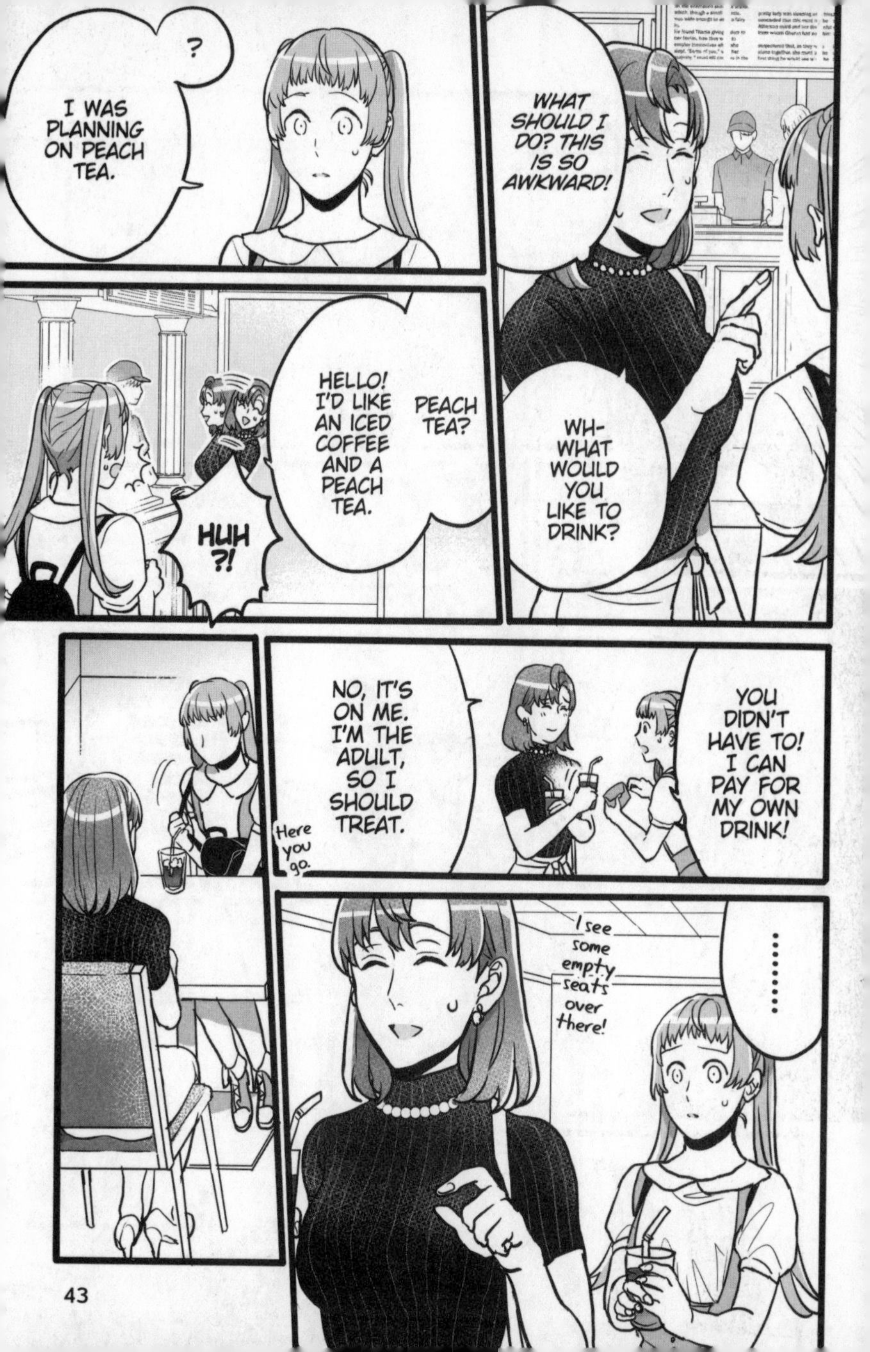
WHAT SHOULD I DO? THIS IS SO AWKWARD!
WH-WHAT WOULD YOU LIKE TO DRINK?
?
I WAS PLANNING ON PEACH TEA.
PEACH TEA?
HELLO! I'D LIKE AN ICED COFFEE AND A PEACH TEA.
HUH?!
YOU DIDN'T HAVE TO! I CAN PAY FOR MY OWN DRINK!
NO, IT'S ON ME. I'M THE ADULT, SO I SHOULD TREAT.
Here you go.
....
I see some empty seats over there!

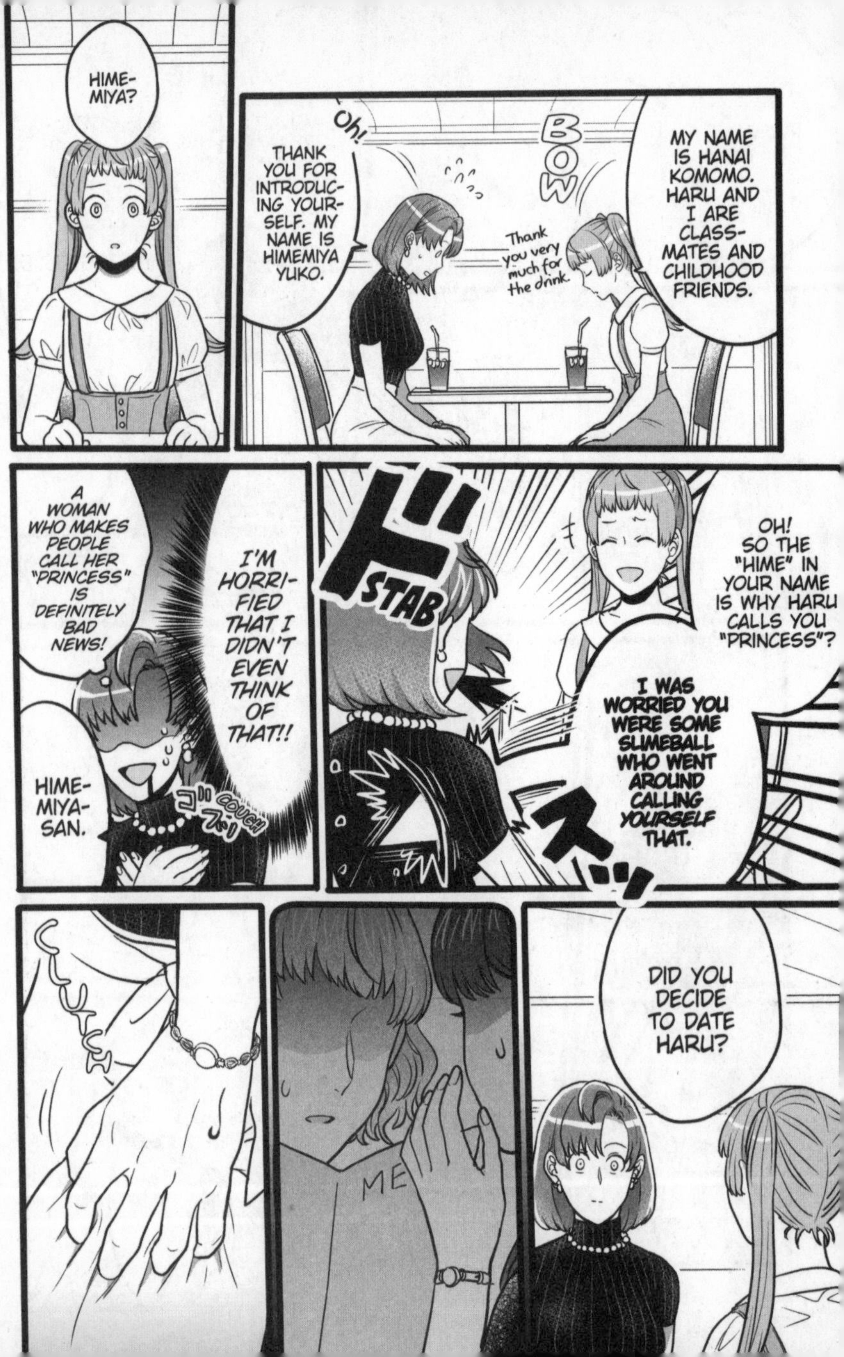
MY NAME IS HANAI KOMOMO. HARU AND I ARE CLASSMATES AND CHILDHOOD FRIENDS.
BOW
Thank you very much for the drink.
Oh!
THANK YOU FOR INTRODUCING YOURSELF. MY NAME IS HIMEMIYA YUKO.
HIME-MIYA?
OH! SO THE "HIME" IN YOUR NAME IS WHY HARU CALLS YOU "PRINCESS"?
I WAS WORRIED YOU WERE SOME SLIMEBALL WHO WENT AROUND CALLING *YOURSELF* THAT.
STAB
I'M HORRIFIED THAT I DIDN'T EVEN THINK OF THAT!!
A WOMAN WHO MAKES PEOPLE CALL HER "PRINCESS" IS DEFINITELY BAD NEWS!
HIME-MIYA-SAN.
COUGH
DID YOU DECIDE TO DATE HARU?
ME
CLUTCH

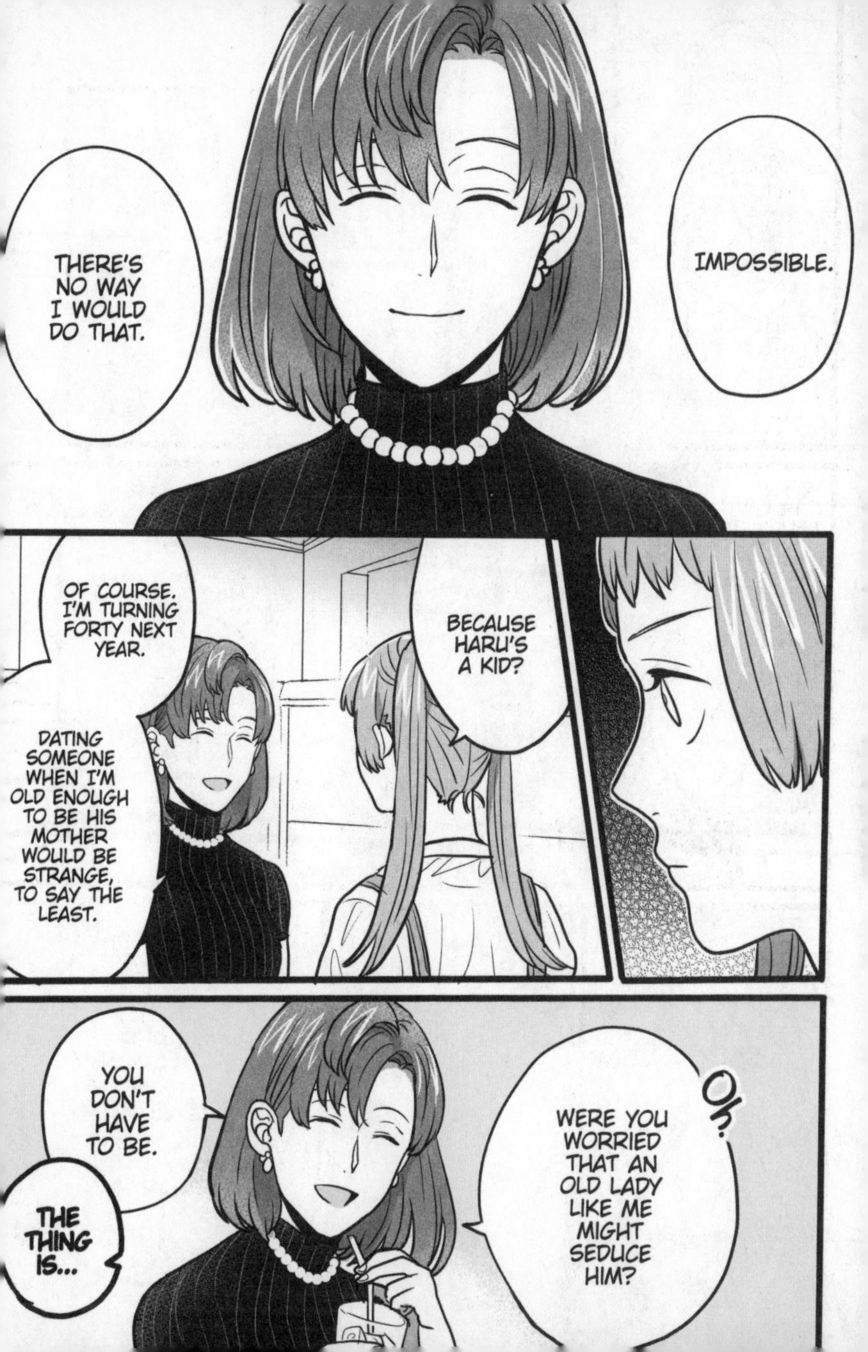
IMPOSSIBLE.
THERE'S NO WAY I WOULD DO THAT.
BECAUSE HARU'S A KID?
OF COURSE. I'M TURNING FORTY NEXT YEAR.
DATING SOMEONE WHEN I'M OLD ENOUGH TO BE HIS MOTHER WOULD BE STRANGE, TO SAY THE LEAST.
Oh.
WERE YOU WORRIED THAT AN OLD LADY LIKE ME MIGHT SEDUCE HIM?
YOU DON'T HAVE TO BE.
THE THING IS...

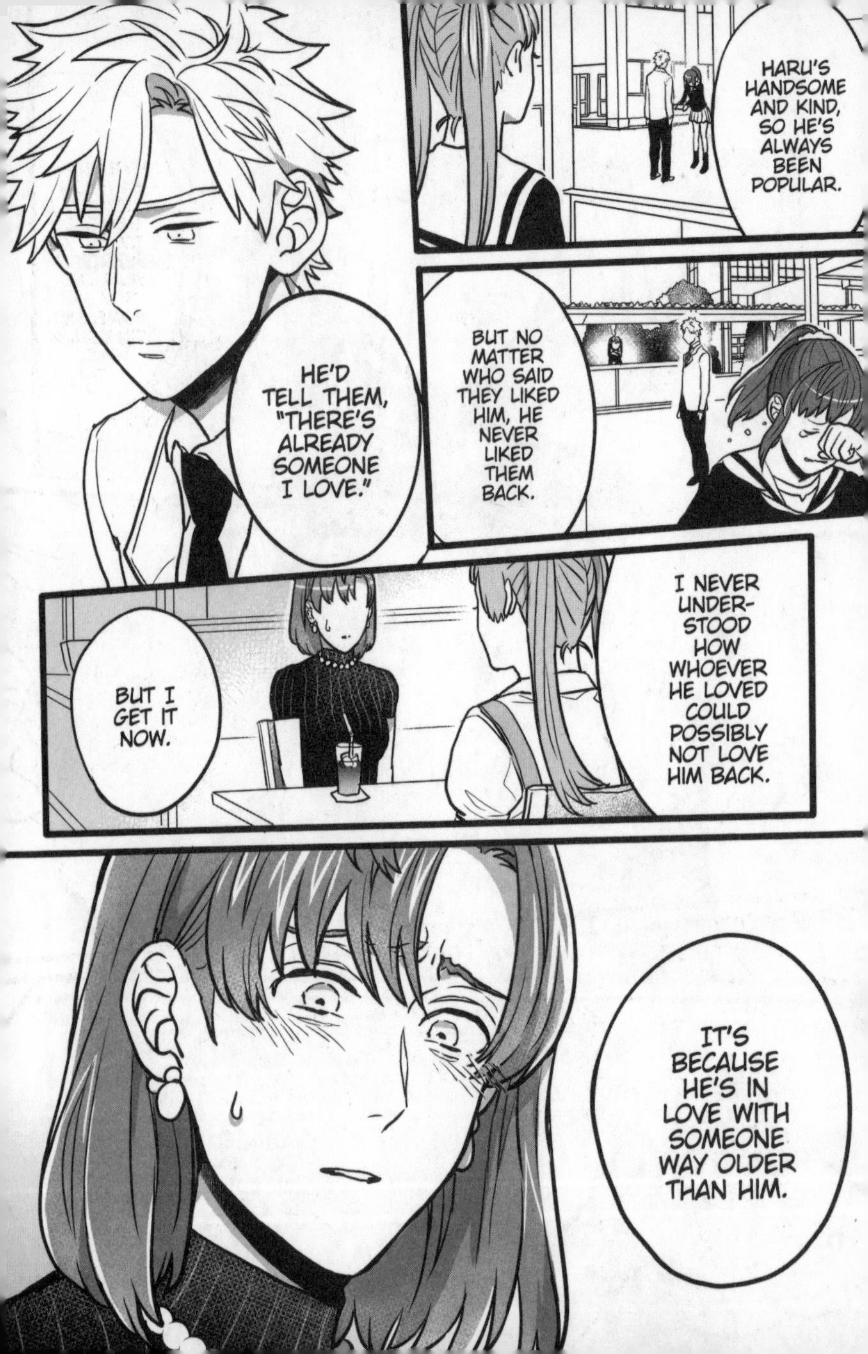
HARU'S HANDSOME AND KIND, SO HE'S ALWAYS BEEN POPULAR.
BUT NO MATTER WHO SAID THEY LIKED HIM, HE NEVER LIKED THEM BACK.
HE'D TELL THEM, "THERE'S ALREADY SOMEONE I LOVE."
I NEVER UNDER-STOOD HOW WHOEVER HE LOVED COULD POSSIBLY NOT LOVE HIM BACK.
BUT I GET IT NOW.
IT'S BECAUSE HE'S IN LOVE WITH SOMEONE WAY OLDER THAN HIM.

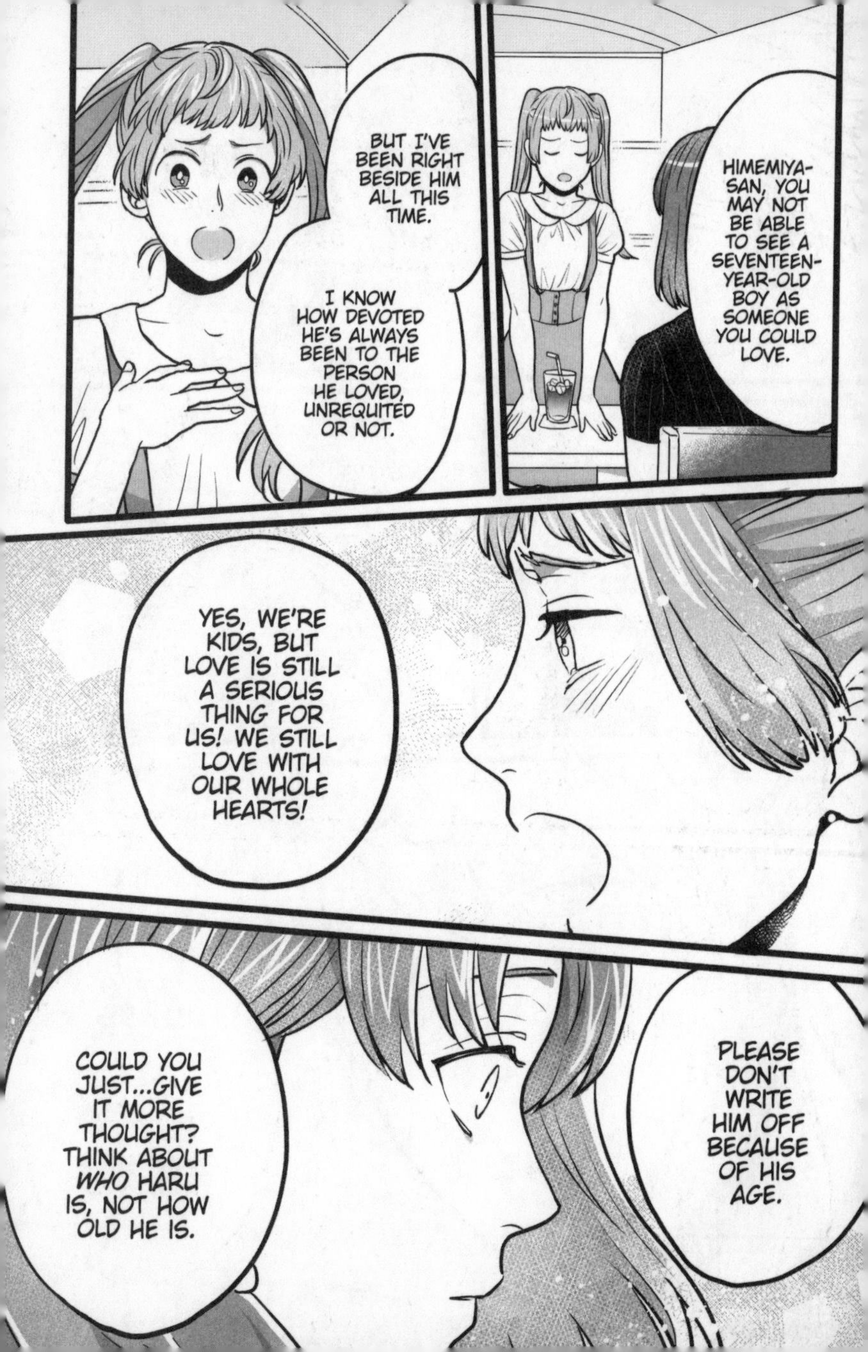
HIMEMIYA-SAN, YOU MAY NOT BE ABLE TO SEE A SEVENTEEN-YEAR-OLD BOY AS SOMEONE YOU COULD LOVE.
BUT I'VE BEEN RIGHT BESIDE HIM ALL THIS TIME.
I KNOW HOW DEVOTED HE'S ALWAYS BEEN TO THE PERSON HE LOVED, UNREQUITED OR NOT.
YES, WE'RE KIDS, BUT LOVE IS STILL A SERIOUS THING FOR US! WE STILL LOVE WITH OUR WHOLE HEARTS!
PLEASE DON'T WRITE HIM OFF BECAUSE OF HIS AGE.
COULD YOU JUST...GIVE IT MORE THOUGHT? THINK ABOUT *WHO* HARU IS, NOT HOW OLD HE IS.

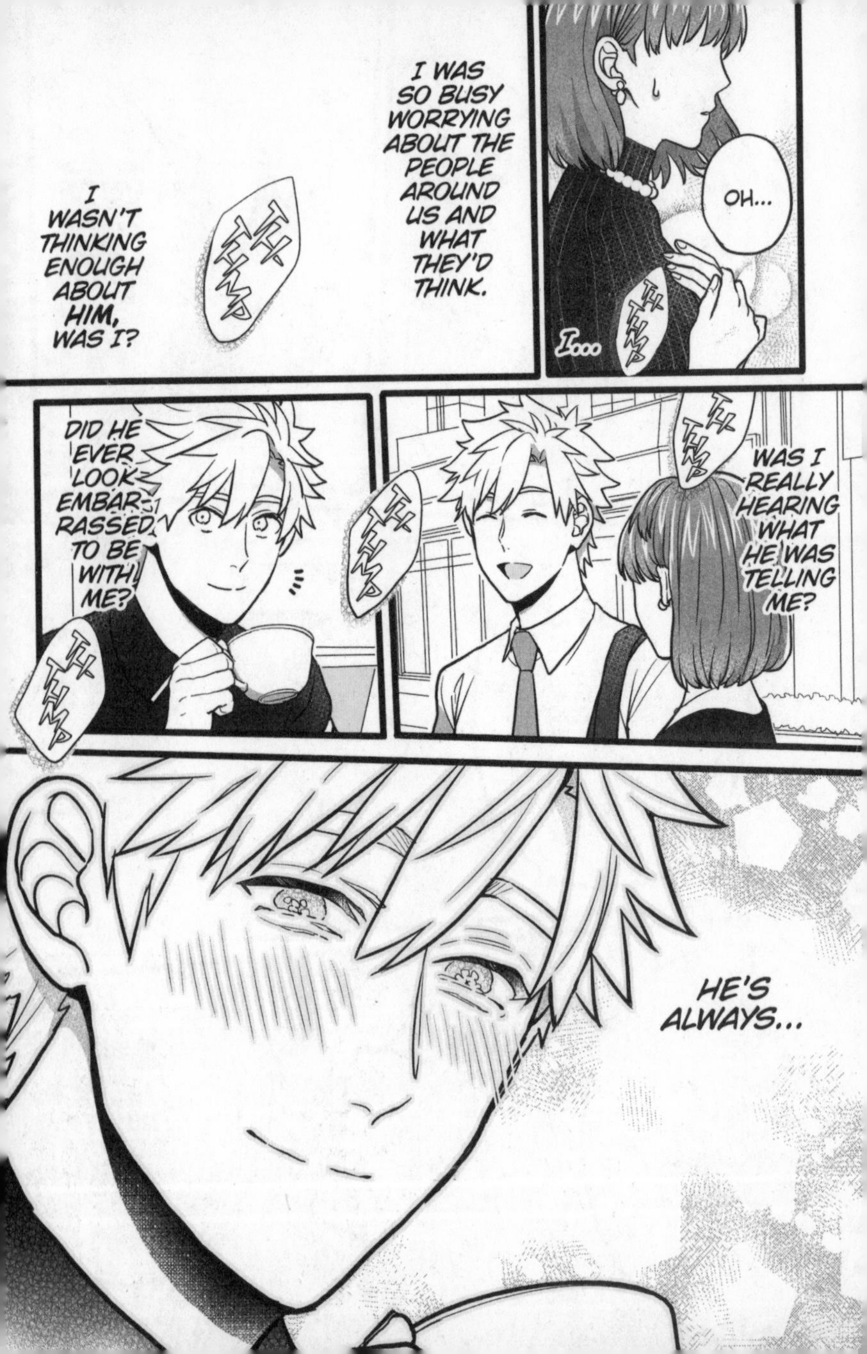
OH...
TH-THMP
I...
I WAS SO BUSY WORRYING ABOUT THE PEOPLE AROUND US AND WHAT THEY'D THINK.
TH-THMP
I WASN'T THINKING ENOUGH ABOUT HIM, WAS I?
TH-THMP
WAS I REALLY HEARING WHAT HE WAS TELLING ME?
TH-THMP
DID HE EVER LOOK EMBARRASSED TO BE WITH ME?
TH-THMP
HE'S ALWAYS...

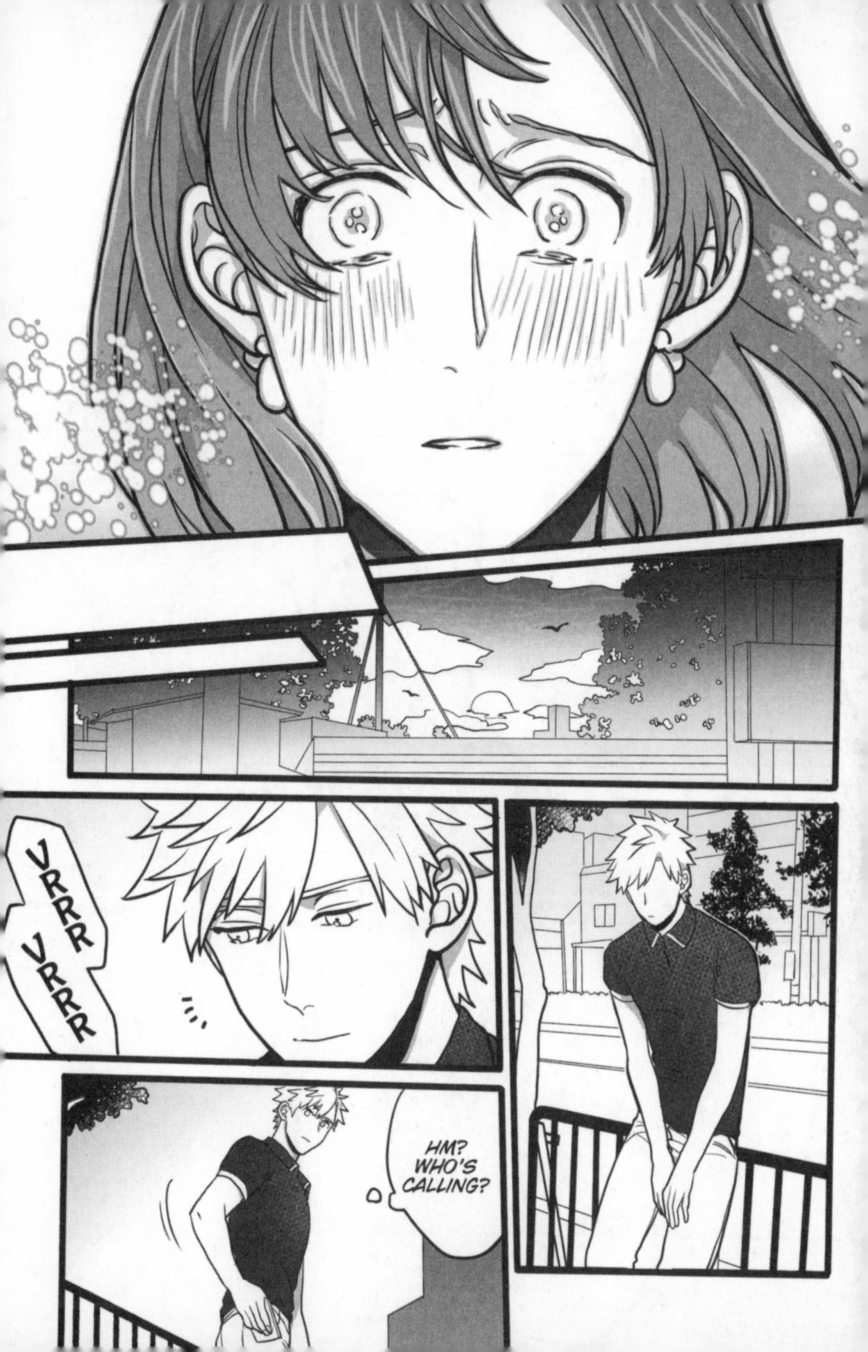
VRRR VRRR
HM? WHO'S CALLING?

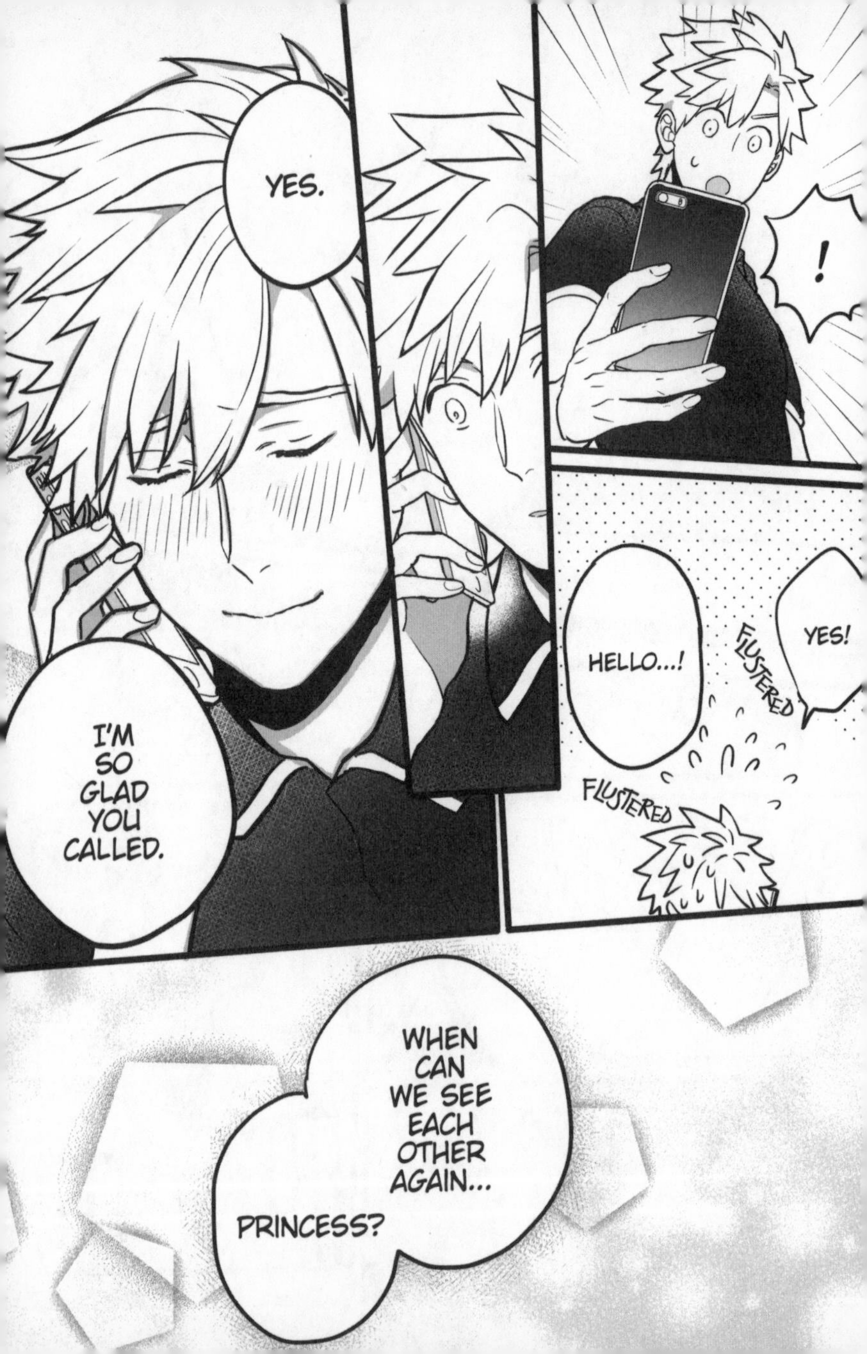
!
YES!
FLUSTERED
HELLO...!
FLUSTERED
YES.
I'M SO GLAD YOU CALLED.
WHEN CAN WE SEE EACH OTHER AGAIN... PRINCESS?

We Swore to
Meet in the Next Life
and That's When
Things Got
Weird!

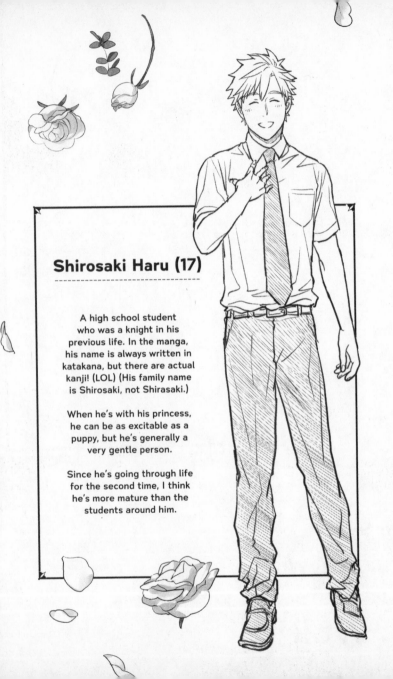

Shirosaki Haru (17)

A high school student who was a knight in his previous life. In the manga, his name is always written in katakana, but there are actual kanji! (LOL) (His family name is Shirosaki, not Shirasaki.)

When he's with his princess, he can be as excitable as a puppy, but he's generally a very gentle person.

Since he's going through life for the second time, I think he's more mature than the students around him.

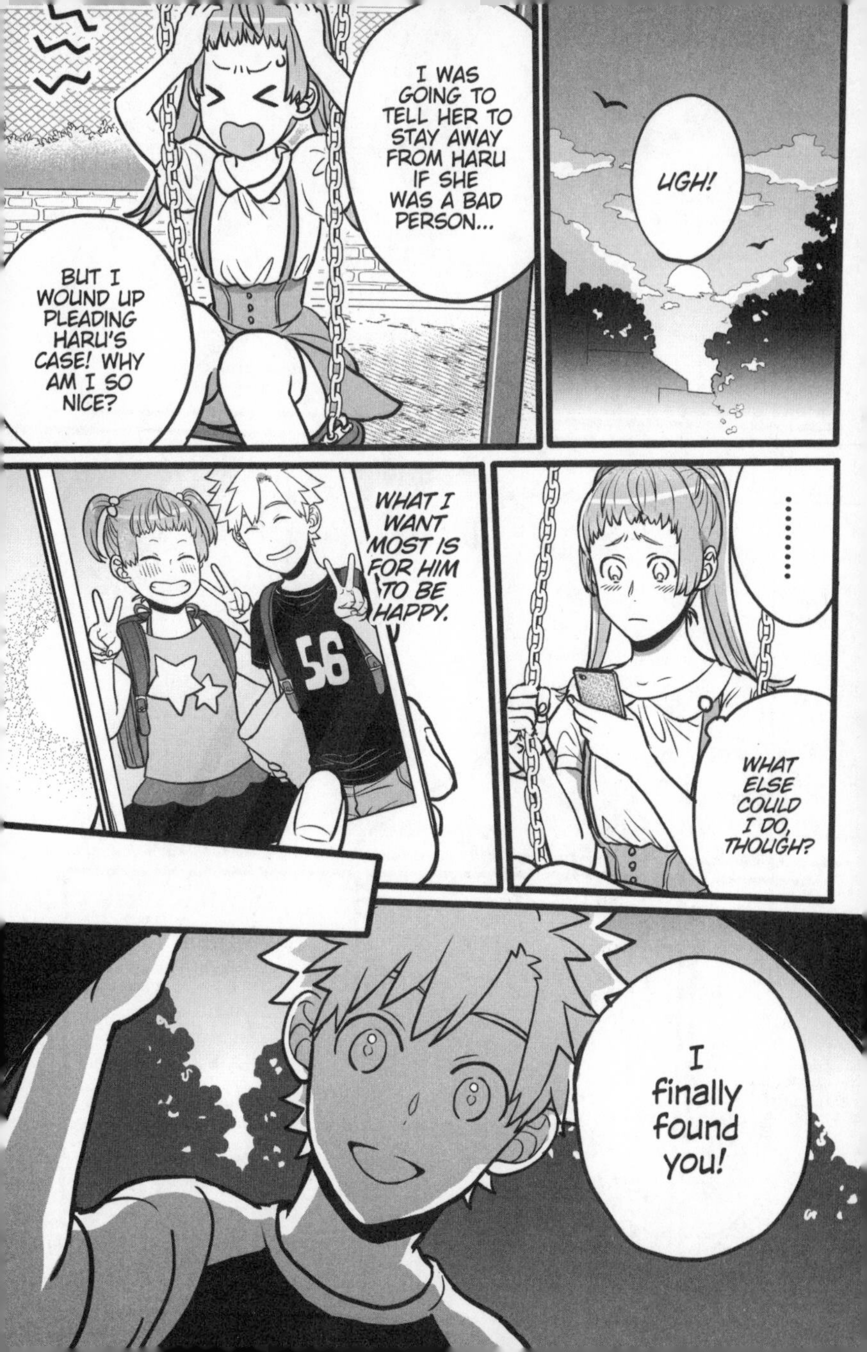
UGH!
I WAS GOING TO TELL HER TO STAY AWAY FROM HARU IF SHE WAS A BAD PERSON...
BUT I WOUND UP PLEADING HARU'S CASE! WHY AM I SO NICE?
....
WHAT ELSE COULD I DO, THOUGH?
WHAT I WANT MOST IS FOR HIM TO BE HAPPY.
I finally found you!

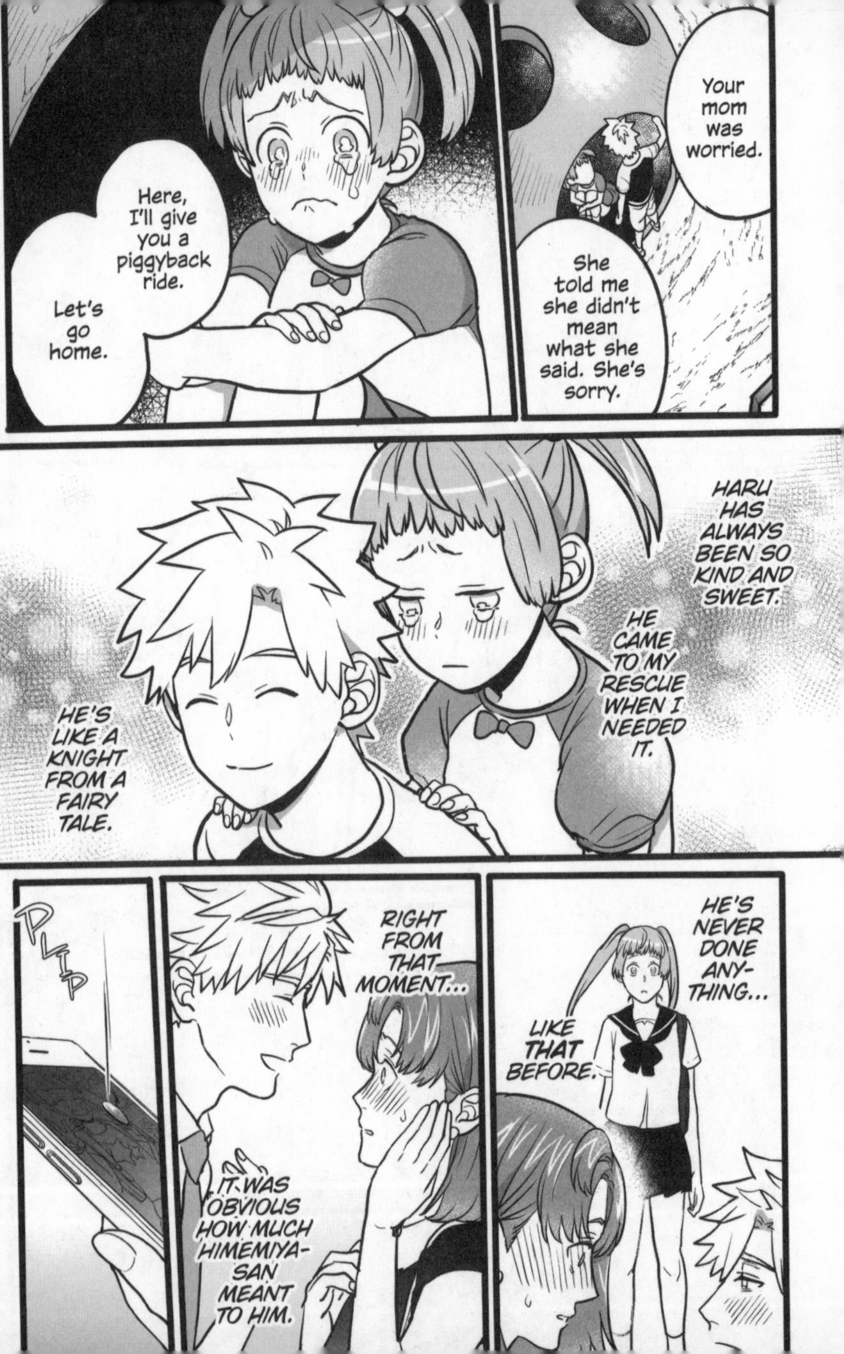
Your mom was worried.
She told me she didn't mean what she said. She's sorry.
Here, I'll give you a piggyback ride.
Let's go home.
HARU HAS ALWAYS BEEN SO KIND AND SWEET.
HE CAME TO MY RESCUE WHEN I NEEDED IT.
HE'S LIKE A KNIGHT FROM A FAIRY TALE.
HE'S NEVER DONE ANY-THING...
LIKE THAT BEFORE.
RIGHT FROM THAT MOMENT...
IT WAS OBVIOUS HOW MUCH HIMEMIYA-SAN MEANT TO HIM.
PLIP

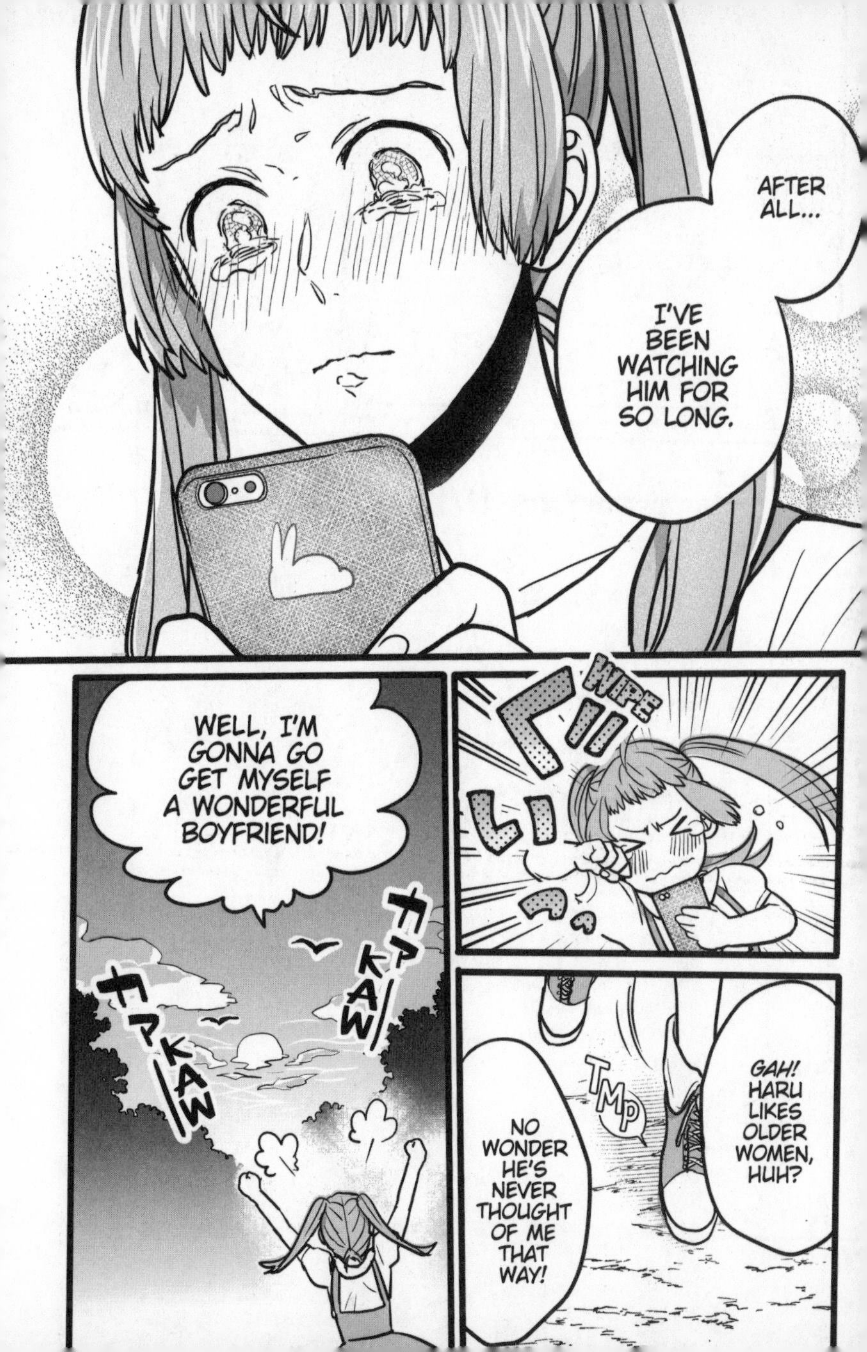
AFTER ALL...
I'VE BEEN WATCHING HIM FOR SO LONG.
WIPE
GAH! HARU LIKES OLDER WOMEN, HUH?
TMP
NO WONDER HE'S NEVER THOUGHT OF ME THAT WAY!
WELL, I'M GONNA GO GET MYSELF A WONDERFUL BOYFRIEND!
KAW
KAW

Hanai Komomo (17)

Haru's classmate and childhood friend. She's been in love with him since she was young, but he's never felt that way about her.

In the beginning, I planned to use the kanji for "tree" in [Ko]momo, but I went with the kanji for "heart" instead. I thought it'd seem more trendy and appropriate.

I decided to draw her with twin ponytails to contrast her youth with Yuko's age, but I wish now that I'd drawn cuter clothes to match that.

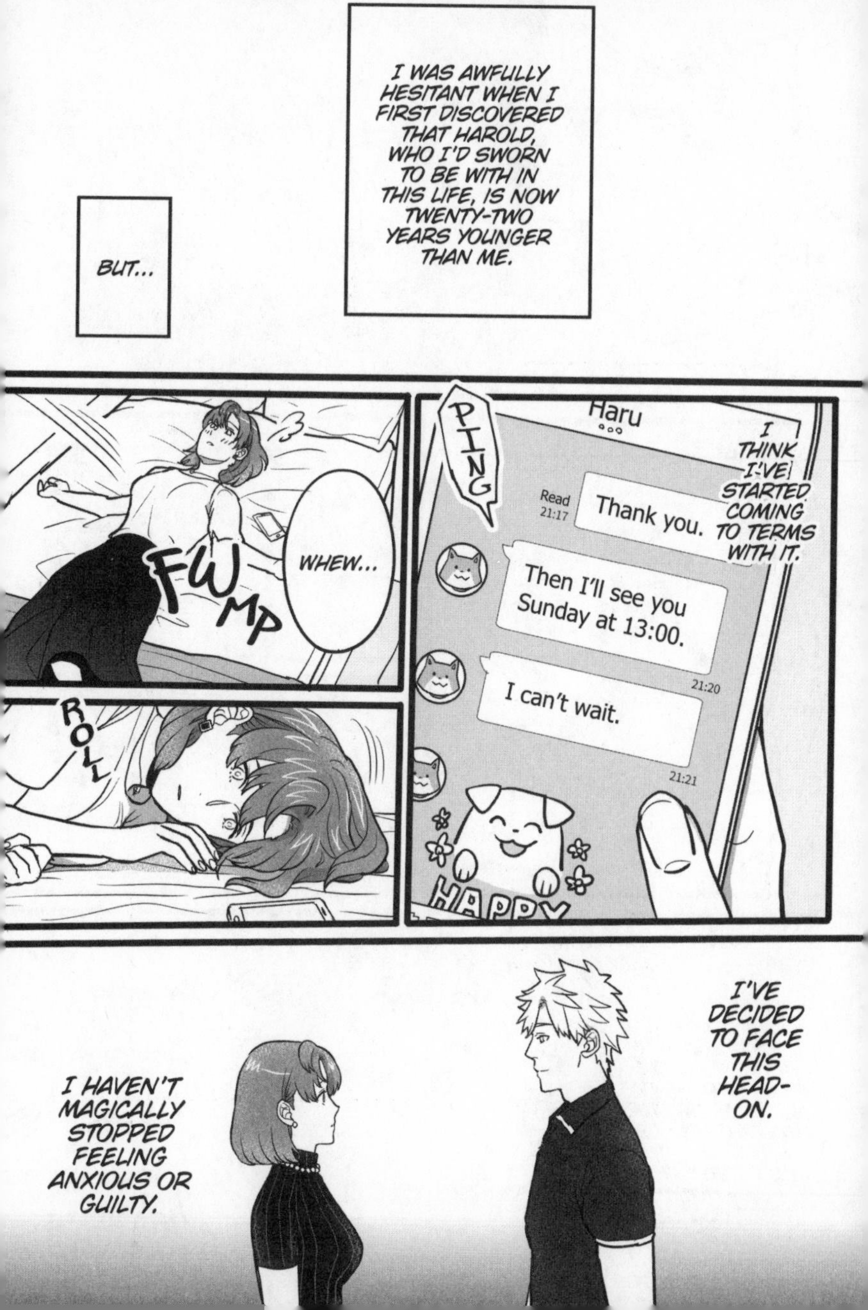
I WAS AWFULLY HESITANT WHEN I FIRST DISCOVERED THAT HAROLD, WHO I'D SWORN TO BE WITH IN THIS LIFE, IS NOW TWENTY-TWO YEARS YOUNGER THAN ME.
BUT...
I THINK I'VE STARTED COMING TO TERMS WITH IT.
PING
Haru
Read 21:17
Thank you.
Then I'll see you Sunday at 13:00.
21:20
I can't wait.
21:21
HAPPY
WHEW...
FWUMP
ROLL
I'VE DECIDED TO FACE THIS HEAD-ON.
I HAVEN'T MAGICALLY STOPPED FEELING ANXIOUS OR GUILTY.

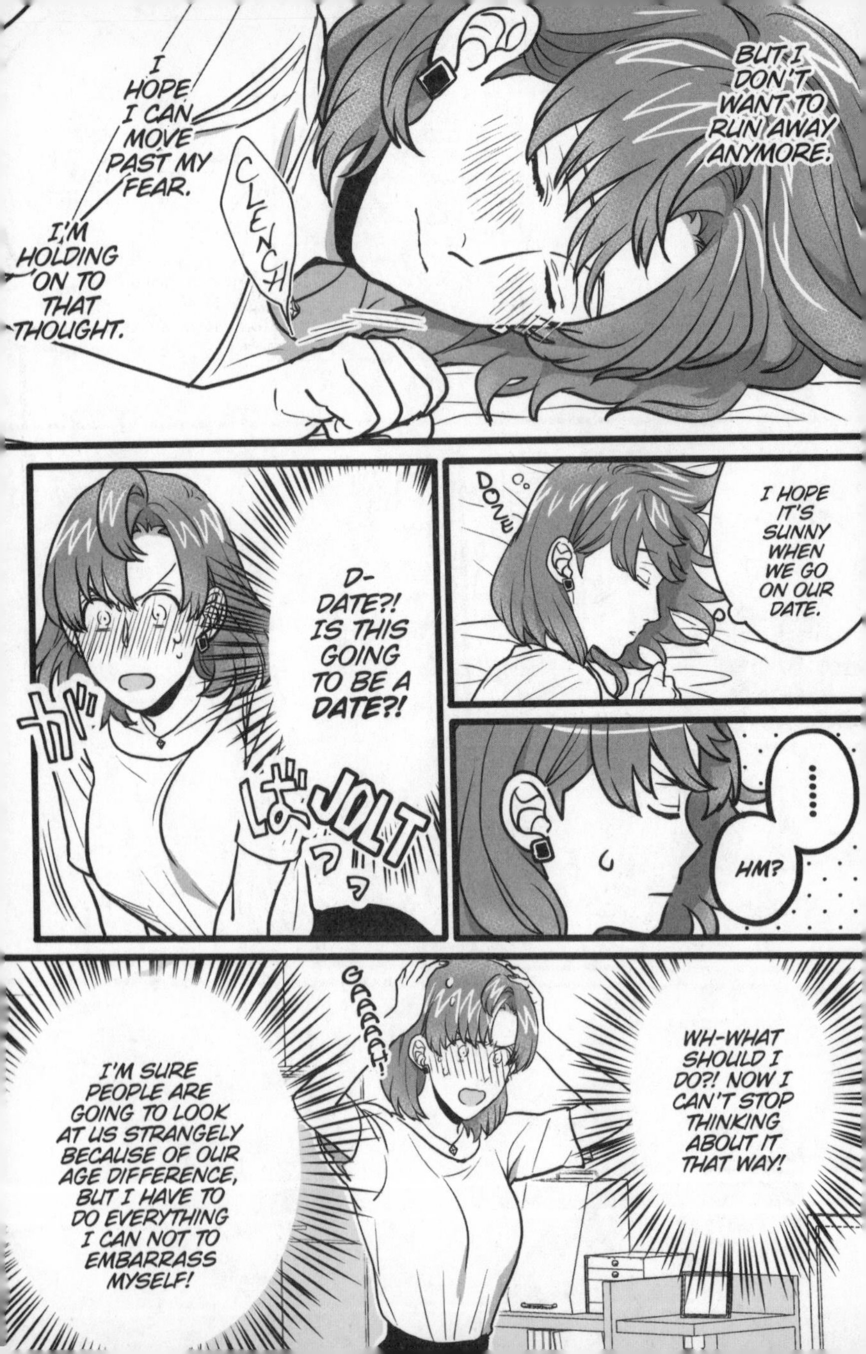
BUT I DON'T WANT TO RUN AWAY ANYMORE.
I HOPE I CAN MOVE PAST MY FEAR.
CLENCH
I'M HOLDING ON TO THAT THOUGHT.
DOZE
I HOPE IT'S SUNNY WHEN WE GO ON OUR DATE.
......
HM?
D-DATE?! IS THIS GOING TO BE A DATE?!
JOLT
WH-WHAT SHOULD I DO?! NOW I CAN'T STOP THINKING ABOUT IT THAT WAY!
I'M SURE PEOPLE ARE GOING TO LOOK AT US STRANGELY BECAUSE OF OUR AGE DIFFERENCE, BUT I HAVE TO DO EVERYTHING I CAN NOT TO EMBARRASS MYSELF!

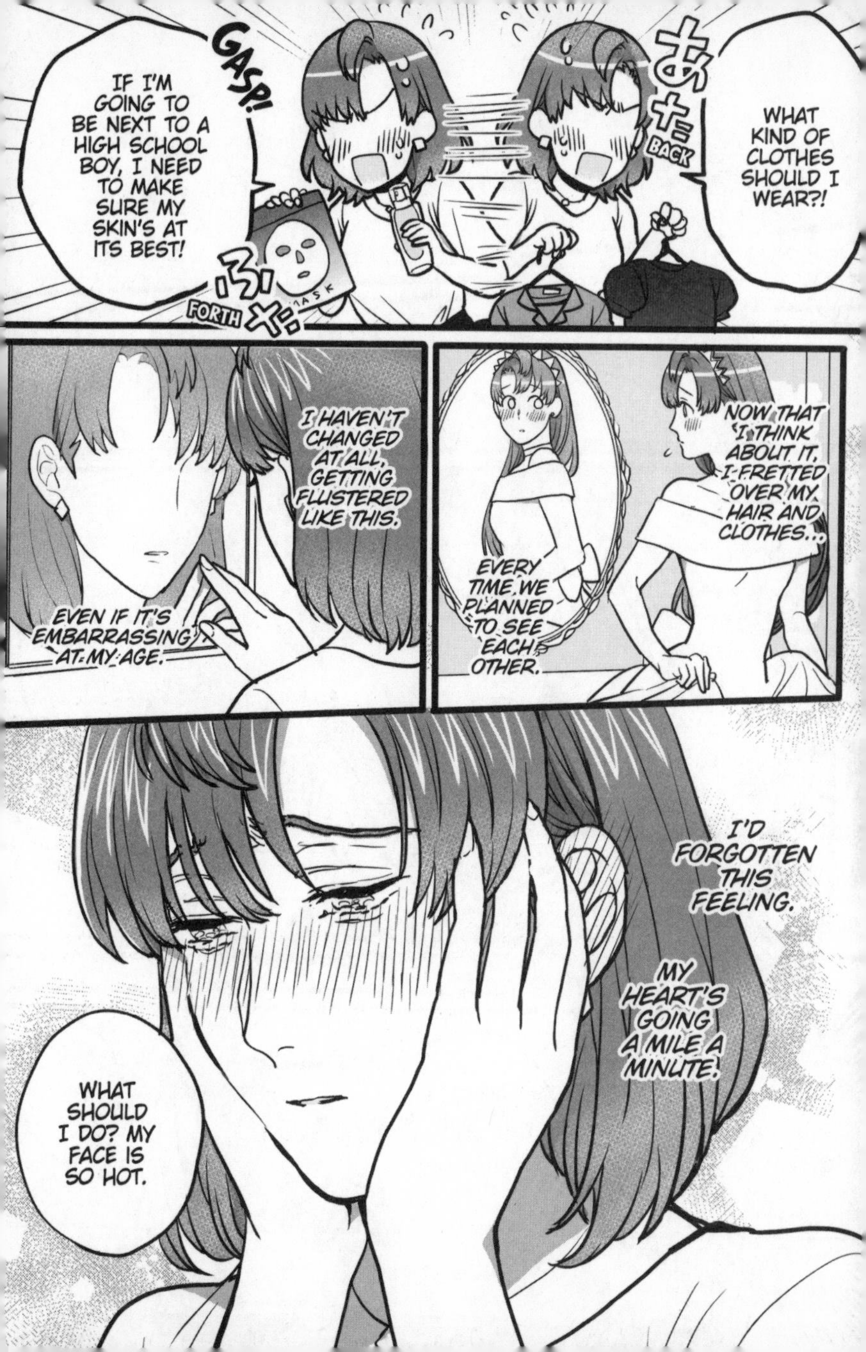
WHAT KIND OF CLOTHES SHOULD I WEAR?!
BACK
GASP!
IF I'M GOING TO BE NEXT TO A HIGH SCHOOL BOY, I NEED TO MAKE SURE MY SKIN'S AT ITS BEST!
MASK
FORTH
NOW THAT I THINK ABOUT IT, I FRETTED OVER MY HAIR AND CLOTHES...
EVERY TIME WE PLANNED TO SEE EACH OTHER.
I HAVEN'T CHANGED AT ALL, GETTING FLUSTERED LIKE THIS.
EVEN IF IT'S EMBARRASSING AT MY AGE.
I'D FORGOTTEN THIS FEELING.
MY HEART'S GOING A MILE A MINUTE.
WHAT SHOULD I DO? MY FACE IS SO HOT.

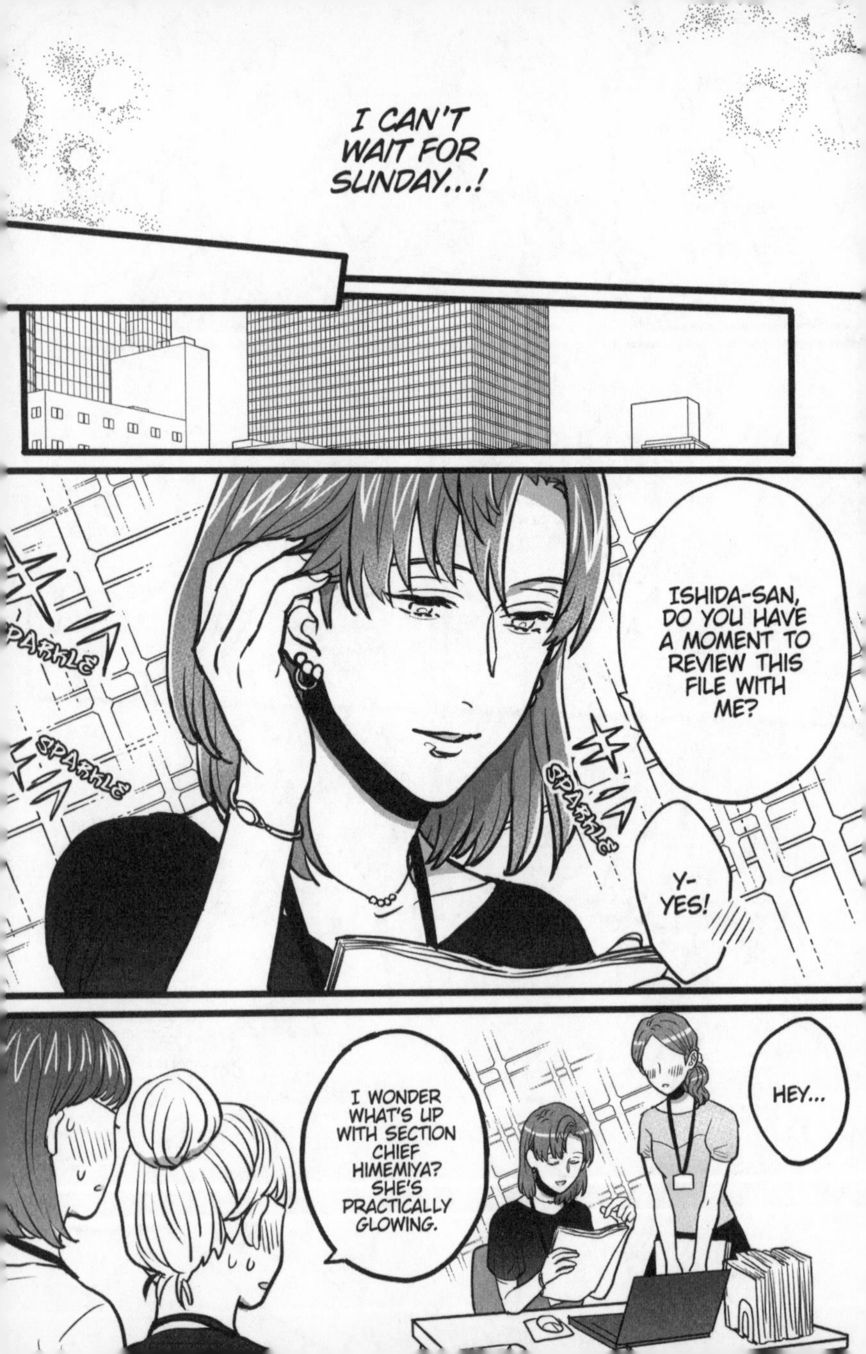
I CAN'T WAIT FOR SUNDAY...!
ISHIDA-SAN, DO YOU HAVE A MOMENT TO REVIEW THIS FILE WITH ME?
Y- YES!
SPARKLE
SPARKLE
SPARKLE
HEY...
I WONDER WHAT'S UP WITH SECTION CHIEF HIMEMIYA? SHE'S PRACTICALLY GLOWING.

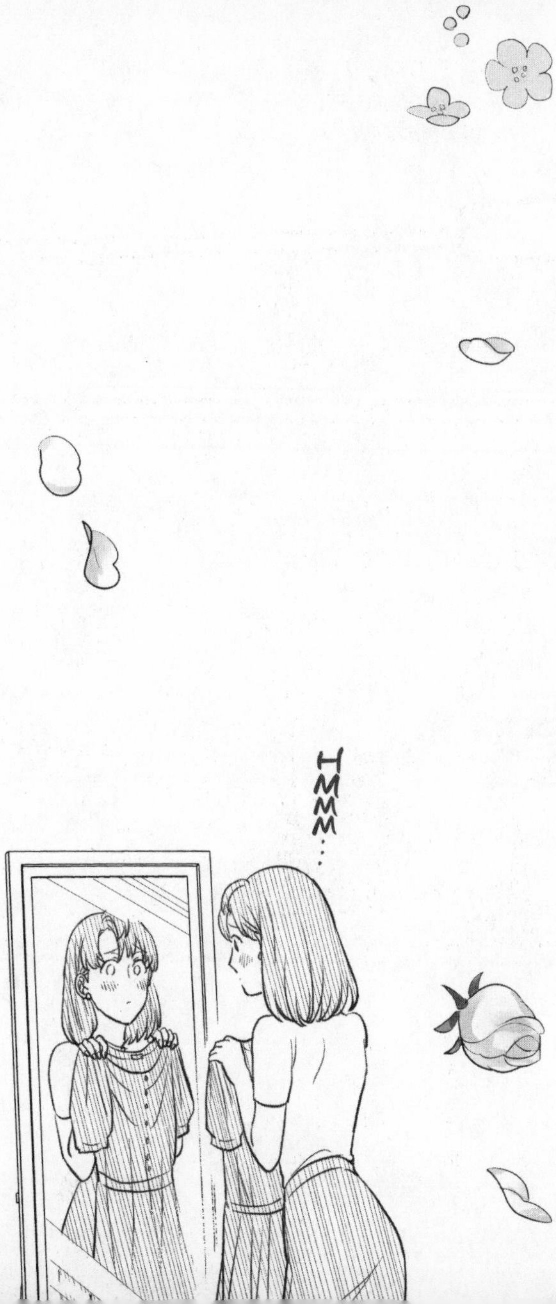
HMMM...

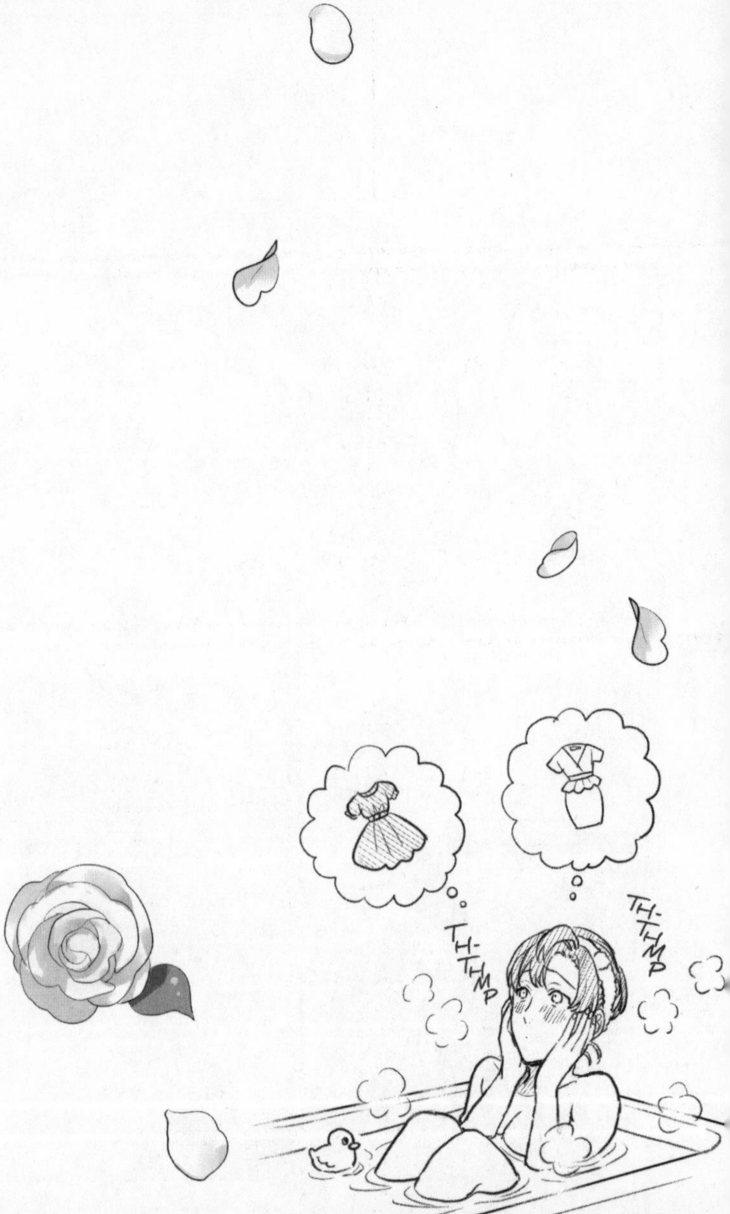
TH-THMP
TH-THMP

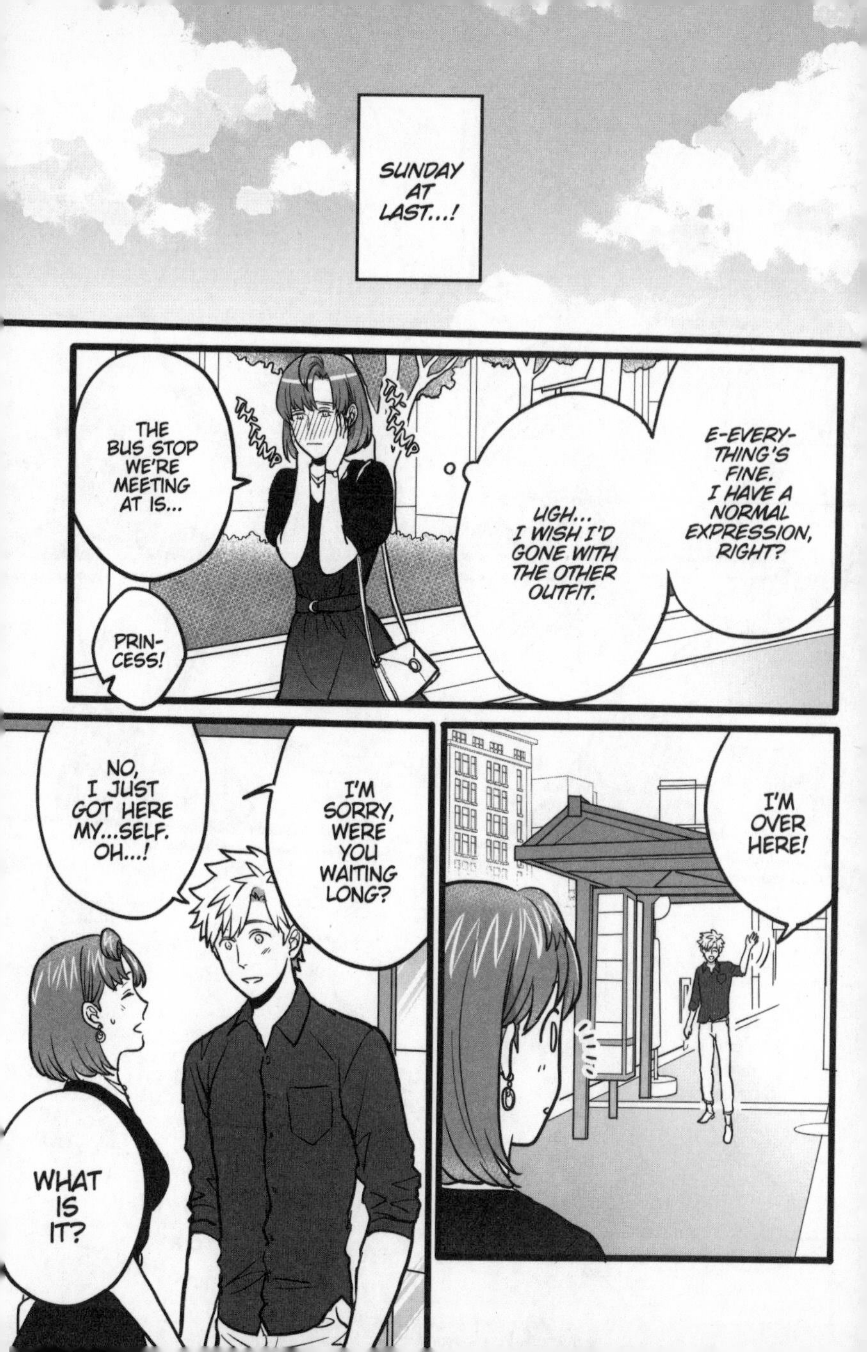
SUNDAY AT LAST...!
THE BUS STOP WE'RE MEETING AT IS...
TH-THMP
TH-THMP
E-EVERY-THING'S FINE. I HAVE A NORMAL EXPRESSION, RIGHT?
UGH... I WISH I'D GONE WITH THE OTHER OUTFIT.
PRIN-CESS!
I'M OVER HERE!
I'M SORRY, WERE YOU WAITING LONG?
NO, I JUST GOT HERE MY...SELF. OH...!
WHAT IS IT?

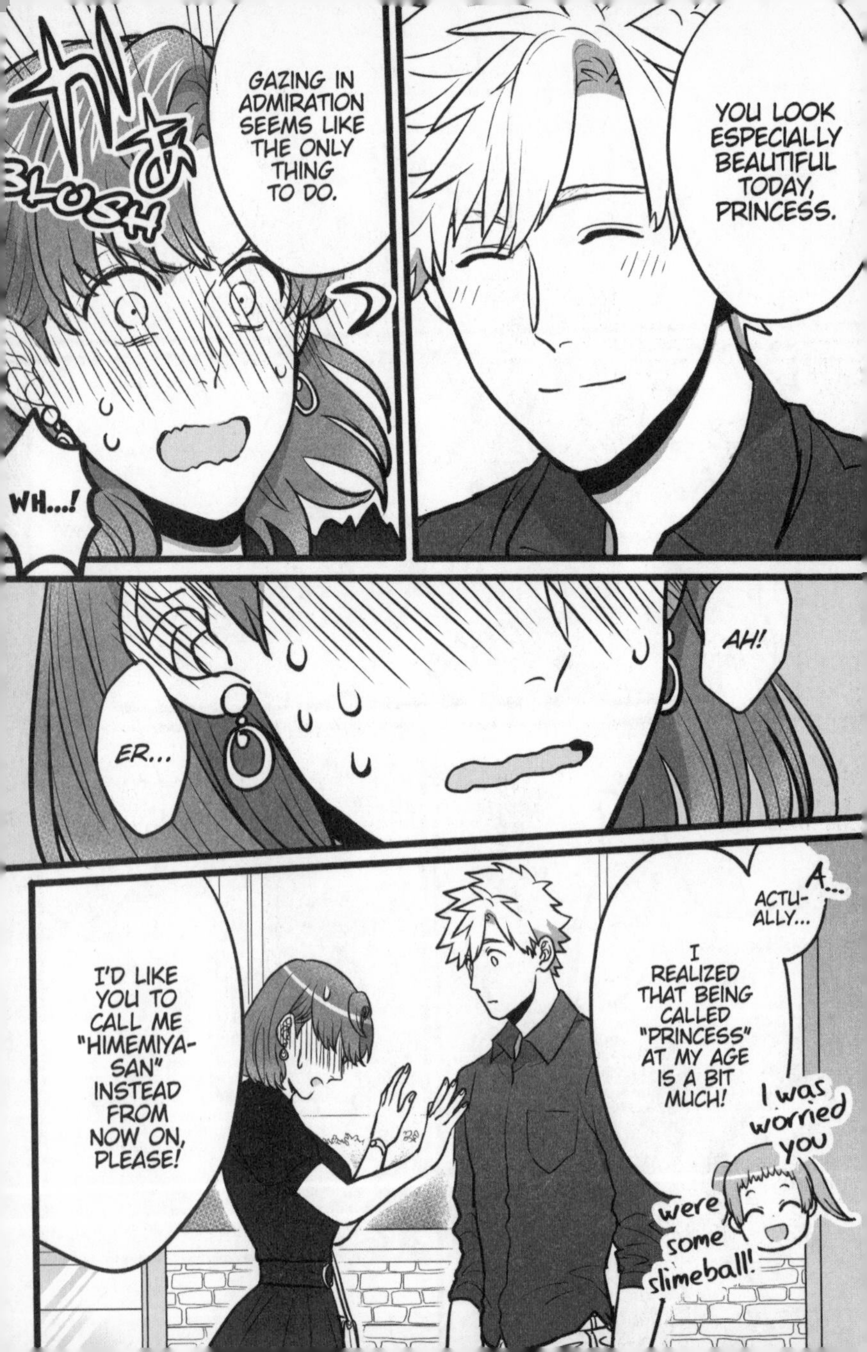
YOU LOOK ESPECIALLY BEAUTIFUL TODAY, PRINCESS.
GAZING IN ADMIRATION SEEMS LIKE THE ONLY THING TO DO.
BLUSH
WH...!
AH!
ER...
A... ACTU-ALLY...
I REALIZED THAT BEING CALLED "PRINCESS" AT MY AGE IS A BIT MUCH!
I'D LIKE YOU TO CALL ME "HIMEMIYA-SAN" INSTEAD FROM NOW ON, PLEASE!
I was worried you were some slimeball!

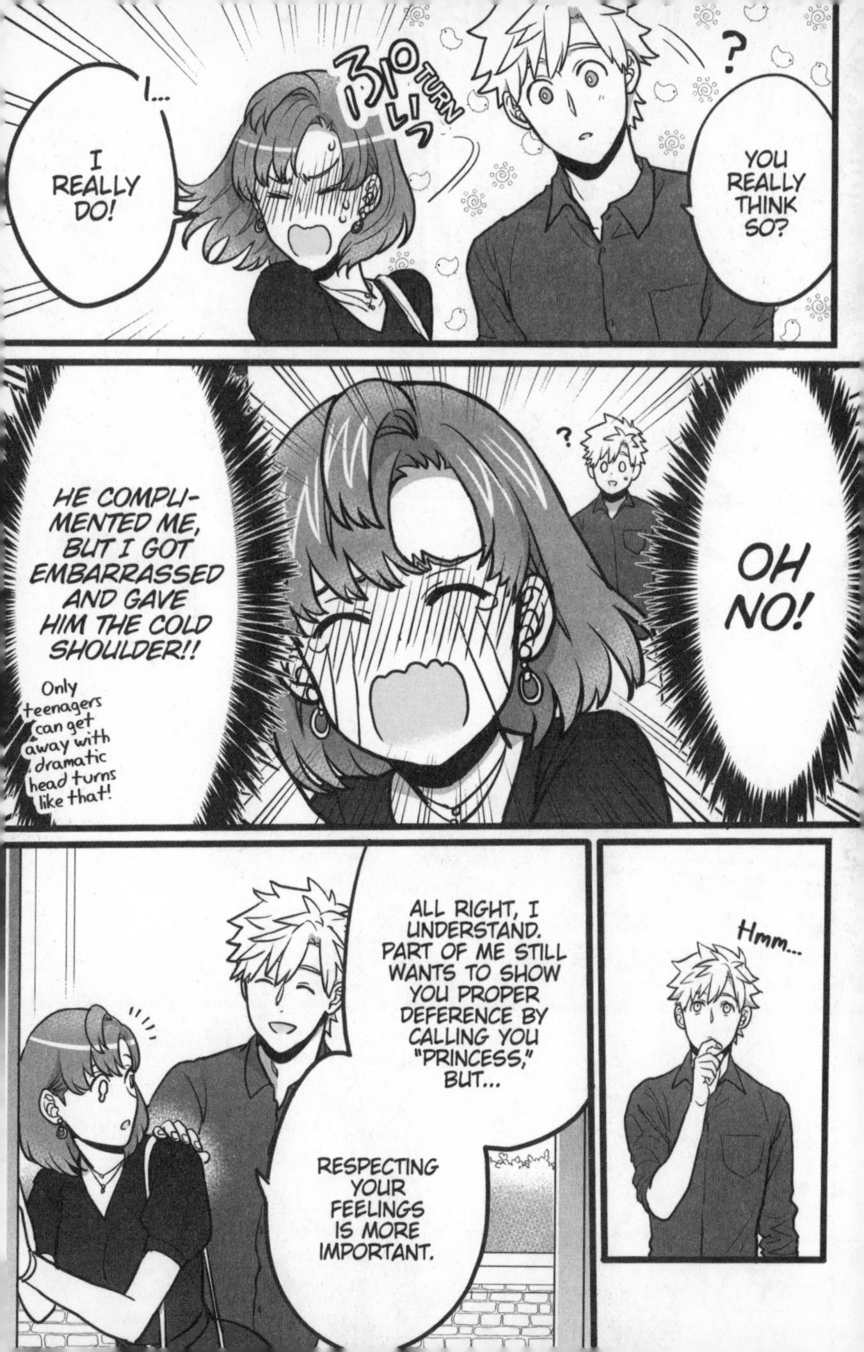
YOU REALLY THINK SO?
TURN
I...
I REALLY DO!
OH NO!
HE COMPLI-MENTED ME, BUT I GOT EMBARRASSED AND GAVE HIM THE COLD SHOULDER!!
Only teenagers can get away with dramatic head turns like that!
Hmm...
ALL RIGHT, I UNDERSTAND. PART OF ME STILL WANTS TO SHOW YOU PROPER DEFERENCE BY CALLING YOU "PRINCESS," BUT...
RESPECTING YOUR FEELINGS IS MORE IMPORTANT.

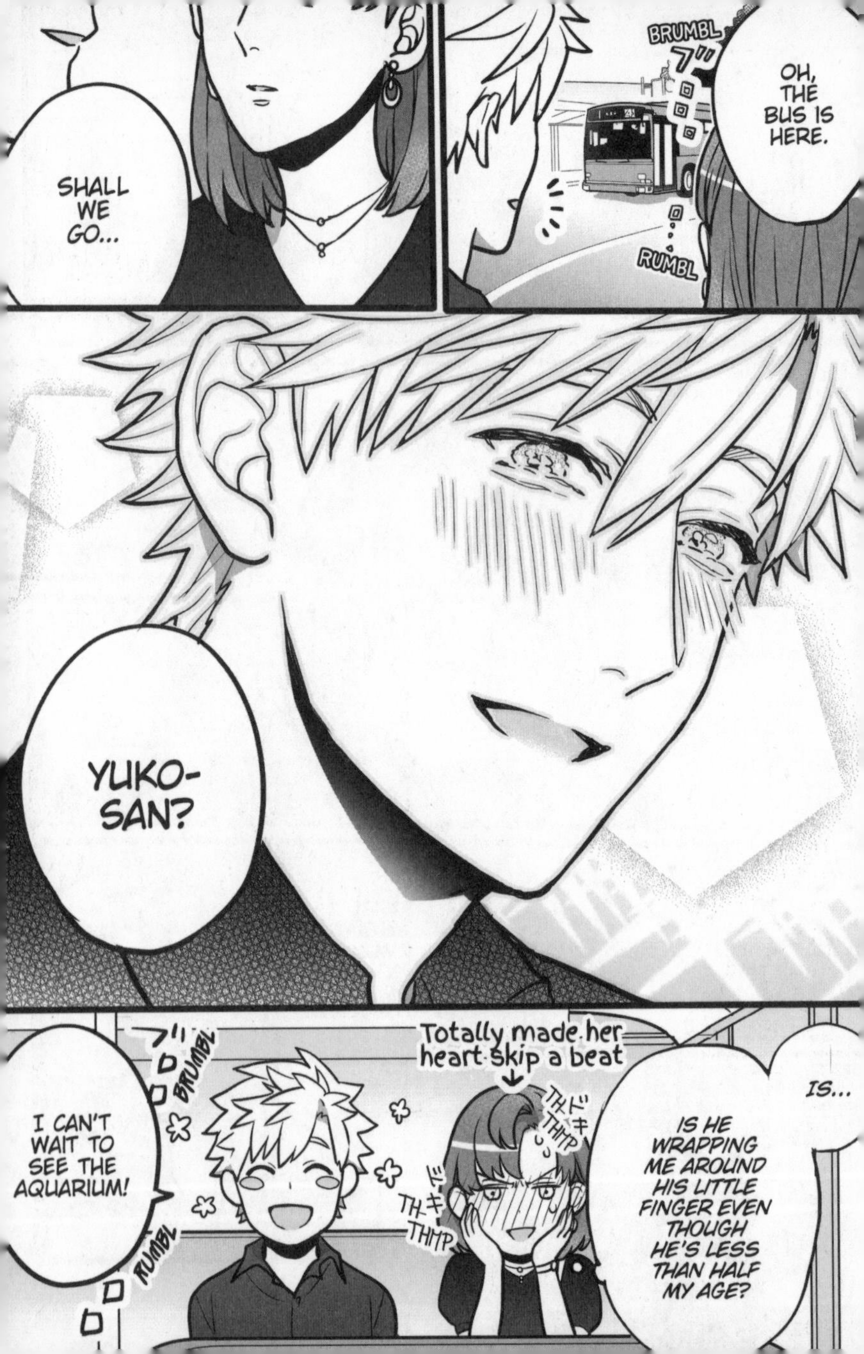
BRUMBL
OH, THE BUS IS HERE.
RUMBL
SHALL WE GO...
YUKO-SAN?
IS...
IS HE WRAPPING ME AROUND HIS LITTLE FINGER EVEN THOUGH HE'S LESS THAN HALF MY AGE?
Totally made her heart skip a beat
THMP THMP
THMP THMP
I CAN'T WAIT TO SEE THE AQUARIUM!
BRUMBL
RUMBL

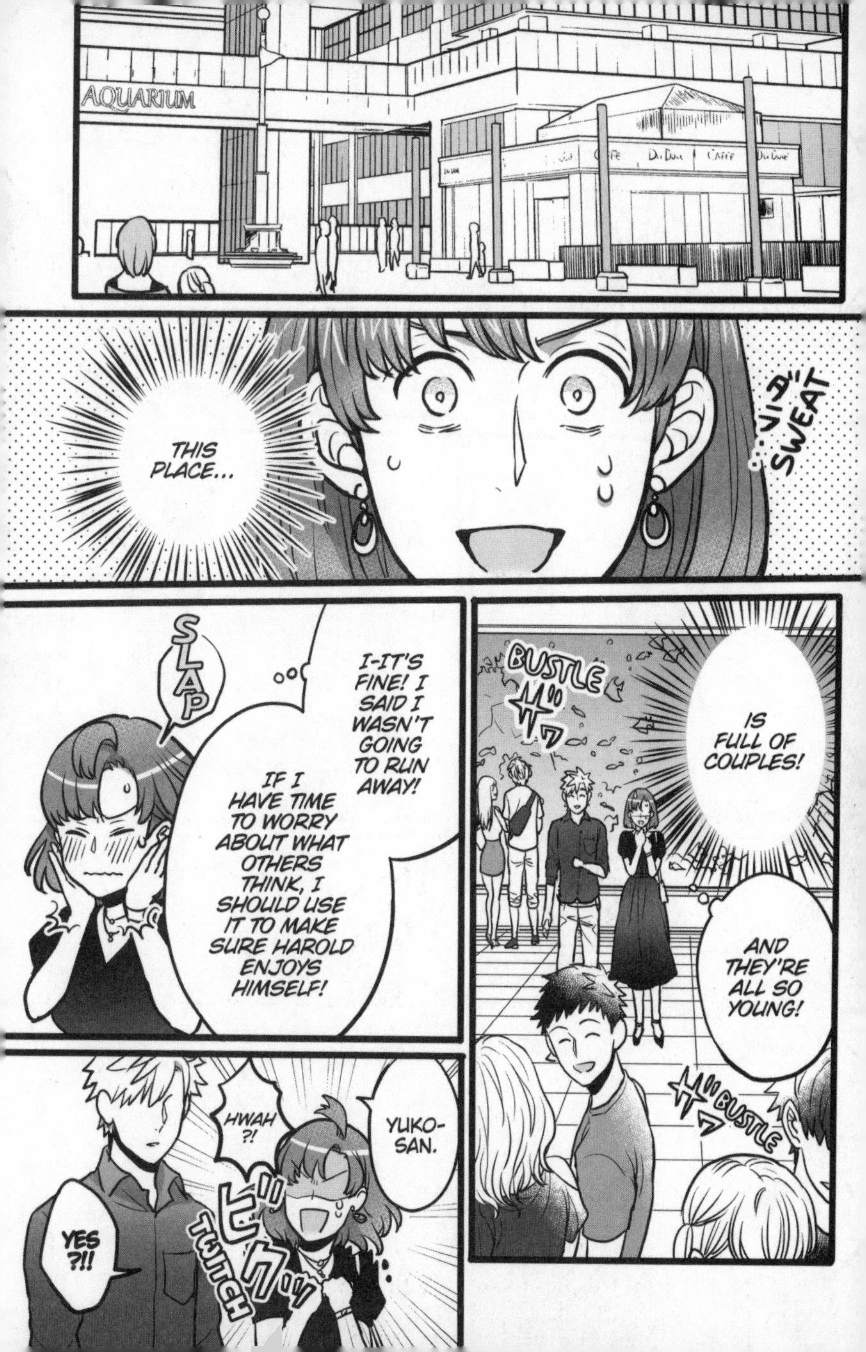
AQUARIUM
THIS PLACE...
SWEAT
IS FULL OF COUPLES!
BUSTLE
AND THEY'RE ALL SO YOUNG!
BUSTLE
SLAP
I-IT'S FINE! I SAID I WASN'T GOING TO RUN AWAY!
IF I HAVE TIME TO WORRY ABOUT WHAT OTHERS THINK, I SHOULD USE IT TO MAKE SURE HAROLD ENJOYS HIMSELF!
YUKO-SAN.
HWAH ?!
TWITCH
YES ?!!

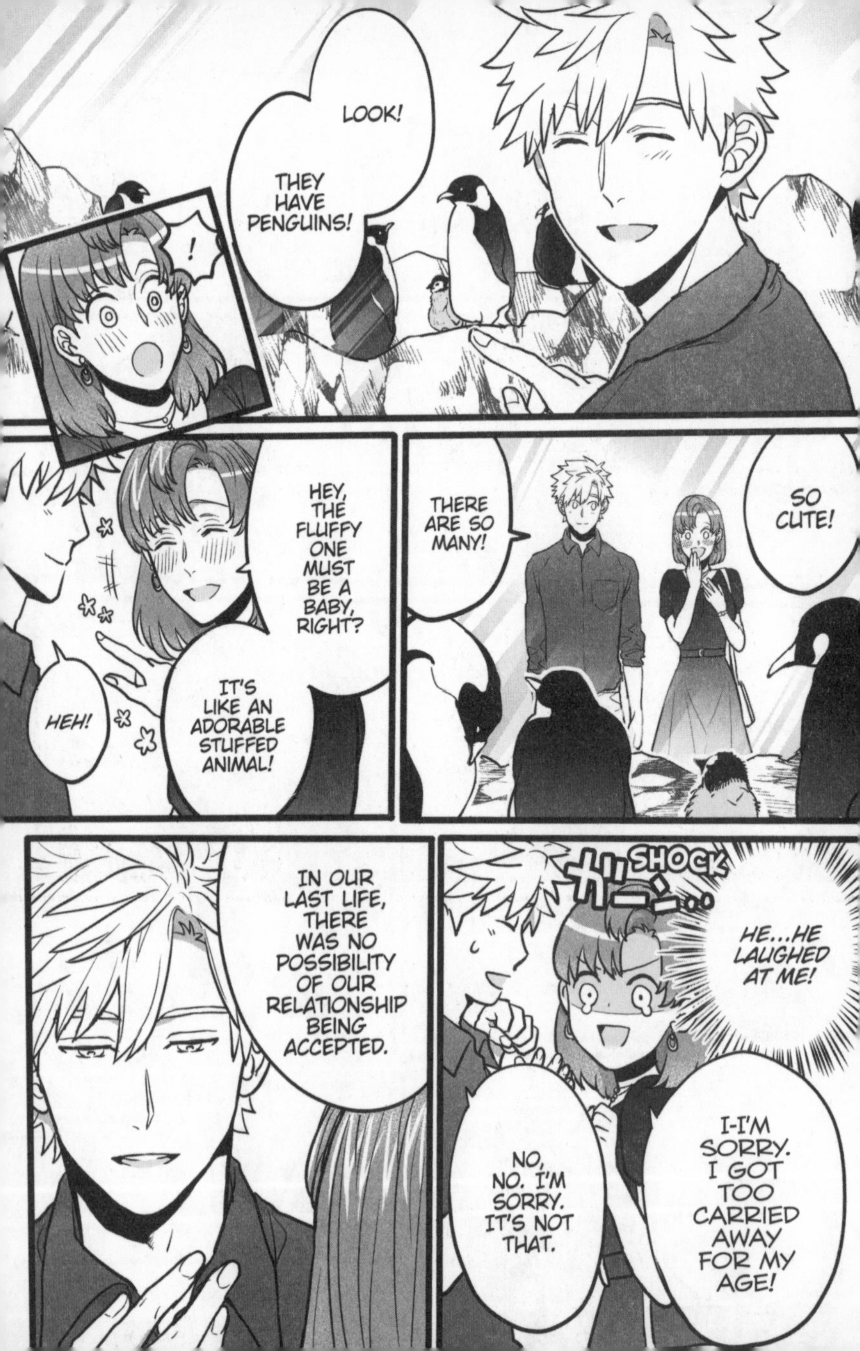
LOOK!
THEY HAVE PENGUINS!
!
SO CUTE!
THERE ARE SO MANY!
HEY, THE FLUFFY ONE MUST BE A BABY, RIGHT?
IT'S LIKE AN ADORABLE STUFFED ANIMAL!
HEH!
SHOCK
HE...HE LAUGHED AT ME!
I-I'M SORRY. I GOT TOO CARRIED AWAY FOR MY AGE!
NO, NO. I'M SORRY. IT'S NOT THAT.
IN OUR LAST LIFE, THERE WAS NO POSSIBILITY OF OUR RELATIONSHIP BEING ACCEPTED.

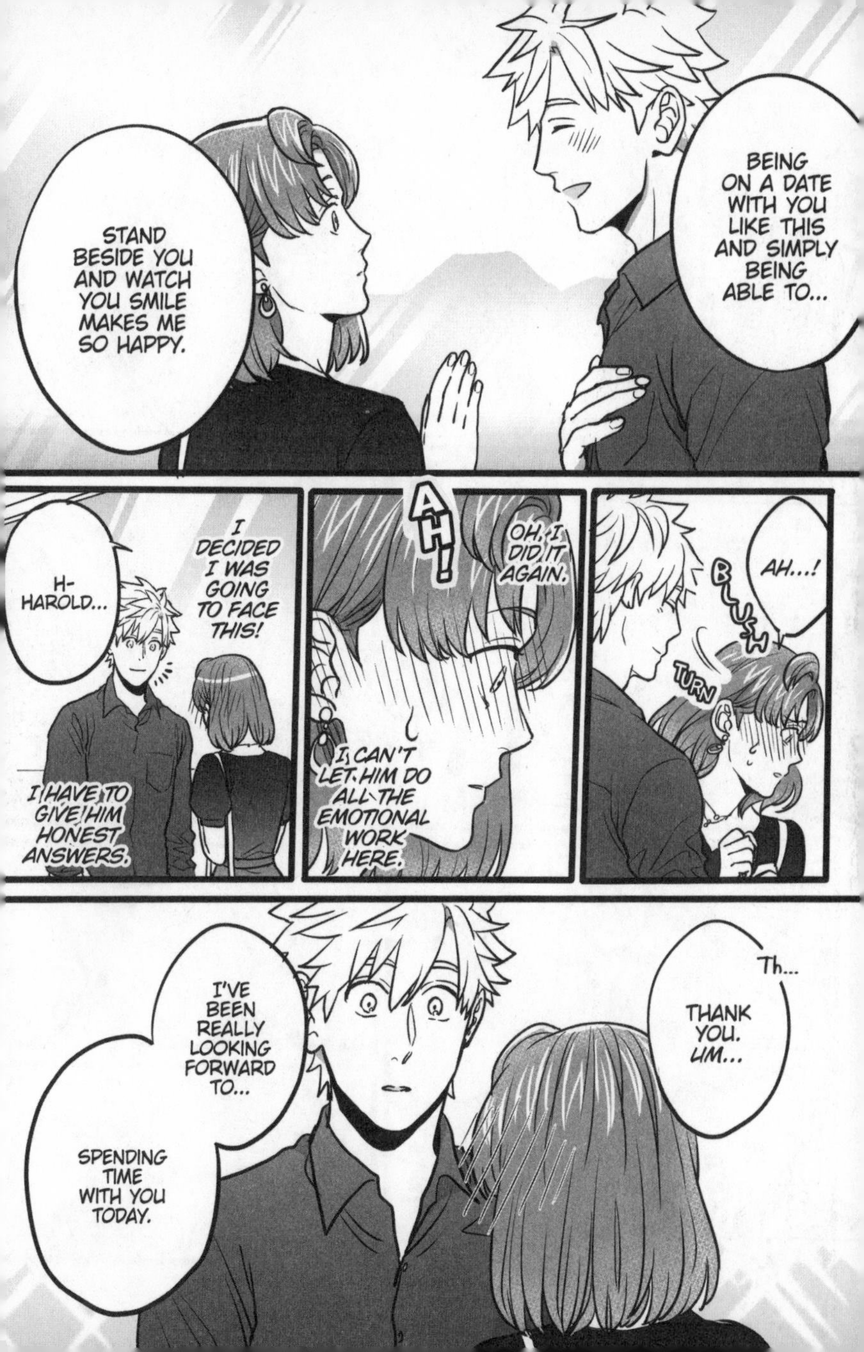
BEING ON A DATE WITH YOU LIKE THIS AND SIMPLY BEING ABLE TO...
STAND BESIDE YOU AND WATCH YOU SMILE MAKES ME SO HAPPY.
AH...!
BLUSH
TURN
AH!
OH, I DID IT AGAIN.
I CAN'T LET HIM DO ALL THE EMOTIONAL WORK HERE.
I DECIDED I WAS GOING TO FACE THIS!
H-HAROLD...
I HAVE TO GIVE HIM HONEST ANSWERS.
Th...
THANK YOU. UM...
I'VE BEEN REALLY LOOKING FORWARD TO...
SPENDING TIME WITH YOU TODAY.

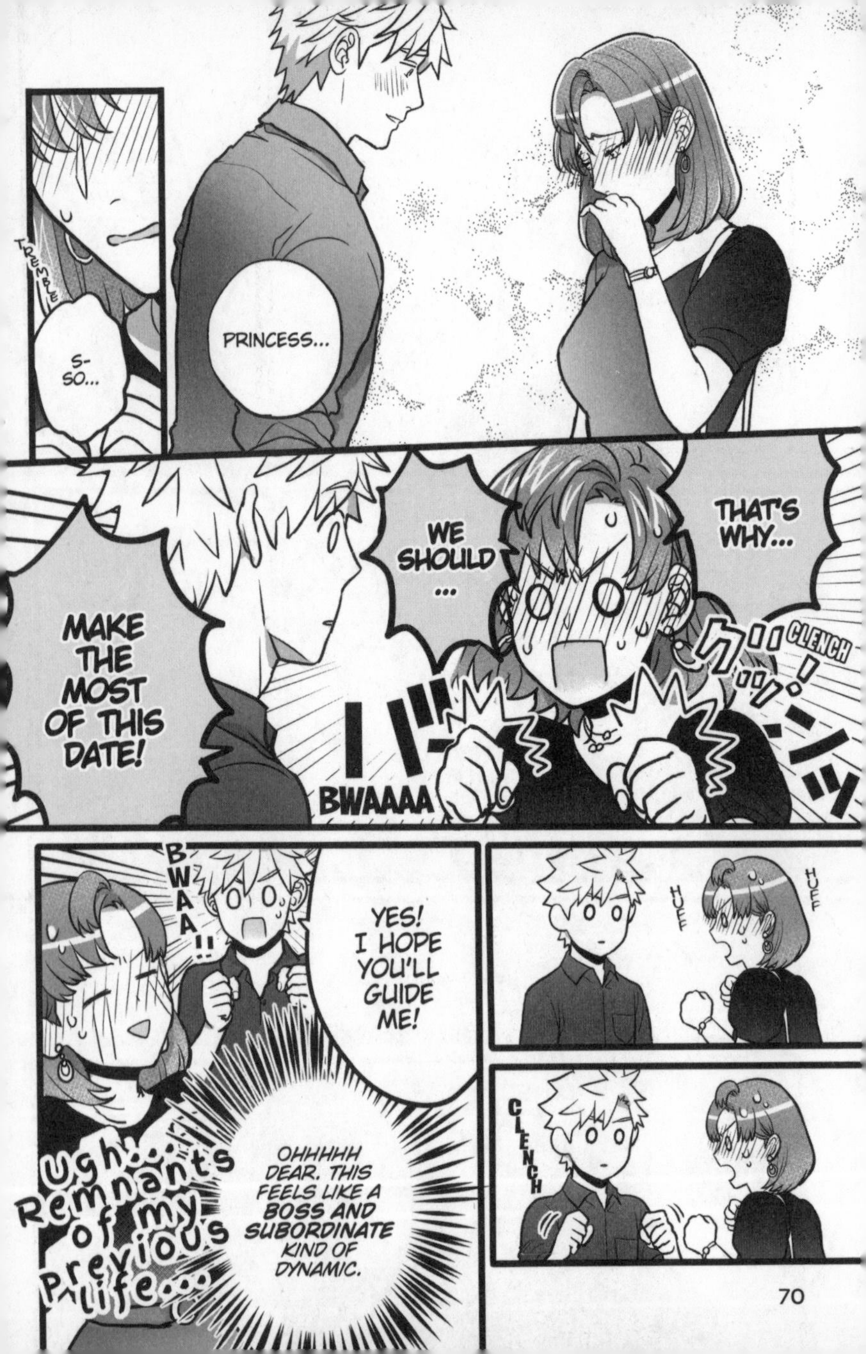
PRINCESS...
TREMBLE
S- SO...
THAT'S WHY...
WE SHOULD ...
CLENCH
MAKE THE MOST OF THIS DATE!
BWAAAA
HUFF
HUFF
CLENCH
YES! I HOPE YOU'LL GUIDE ME!
BWAA!!
OHHHHH DEAR. THIS FEELS LIKE A BOSS AND SUBORDINATE KIND OF DYNAMIC.
Ugh... Remnants of my previous life...

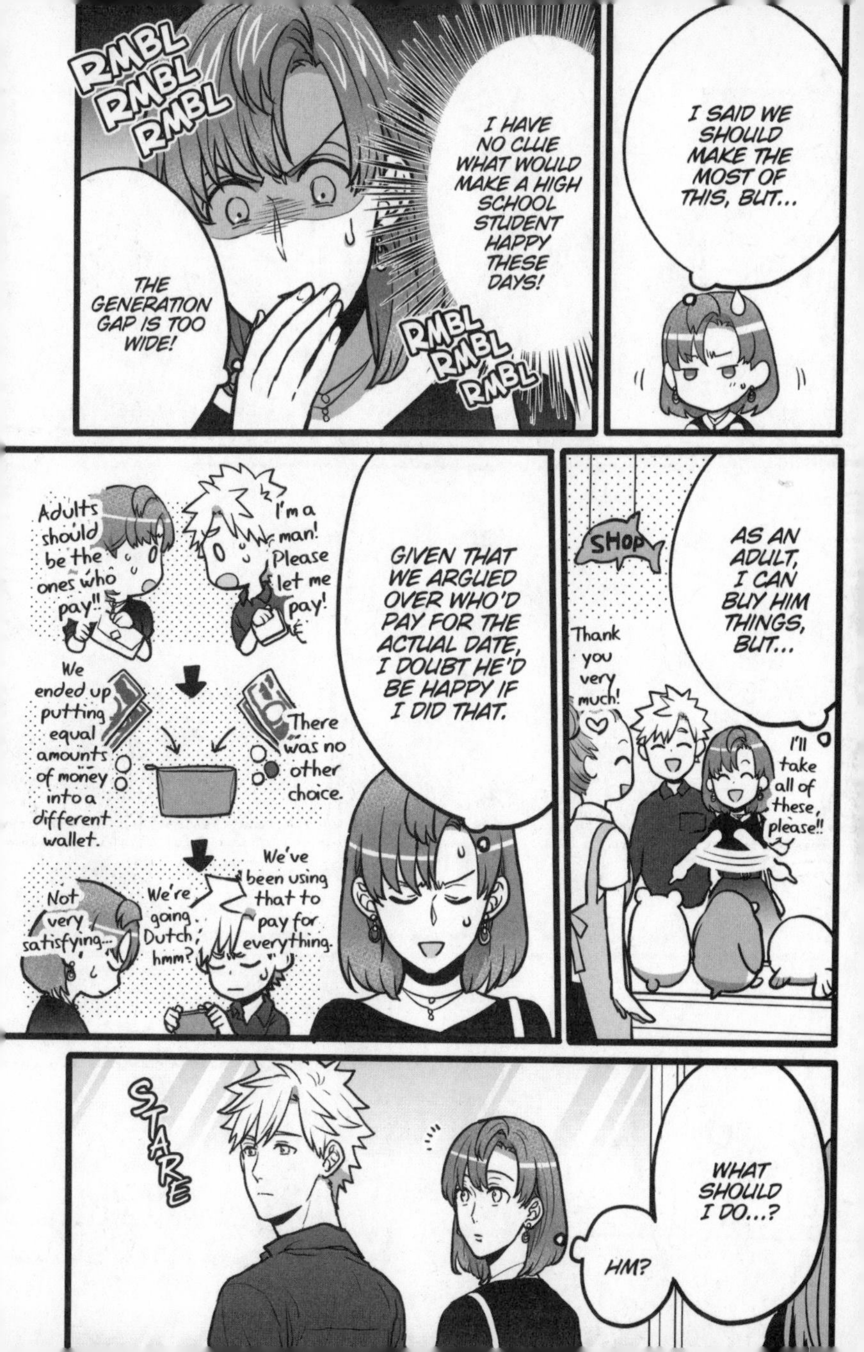
I SAID WE SHOULD MAKE THE MOST OF THIS, BUT...
RMBL RMBL RMBL
I HAVE NO CLUE WHAT WOULD MAKE A HIGH SCHOOL STUDENT HAPPY THESE DAYS!
RMBL RMBL RMBL
THE GENERATION GAP IS TOO WIDE!
AS AN ADULT, I CAN BUY HIM THINGS, BUT...
SHOP
I'll take all of these, please!!
Thank you very much!
GIVEN THAT WE ARGUED OVER WHO'D PAY FOR THE ACTUAL DATE, I DOUBT HE'D BE HAPPY IF I DID THAT.
I'm a man! Please let me pay!
Adults should be the ones who pay!!
There was no other choice.
We ended up putting equal amounts of money into a different wallet.
We've been using that to pay for everything.
We're going Dutch, hmm?
Not very satisfying...
WHAT SHOULD I DO...?
HM?
STARE

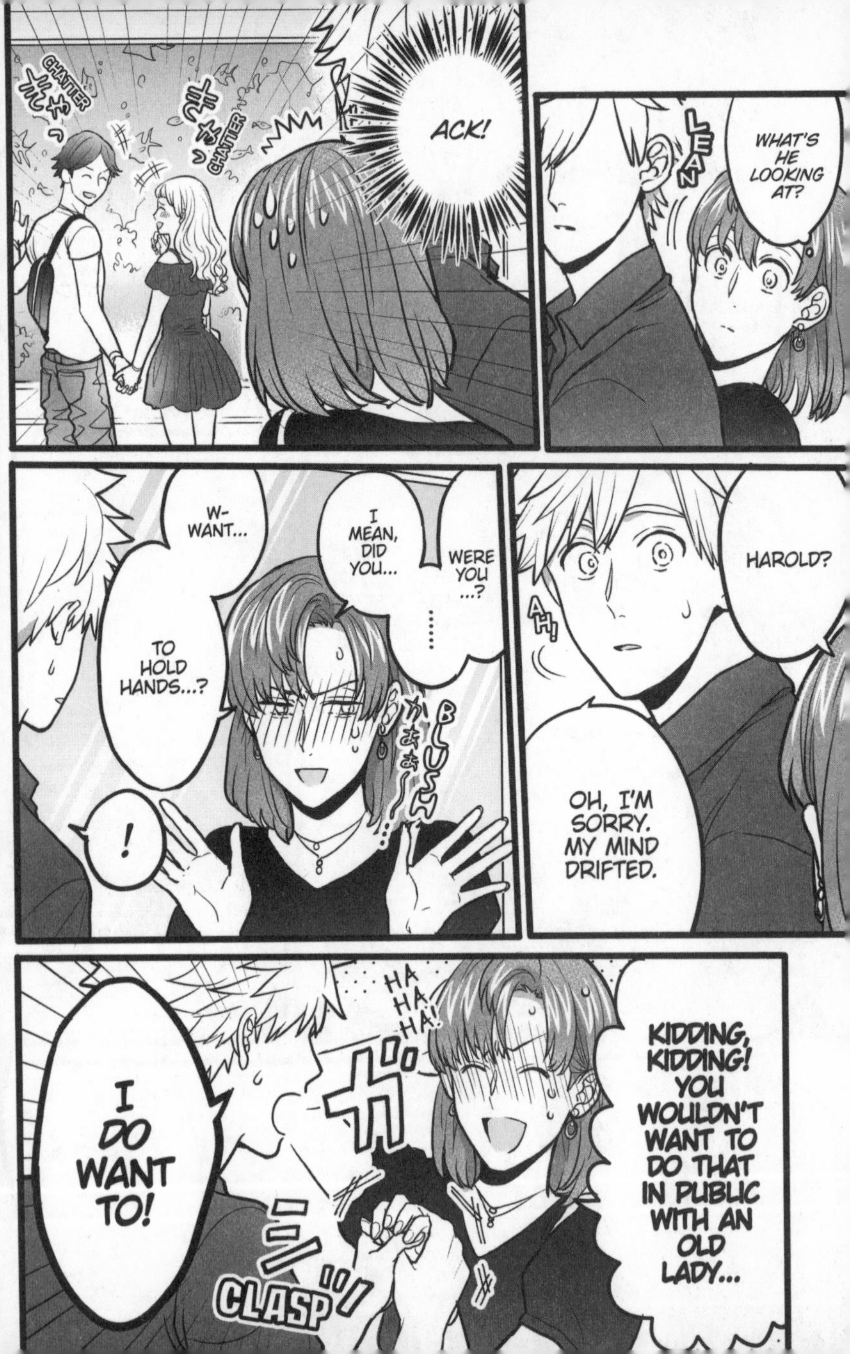
WHAT'S HE LOOKING AT?
LEAN
ACK!
CHATTER
CHATTER
HAROLD?
AH!
OH, I'M SORRY. MY MIND DRIFTED.
I MEAN, DID YOU...
WERE YOU ...?
......
W-WANT...
TO HOLD HANDS...?
BLUSH
!
KIDDING, KIDDING! YOU WOULDN'T WANT TO DO THAT IN PUBLIC WITH AN OLD LADY...
HA HA HA!
I DO WANT TO!
CLASP

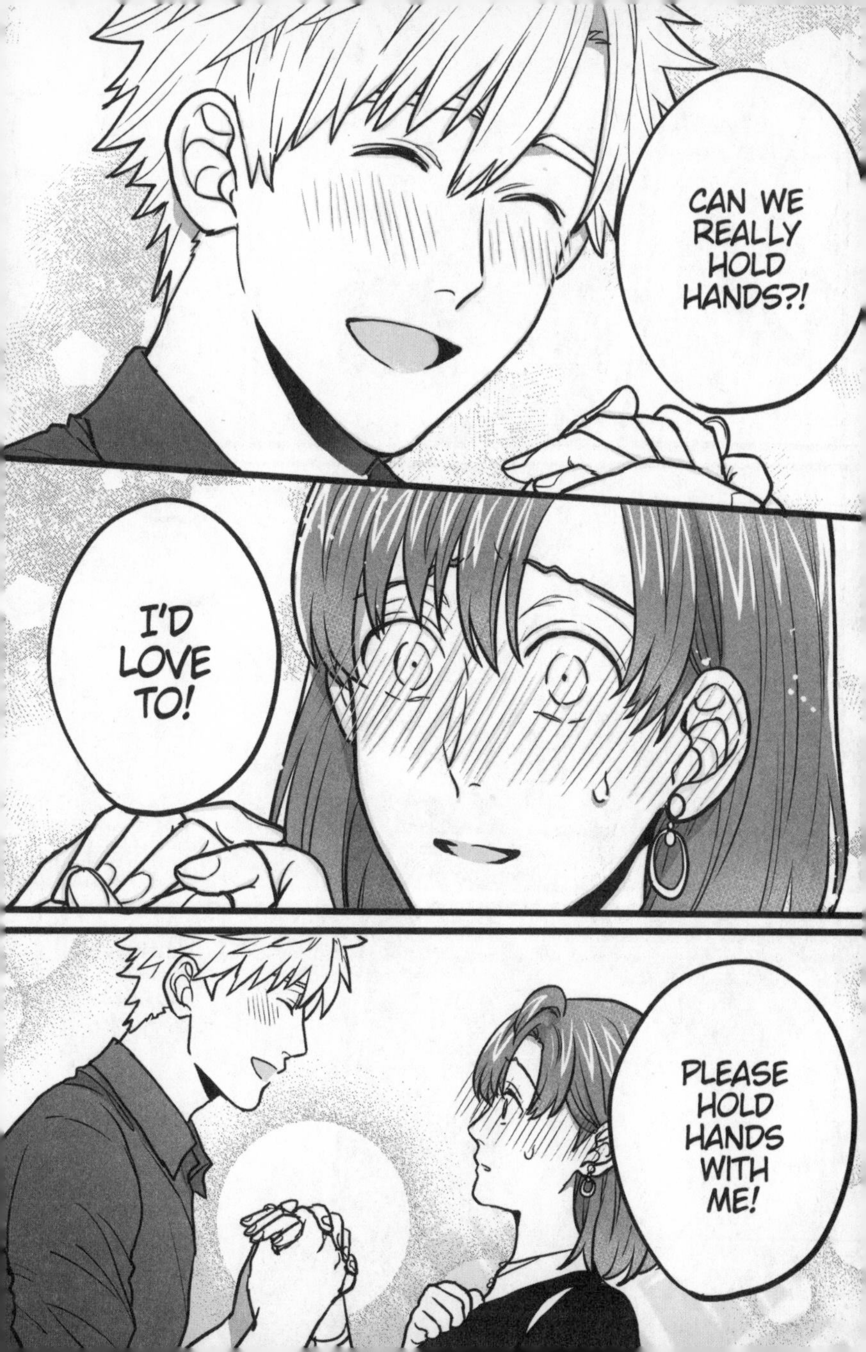
CAN WE REALLY HOLD HANDS?!
I'D LOVE TO!
PLEASE HOLD HANDS WITH ME!

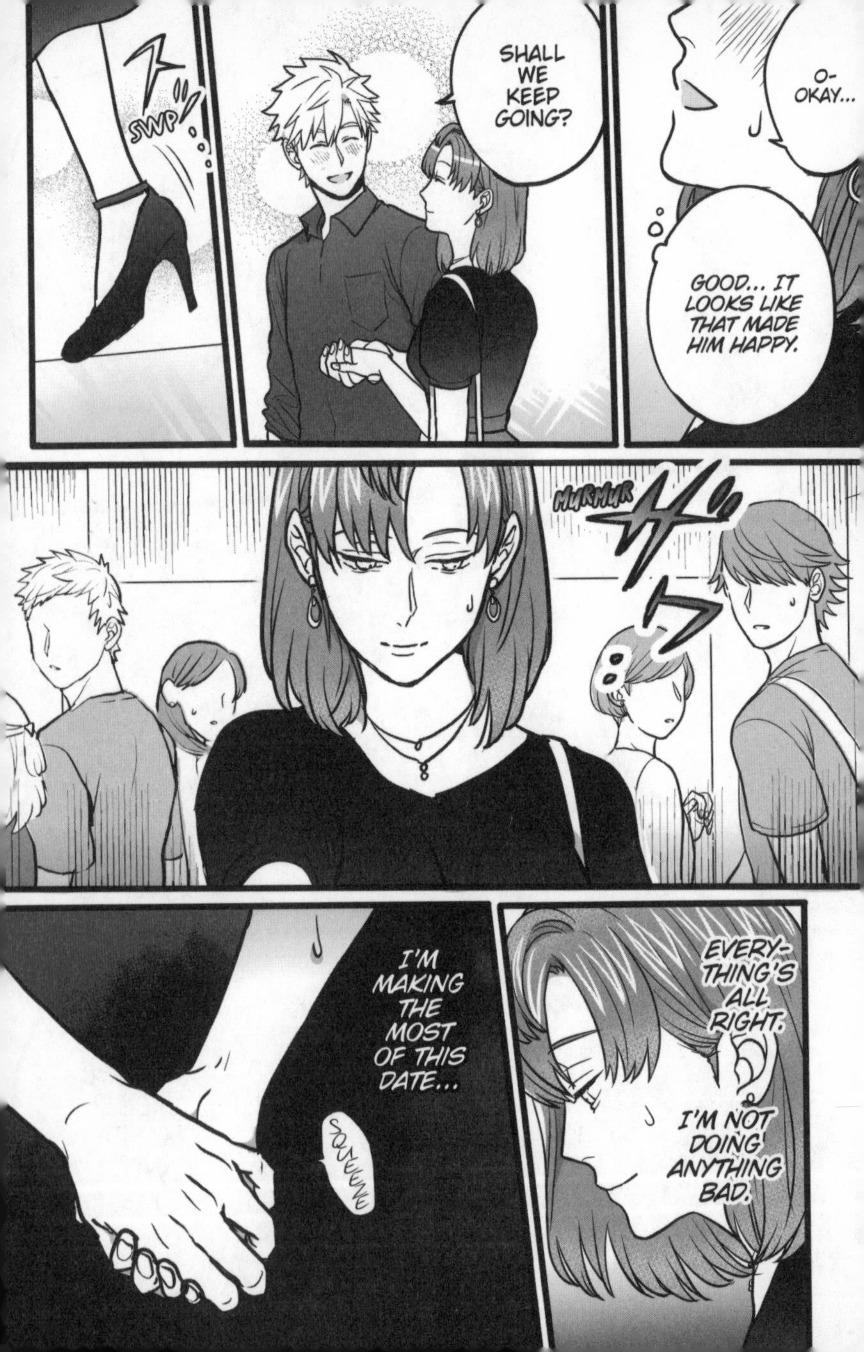
O-OKAY...
GOOD... IT LOOKS LIKE THAT MADE HIM HAPPY.
SHALL WE KEEP GOING?
SWP
MURMUR
EVERY-THING'S ALL RIGHT.
I'M NOT DOING ANYTHING BAD.
I'M MAKING THE MOST OF THIS DATE...
SQUEEEZE

We Swore to Meet in the Next Life **and That's When** Things Got Weird!

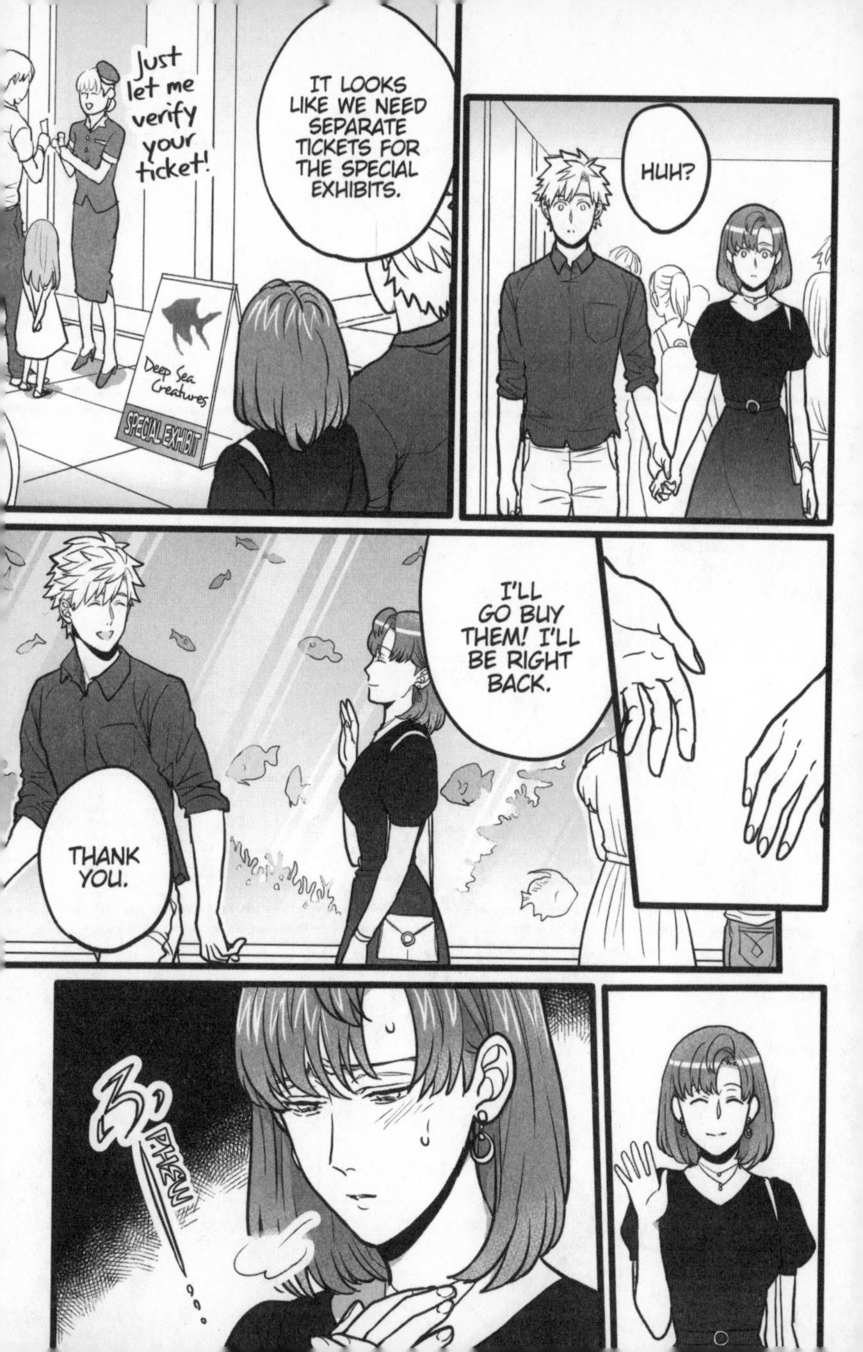
Just let me verify your ticket!
IT LOOKS LIKE WE NEED SEPARATE TICKETS FOR THE SPECIAL EXHIBITS.
Deep Sea Creatures
SPECIAL EXHIBIT
HUH?
I'LL GO BUY THEM! I'LL BE RIGHT BACK.
THANK YOU.
PHEW

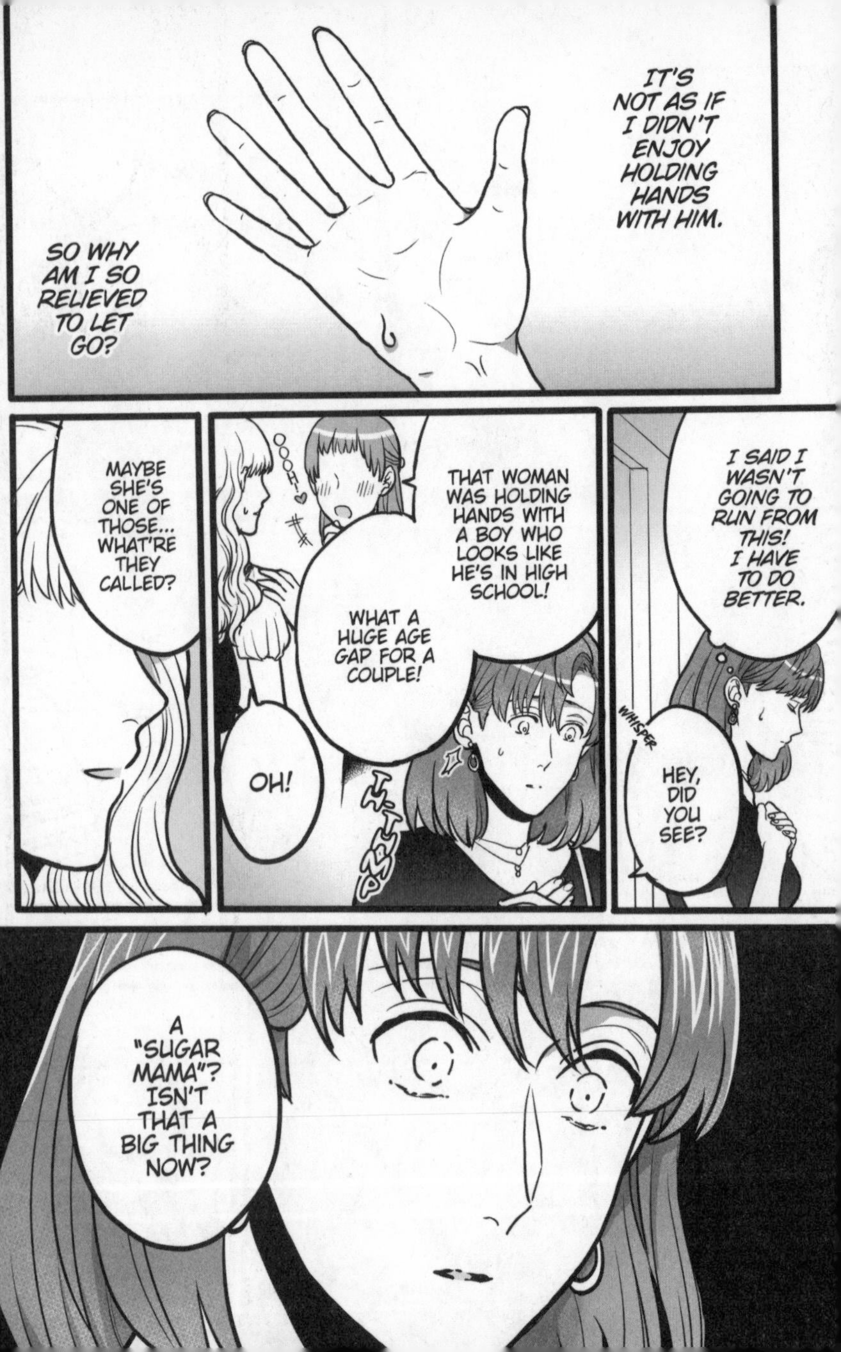
IT'S NOT AS IF I DIDN'T ENJOY HOLDING HANDS WITH HIM.
SO WHY AM I SO RELIEVED TO LET GO?
I SAID I WASN'T GOING TO RUN FROM THIS! I HAVE TO DO BETTER.
WHISPER
HEY, DID YOU SEE?
OOOH! ♥
THAT WOMAN WAS HOLDING HANDS WITH A BOY WHO LOOKS LIKE HE'S IN HIGH SCHOOL!
WHAT A HUGE AGE GAP FOR A COUPLE!
OH!
MAYBE SHE'S ONE OF THOSE... WHAT'RE THEY CALLED?
A "SUGAR MAMA"? ISN'T THAT A BIG THING NOW?

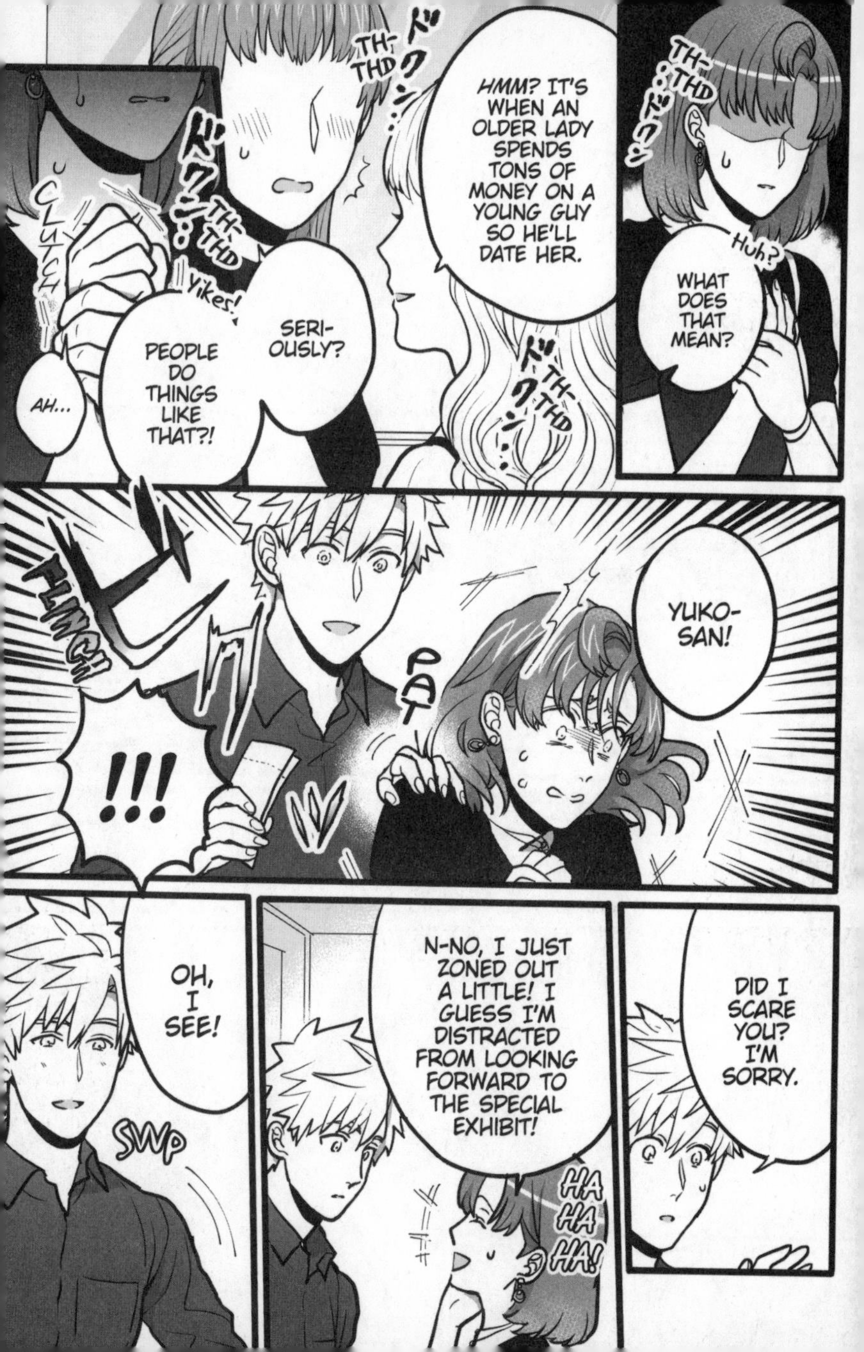
TH-THD
Huh?
WHAT DOES THAT MEAN?
TH-THD
HMM? IT'S WHEN AN OLDER LADY SPENDS TONS OF MONEY ON A YOUNG GUY SO HE'LL DATE HER.
TH-THD
TH-THD
SERI-OUSLY?
yikes!
PEOPLE DO THINGS LIKE THAT?!
CLUTCH
AH...
YUKO-SAN!
PAT
FLINCH!!
!!!
DID I SCARE YOU? I'M SORRY.
N-NO, I JUST ZONED OUT A LITTLE! I GUESS I'M DISTRACTED FROM LOOKING FORWARD TO THE SPECIAL EXHIBIT!
HA HA HA!
OH, I SEE!
SWP

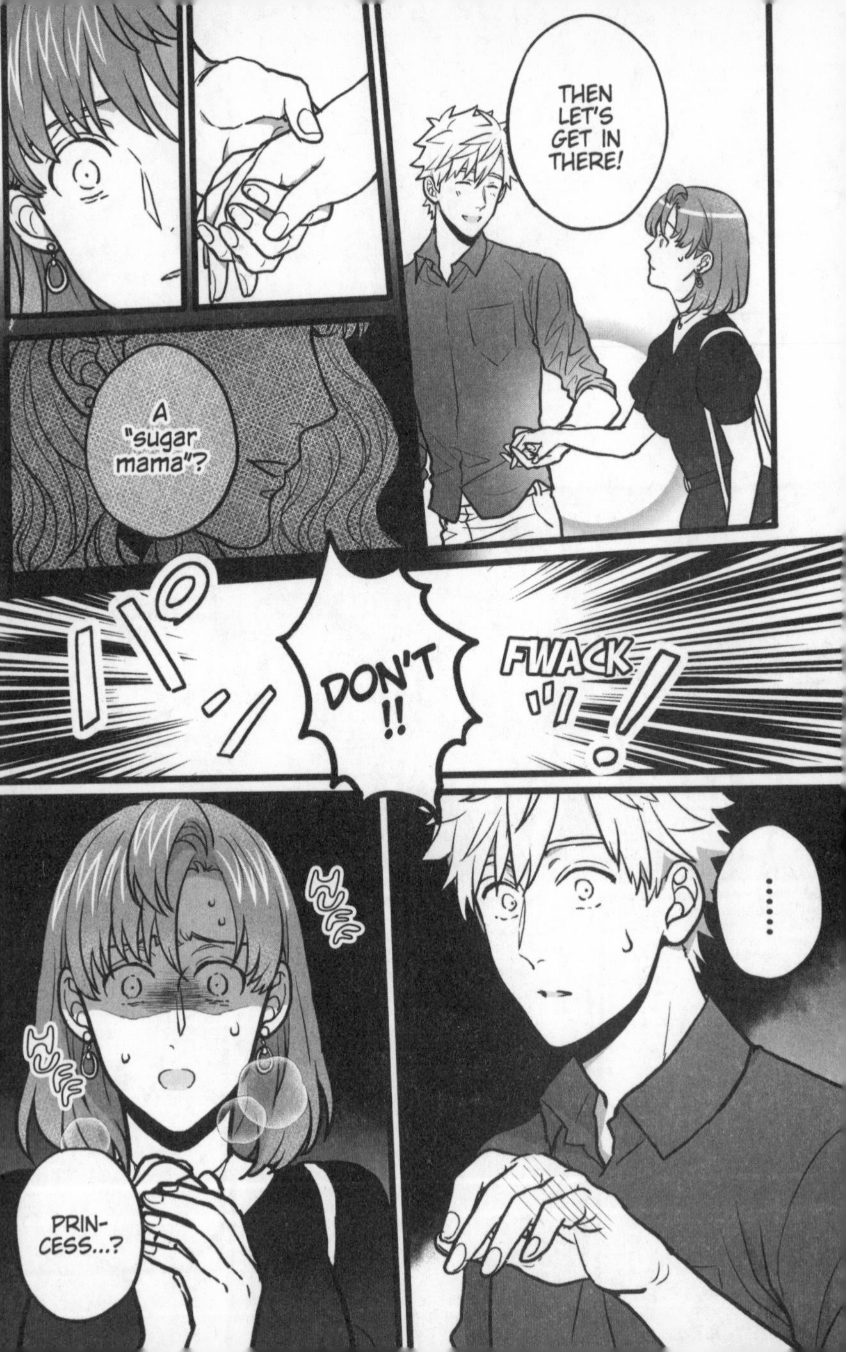
THEN LET'S GET IN THERE!
A "sugar mama"?
FWACK
DON'T!!
......
HUFF
HUFF
PRIN-CESS...?

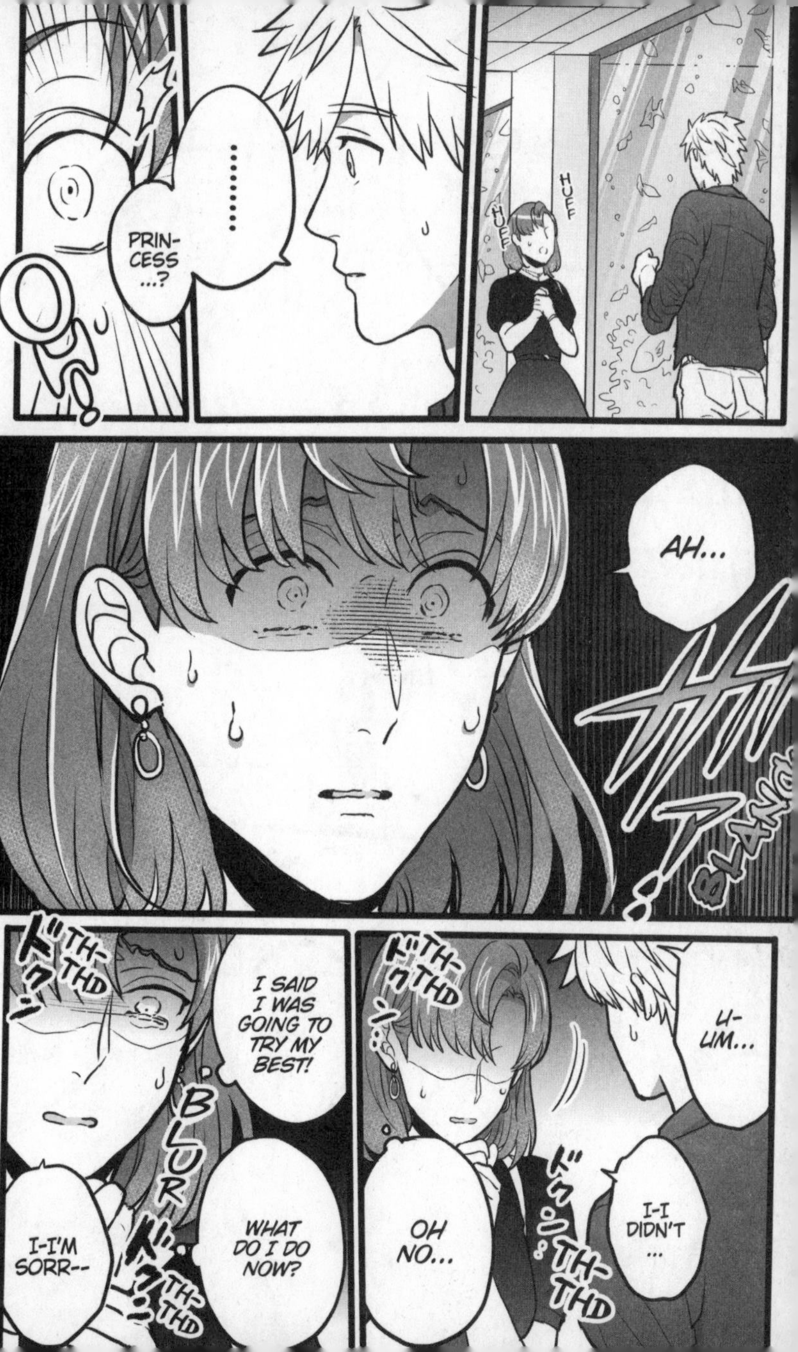
HUFF
HUFF
......
PRINCESS...?
AH...
TH-THD
U-UM...
I-I DIDN'T...
OH NO...
TH-THD
TH-THD
I SAID I WAS GOING TO TRY MY BEST!
BLUR
WHAT DO I DO NOW?
I-I'M SORR--
TH-THD

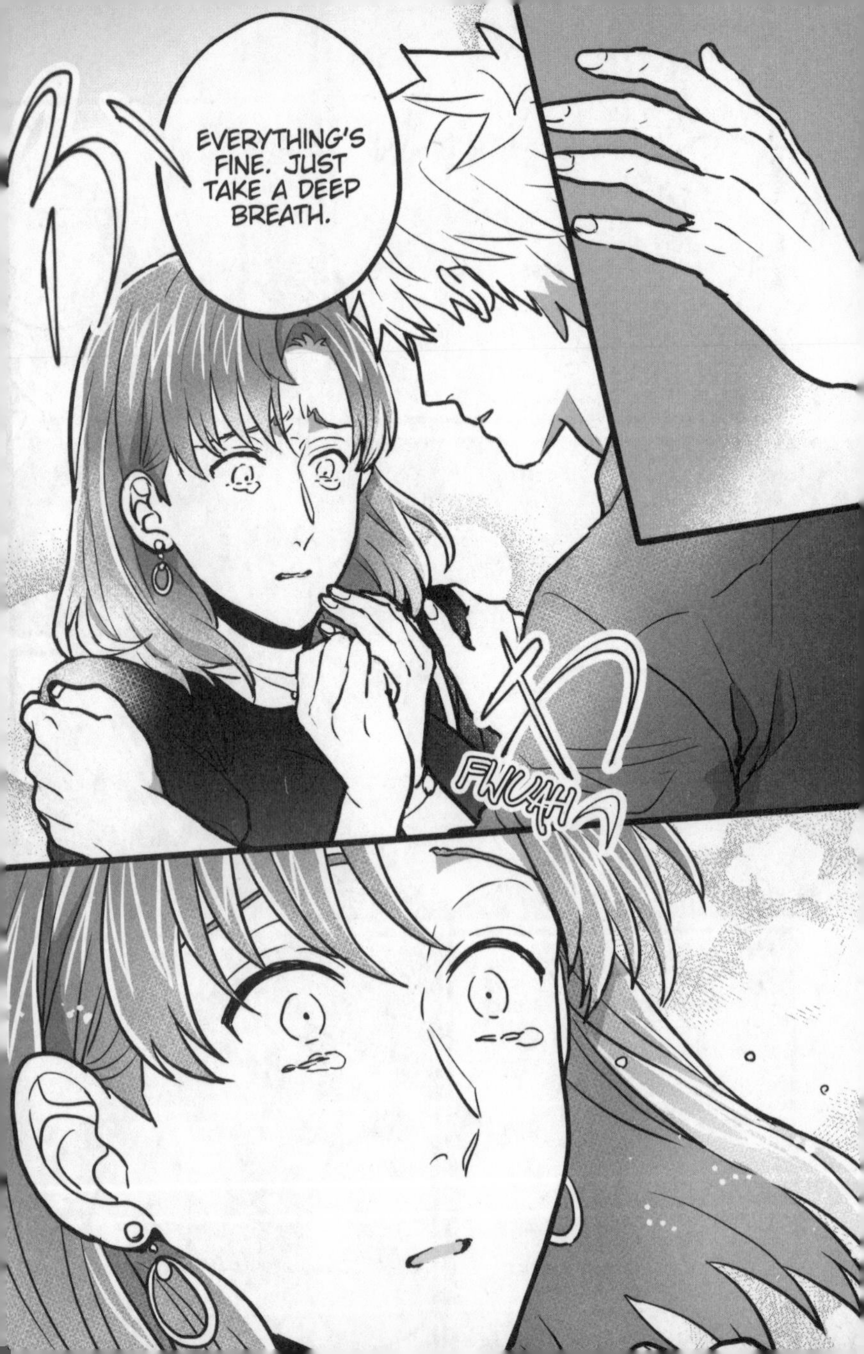
EVERYTHING'S FINE. JUST TAKE A DEEP BREATH.
FWUAH

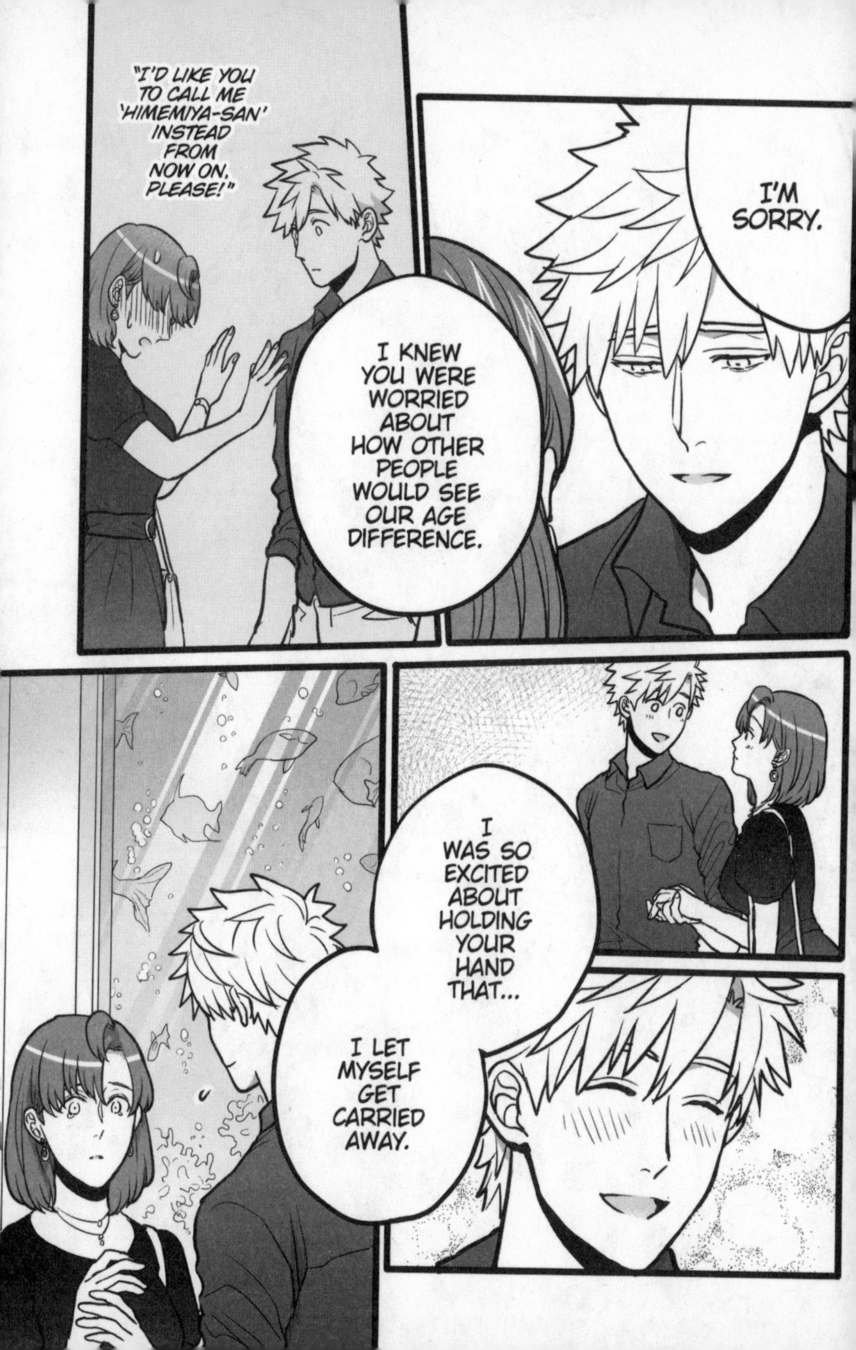
I'M SORRY.
I KNEW YOU WERE WORRIED ABOUT HOW OTHER PEOPLE WOULD SEE OUR AGE DIFFERENCE.
"I'D LIKE YOU TO CALL ME 'HIMEMIYA-SAN' INSTEAD FROM NOW ON. PLEASE!"
I WAS SO EXCITED ABOUT HOLDING YOUR HAND THAT...
I LET MYSELF GET CARRIED AWAY.

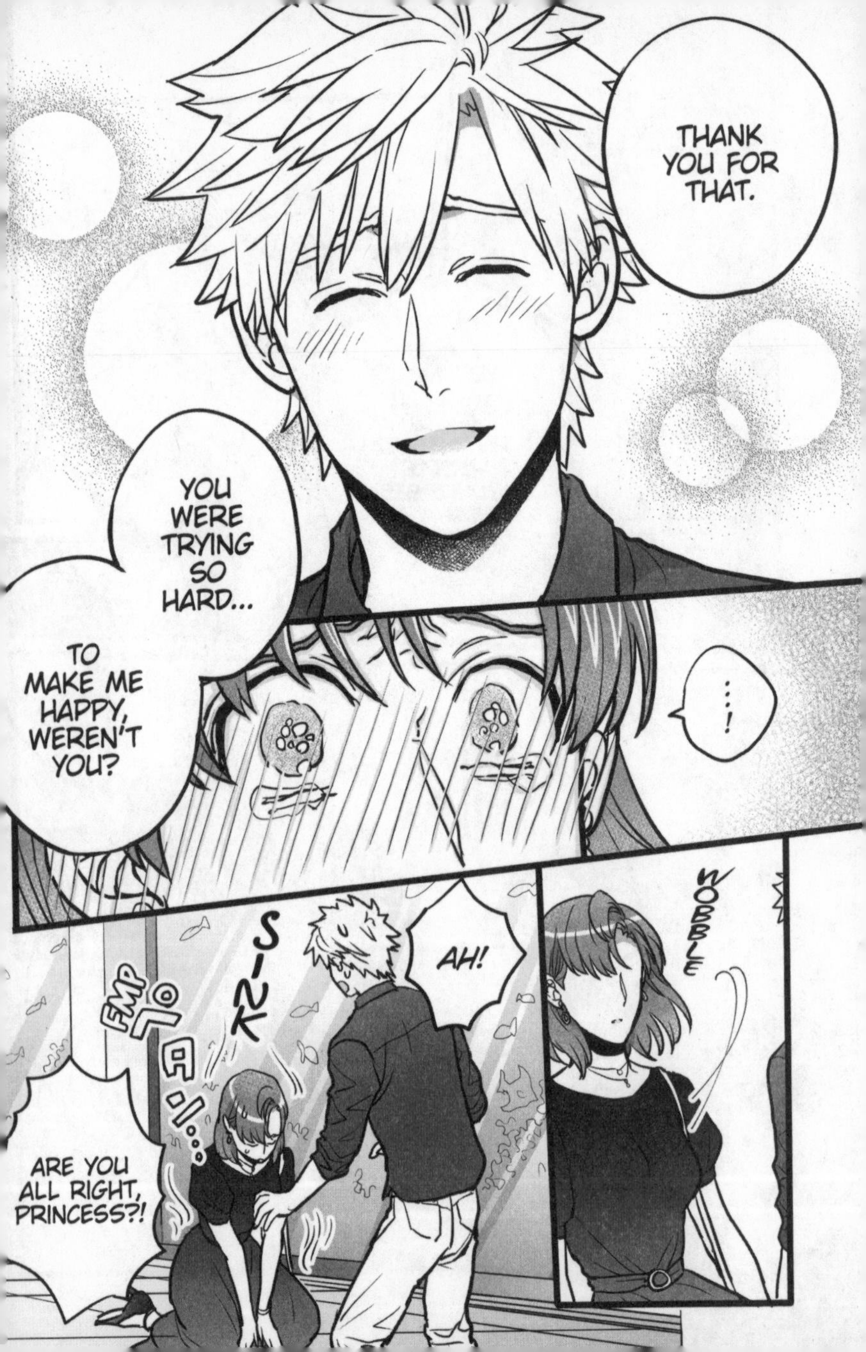
THANK YOU FOR THAT.
YOU WERE TRYING SO HARD...
TO MAKE ME HAPPY, WEREN'T YOU?
...!
WOBBLE
AH!
SINK
FMP
ARE YOU ALL RIGHT, PRINCESS?!

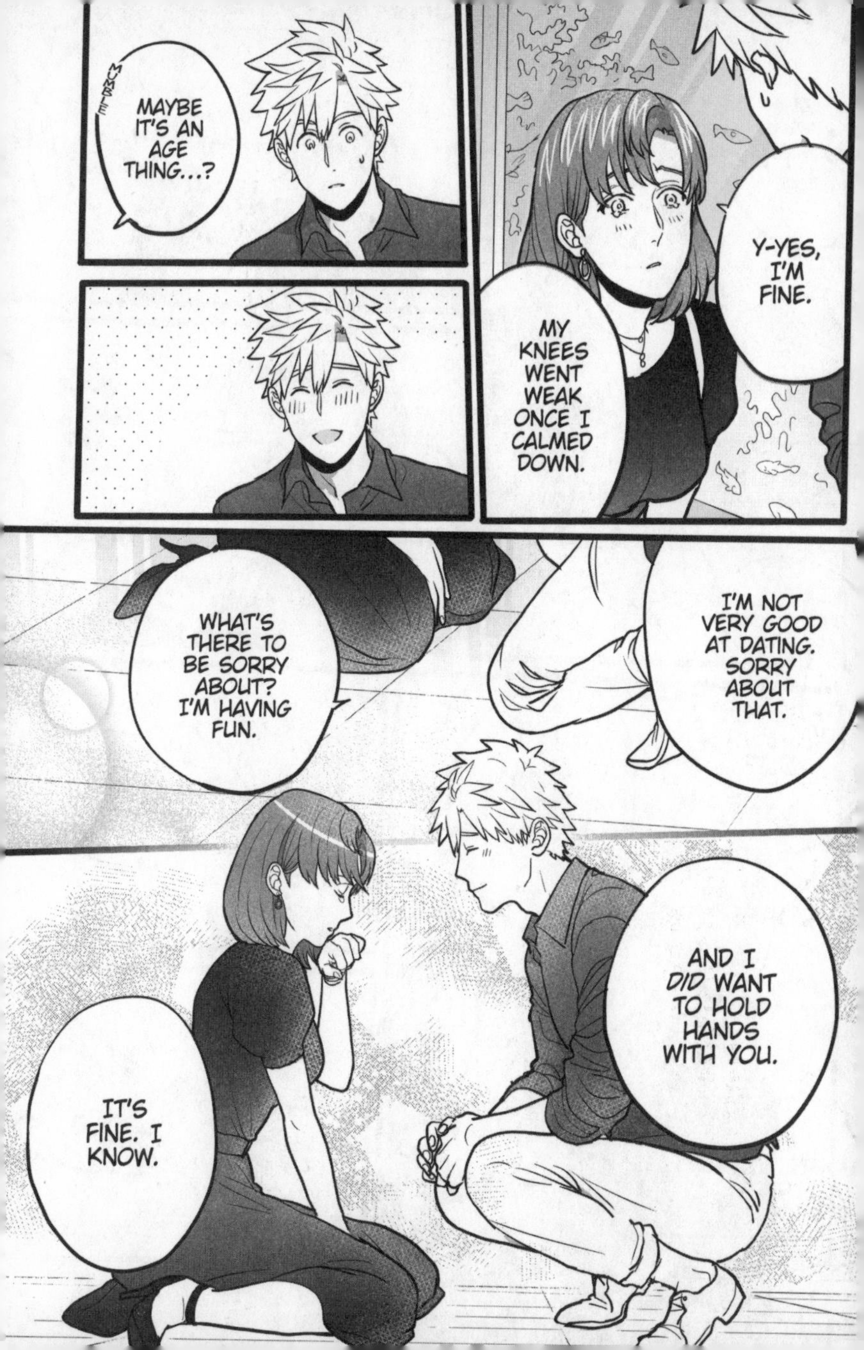
Y-YES, I'M FINE.
MY KNEES WENT WEAK ONCE I CALMED DOWN.
MUMBLE
MAYBE IT'S AN AGE THING...?
I'M NOT VERY GOOD AT DATING. SORRY ABOUT THAT.
WHAT'S THERE TO BE SORRY ABOUT? I'M HAVING FUN.
AND I *DID* WANT TO HOLD HANDS WITH YOU.
IT'S FINE. I KNOW.

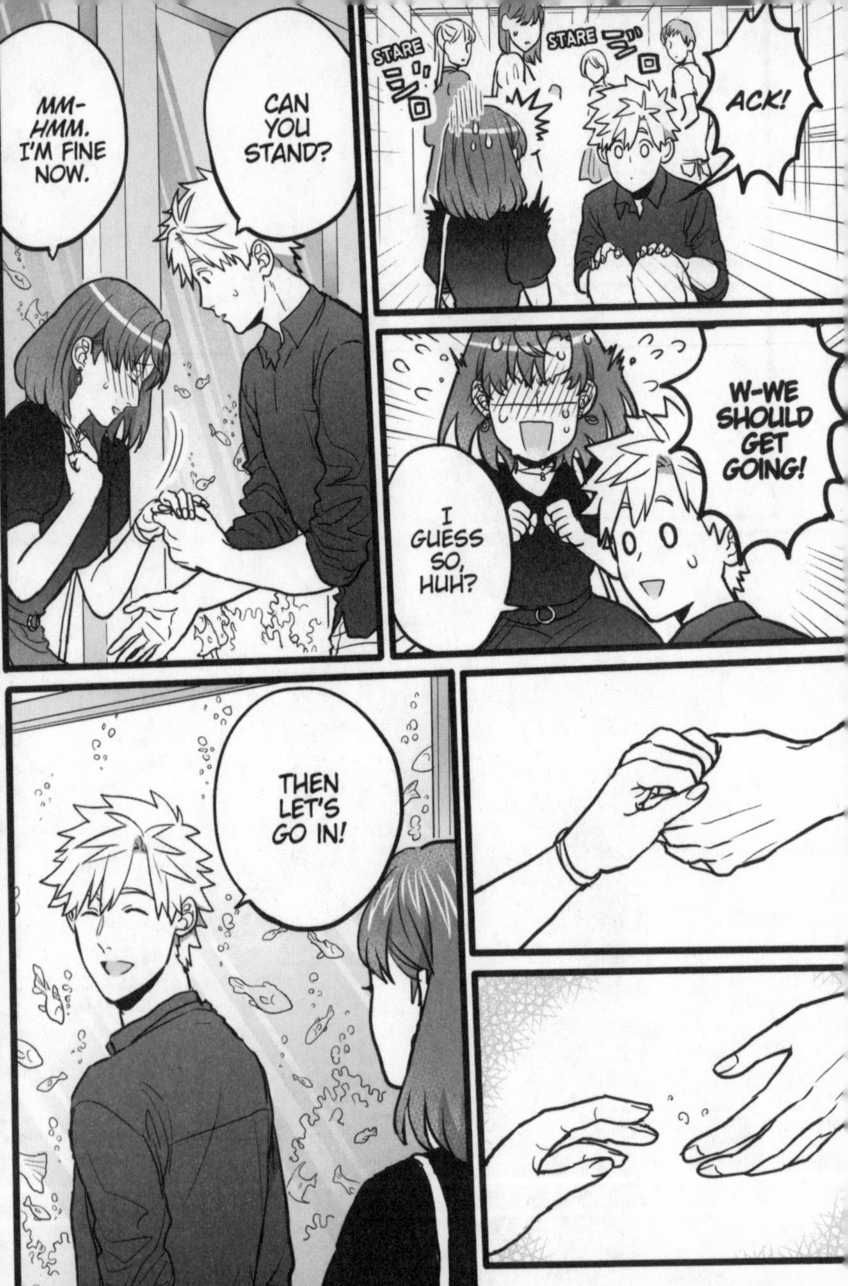
STARE
STARE
ACK!
W-WE SHOULD GET GOING!
I GUESS SO, HUH?
CAN YOU STAND?
MM-HMM. I'M FINE NOW.
THEN LET'S GO IN!

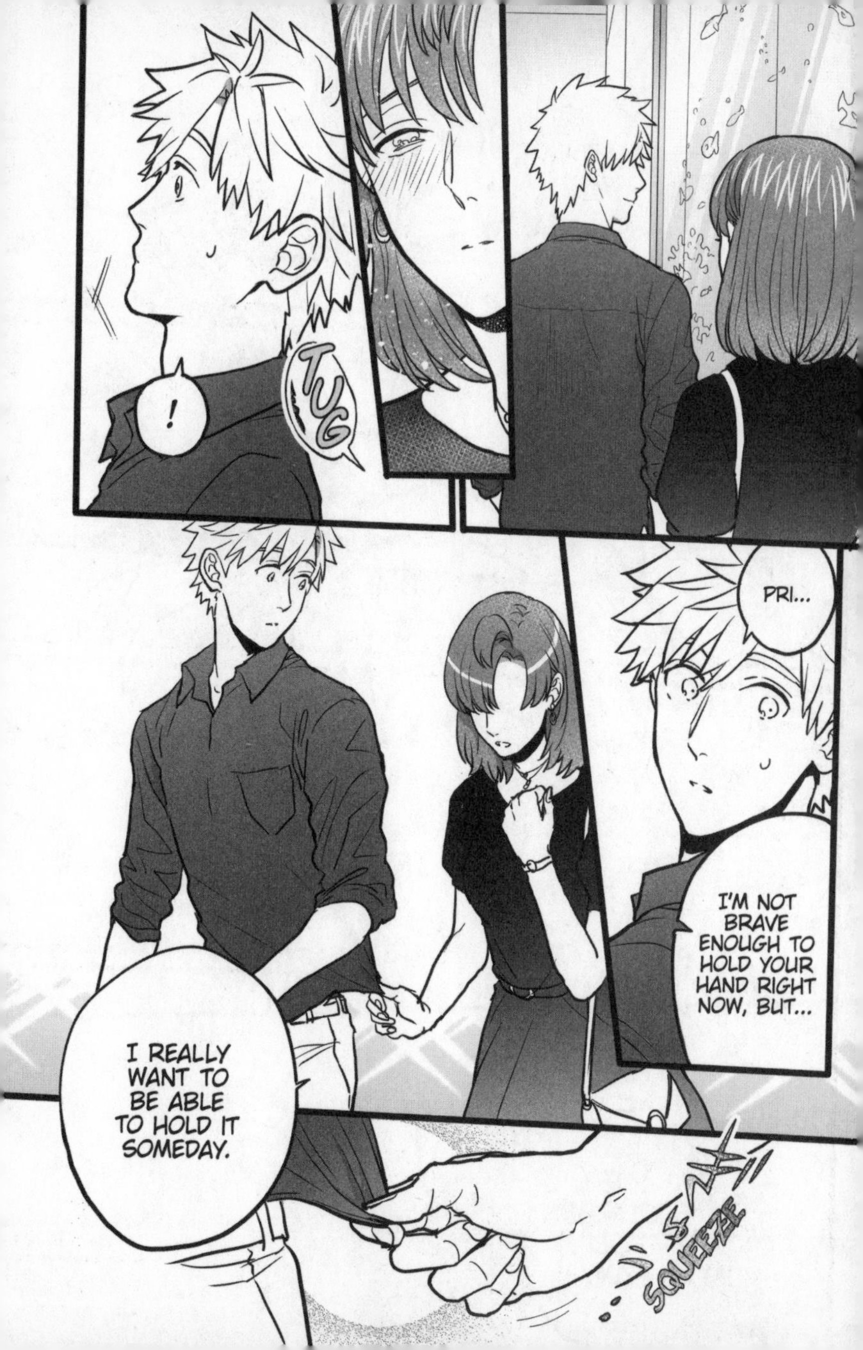

TUG
!
PRI...
I'M NOT BRAVE ENOUGH TO HOLD YOUR HAND RIGHT NOW, BUT...
I REALLY WANT TO BE ABLE TO HOLD IT SOMEDAY.
SQUEEZE

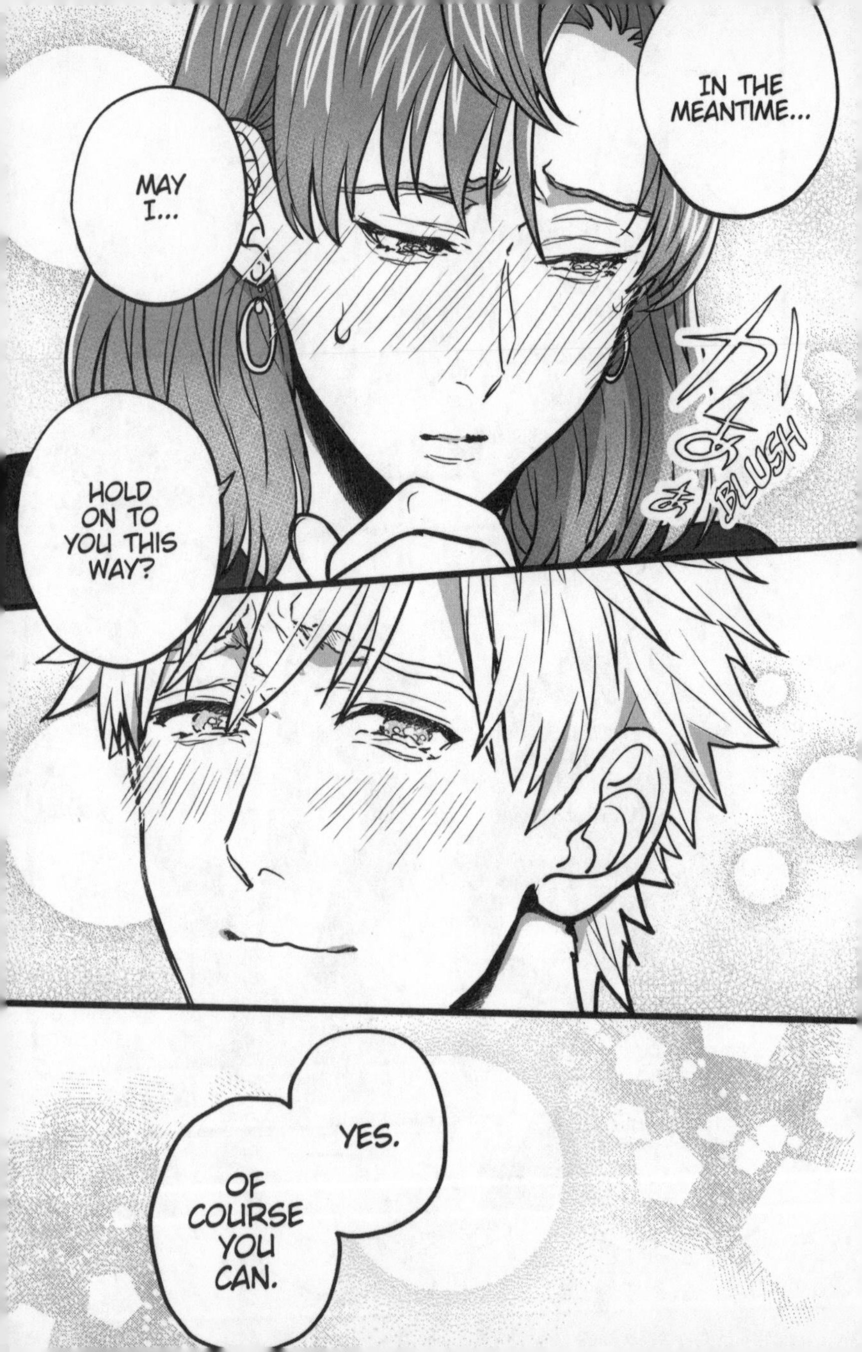
IN THE MEANTIME...
MAY I...
HOLD ON TO YOU THIS WAY?
BLUSH
YES.
OF COURSE YOU CAN.

We Swore to Meet in the Next Life **and That's When** Things Got **Weird!**

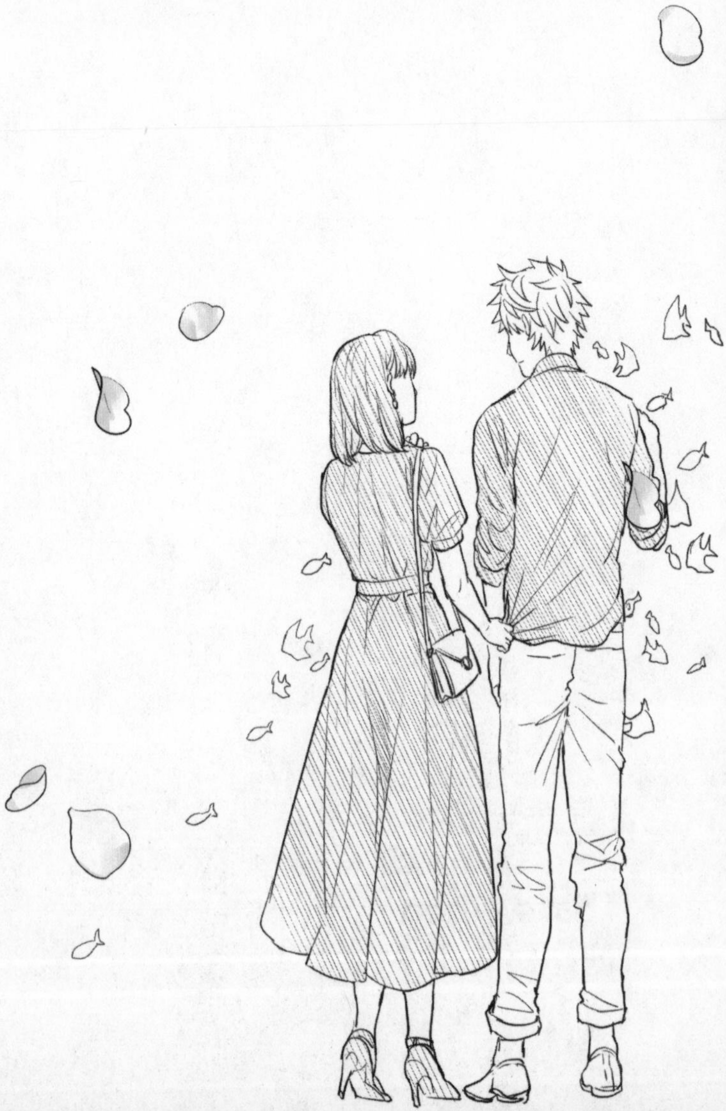

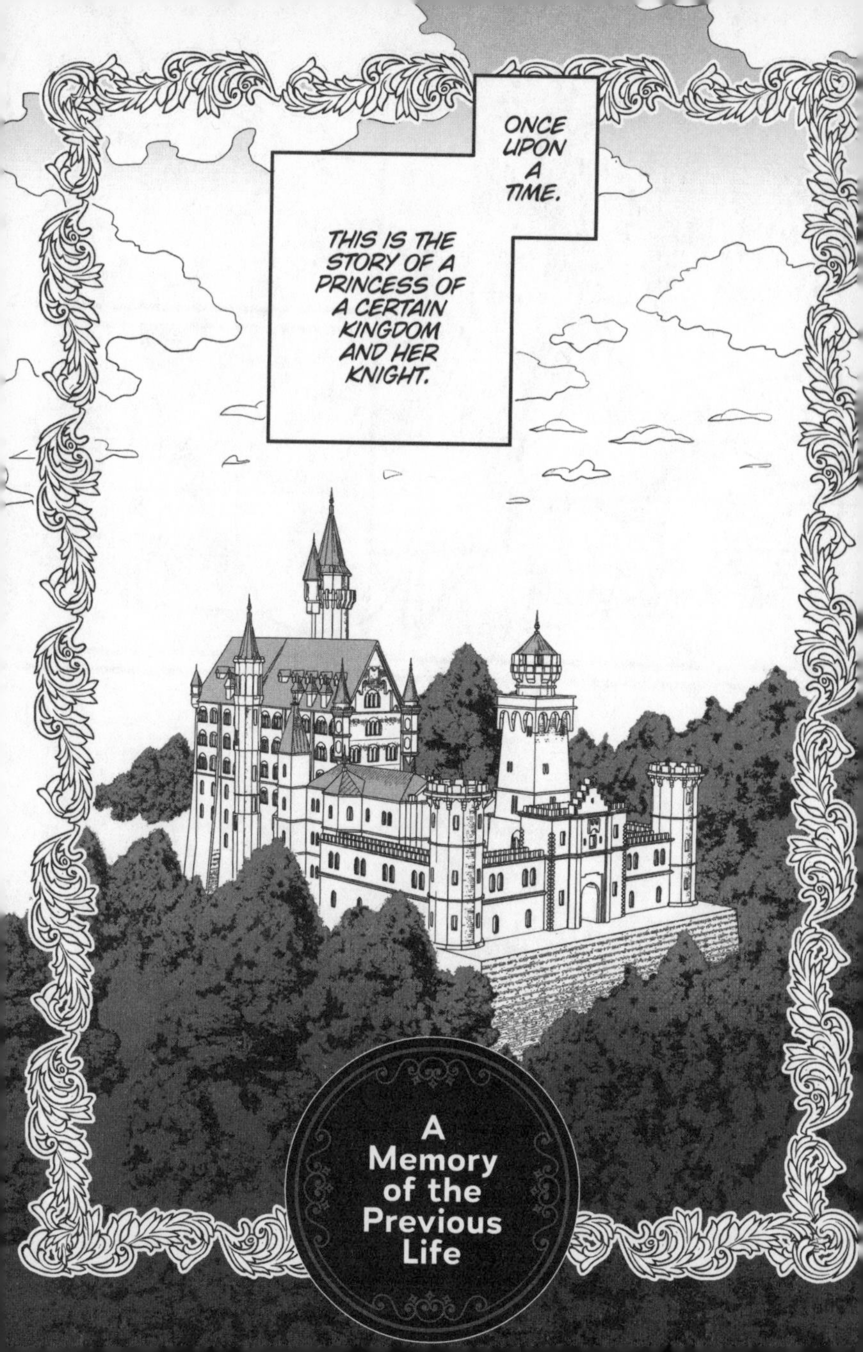
ONCE UPON A TIME.
THIS IS THE STORY OF A PRINCESS OF A CERTAIN KINGDOM AND HER KNIGHT.
A Memory of the Previous Life

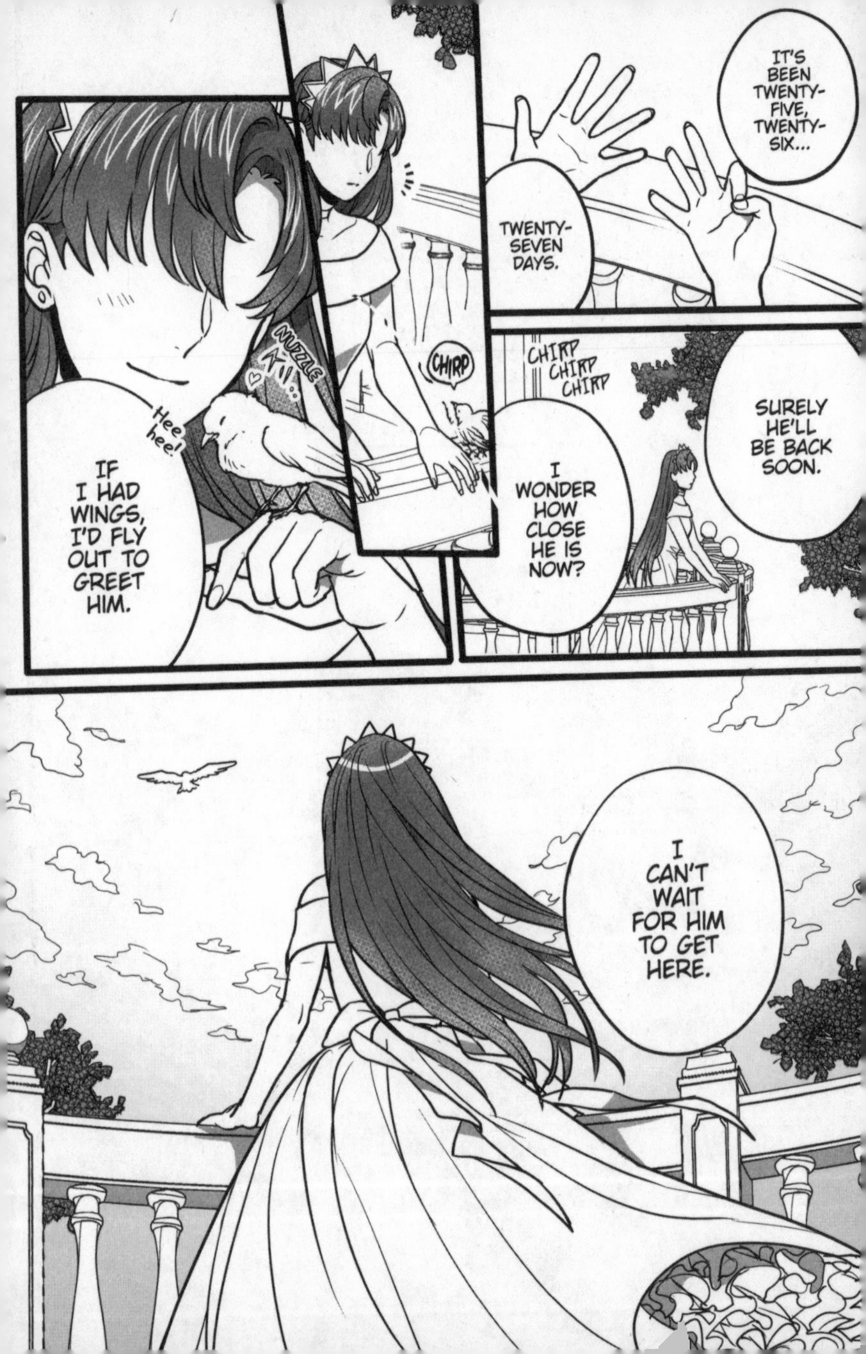
IT'S BEEN TWENTY-FIVE, TWENTY-SIX...
TWENTY-SEVEN DAYS.
CHIRP CHIRP CHIRP
SURELY HE'LL BE BACK SOON.
I WONDER HOW CLOSE HE IS NOW?
CHIRP
NUZZLE
Hee hee!
IF I HAD WINGS, I'D FLY OUT TO GREET HIM.
I CAN'T WAIT FOR HIM TO GET HERE.

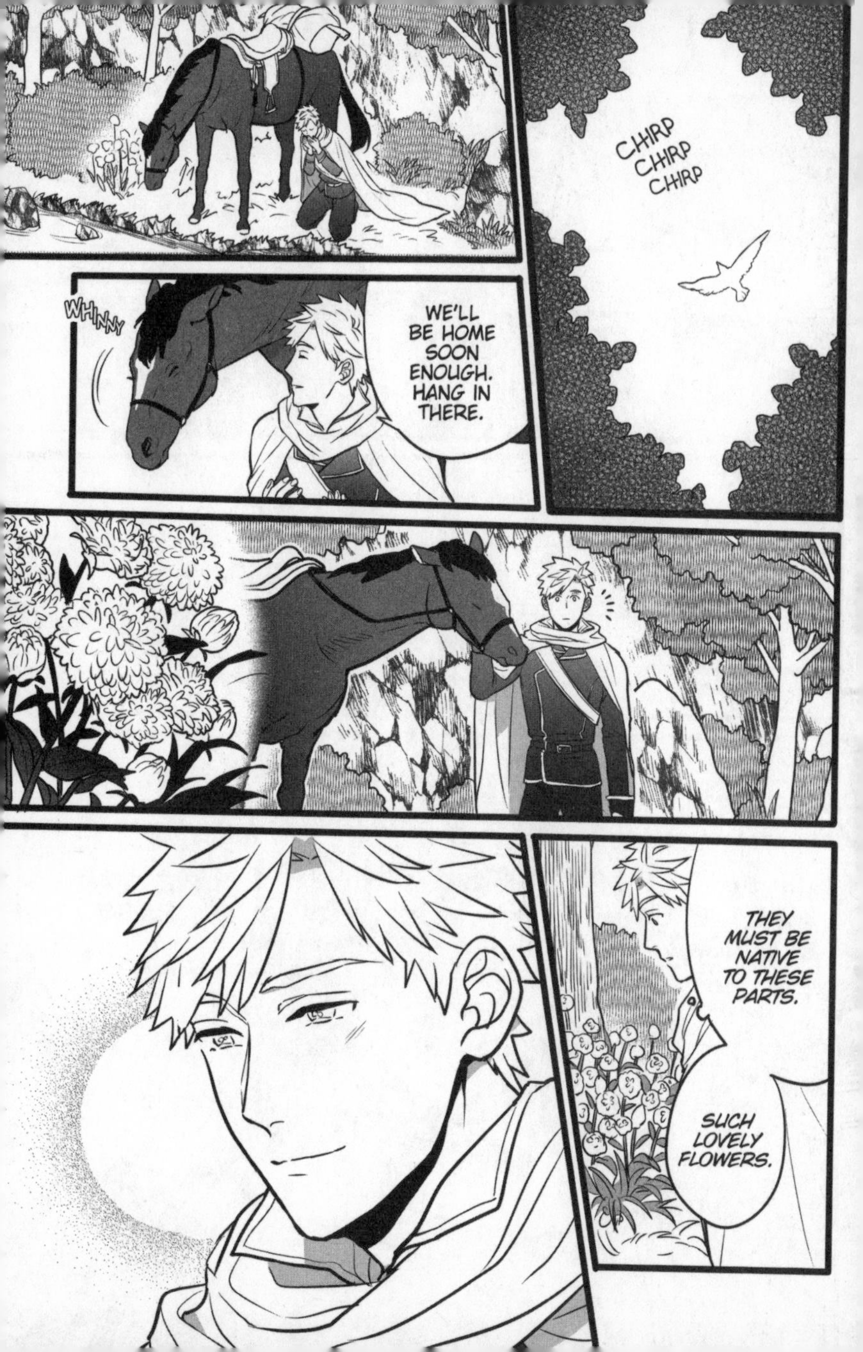
CHIRP CHIRP CHIRP
WE'LL BE HOME SOON ENOUGH. HANG IN THERE.
WHINNY
THEY MUST BE NATIVE TO THESE PARTS.
SUCH LOVELY FLOWERS.

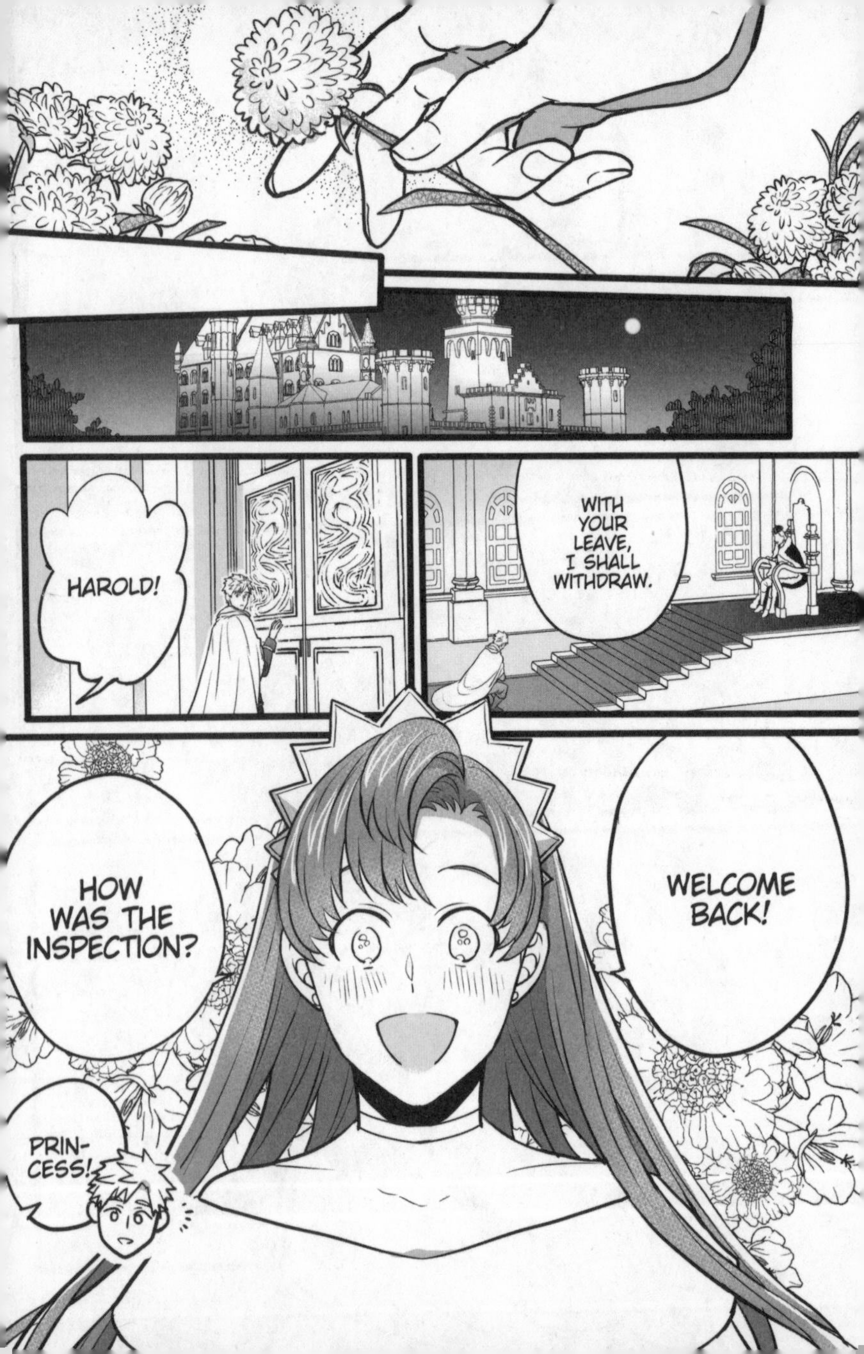
WITH YOUR LEAVE, I SHALL WITHDRAW.
HAROLD!
WELCOME BACK!
HOW WAS THE INSPECTION?
PRIN-CESS!

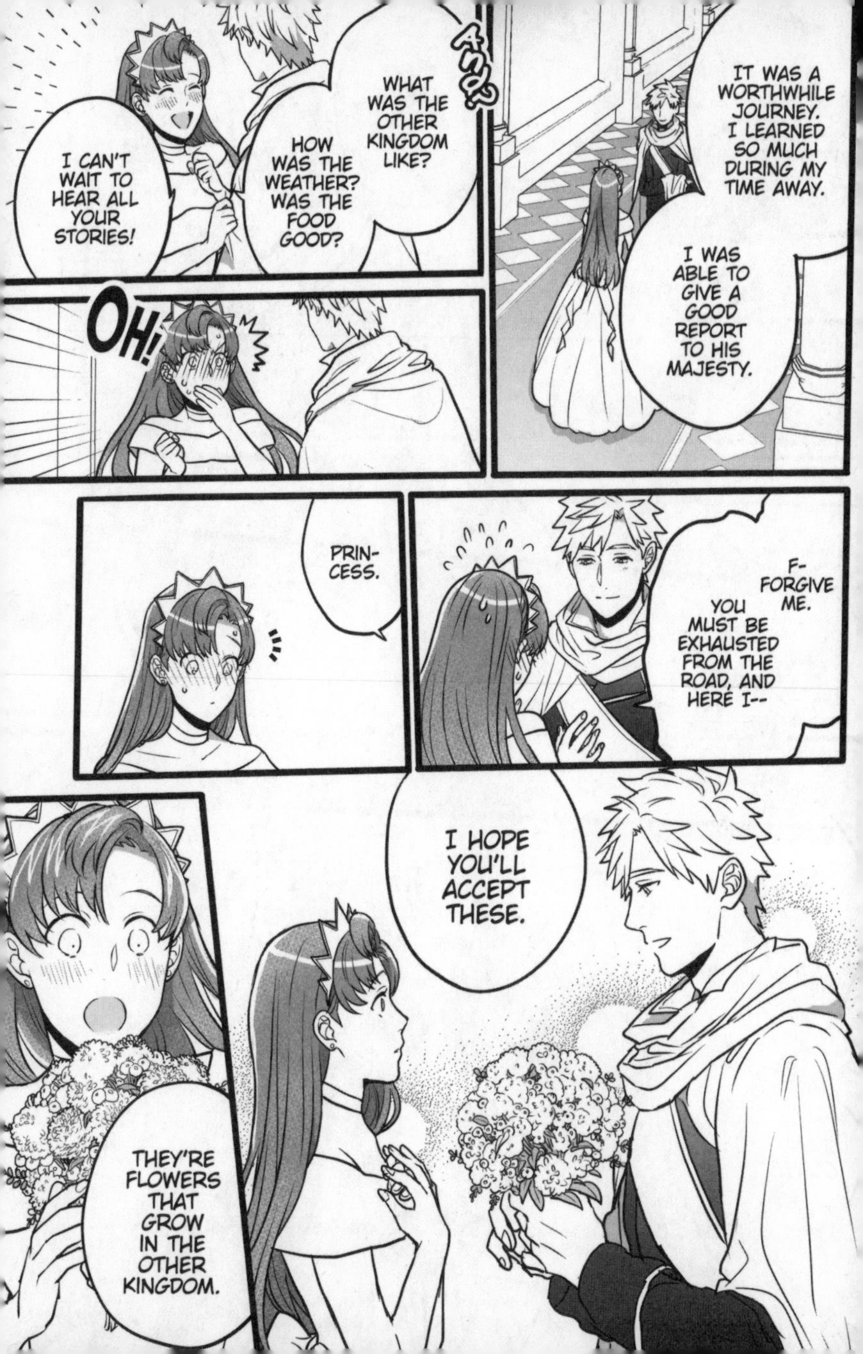
IT WAS A WORTHWHILE JOURNEY. I LEARNED SO MUCH DURING MY TIME AWAY.
I WAS ABLE TO GIVE A GOOD REPORT TO HIS MAJESTY.
And?
WHAT WAS THE OTHER KINGDOM LIKE?
HOW WAS THE WEATHER? WAS THE FOOD GOOD?
I CAN'T WAIT TO HEAR ALL YOUR STORIES!
OH!
F- FORGIVE ME.
YOU MUST BE EXHAUSTED FROM THE ROAD, AND HERE I--
PRIN- CESS.
I HOPE YOU'LL ACCEPT THESE.
THEY'RE FLOWERS THAT GROW IN THE OTHER KINGDOM.

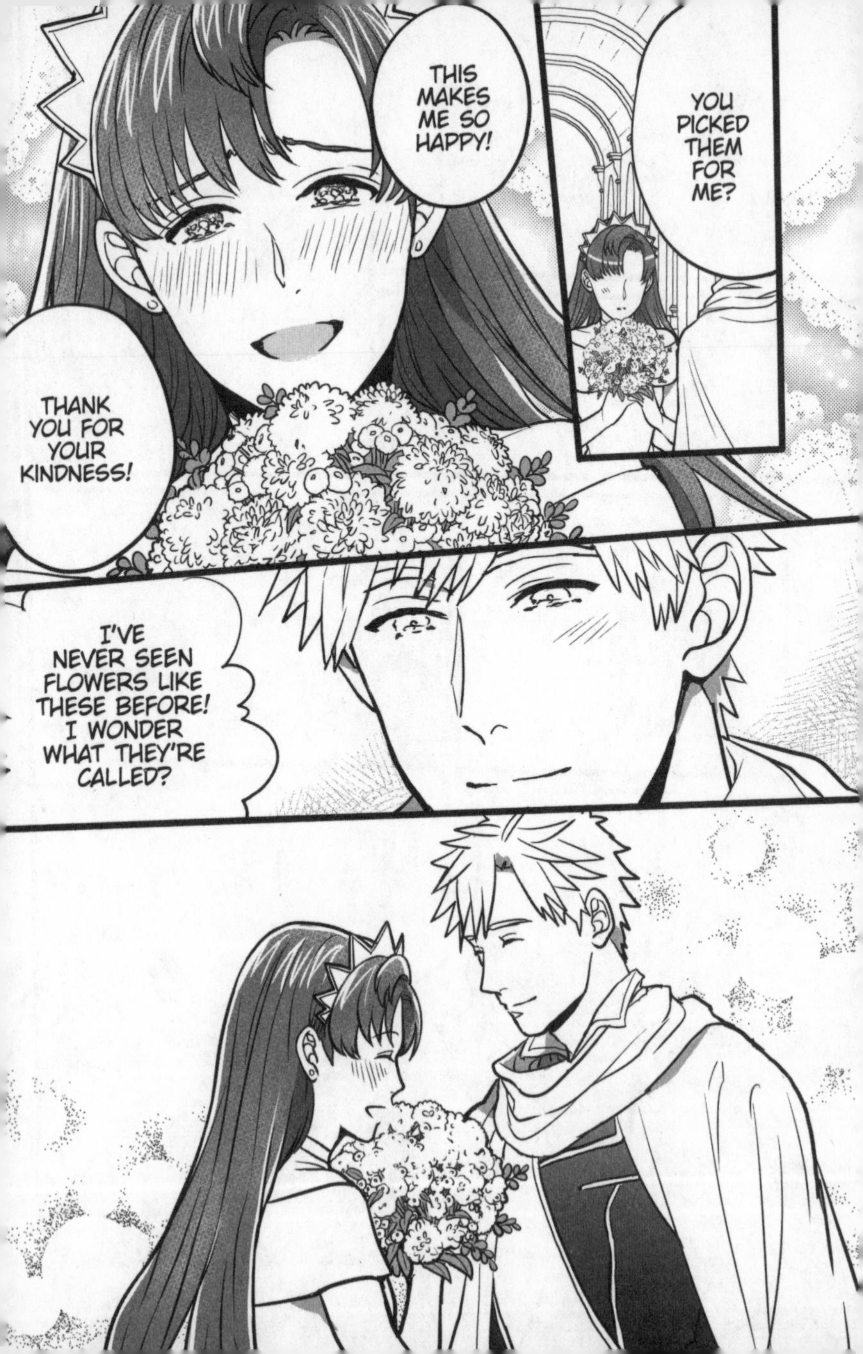
YOU PICKED THEM FOR ME?
THIS MAKES ME SO HAPPY!
THANK YOU FOR YOUR KINDNESS!
I'VE NEVER SEEN FLOWERS LIKE THESE BEFORE! I WONDER WHAT THEY'RE CALLED?

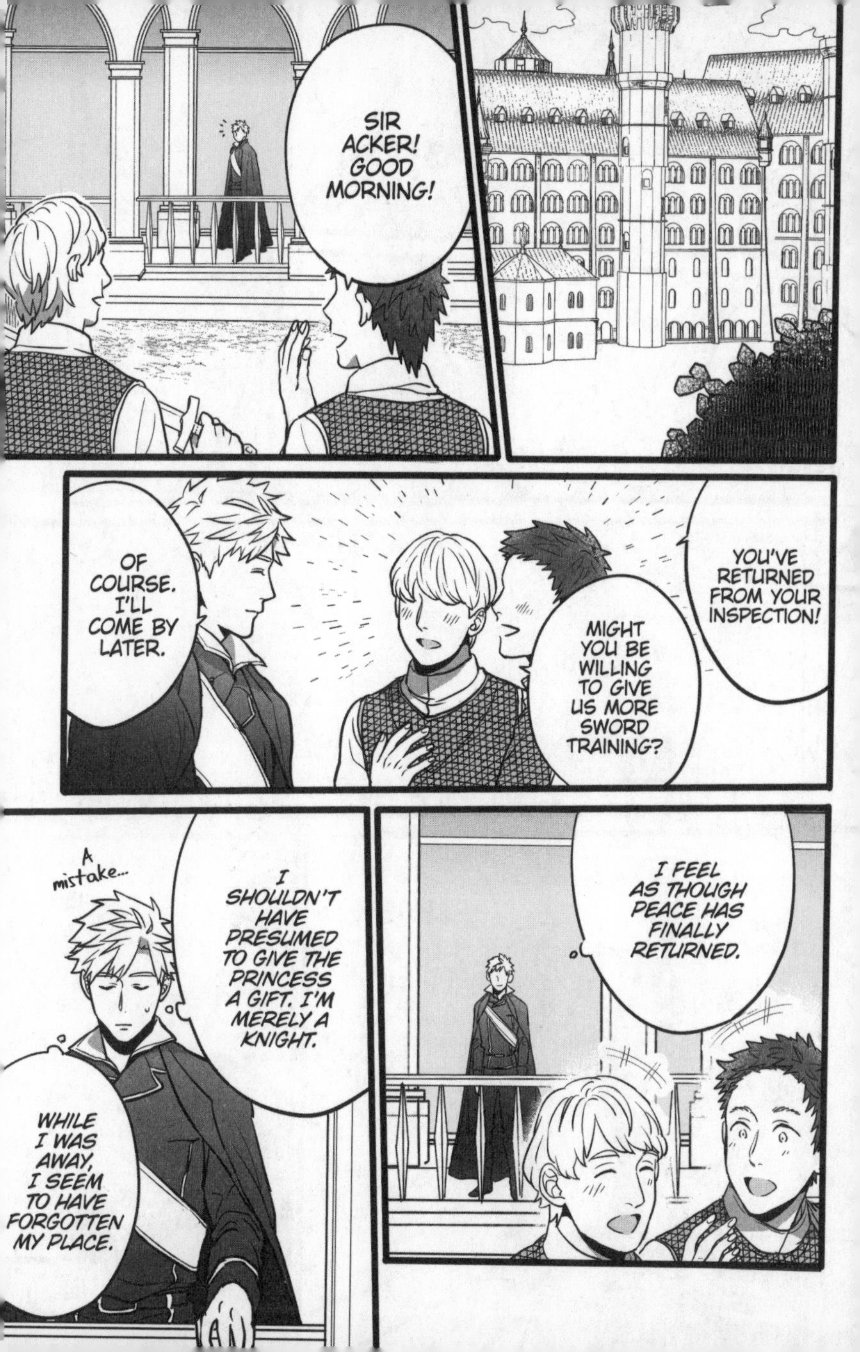
SIR ACKER! GOOD MORNING!
YOU'VE RETURNED FROM YOUR INSPECTION!
MIGHT YOU BE WILLING TO GIVE US MORE SWORD TRAINING?
OF COURSE. I'LL COME BY LATER.
I FEEL AS THOUGH PEACE HAS FINALLY RETURNED.
I SHOULDN'T HAVE PRESUMED TO GIVE THE PRINCESS A GIFT. I'M MERELY A KNIGHT.
A mistake...
WHILE I WAS AWAY, I SEEM TO HAVE FORGOTTEN MY PLACE.

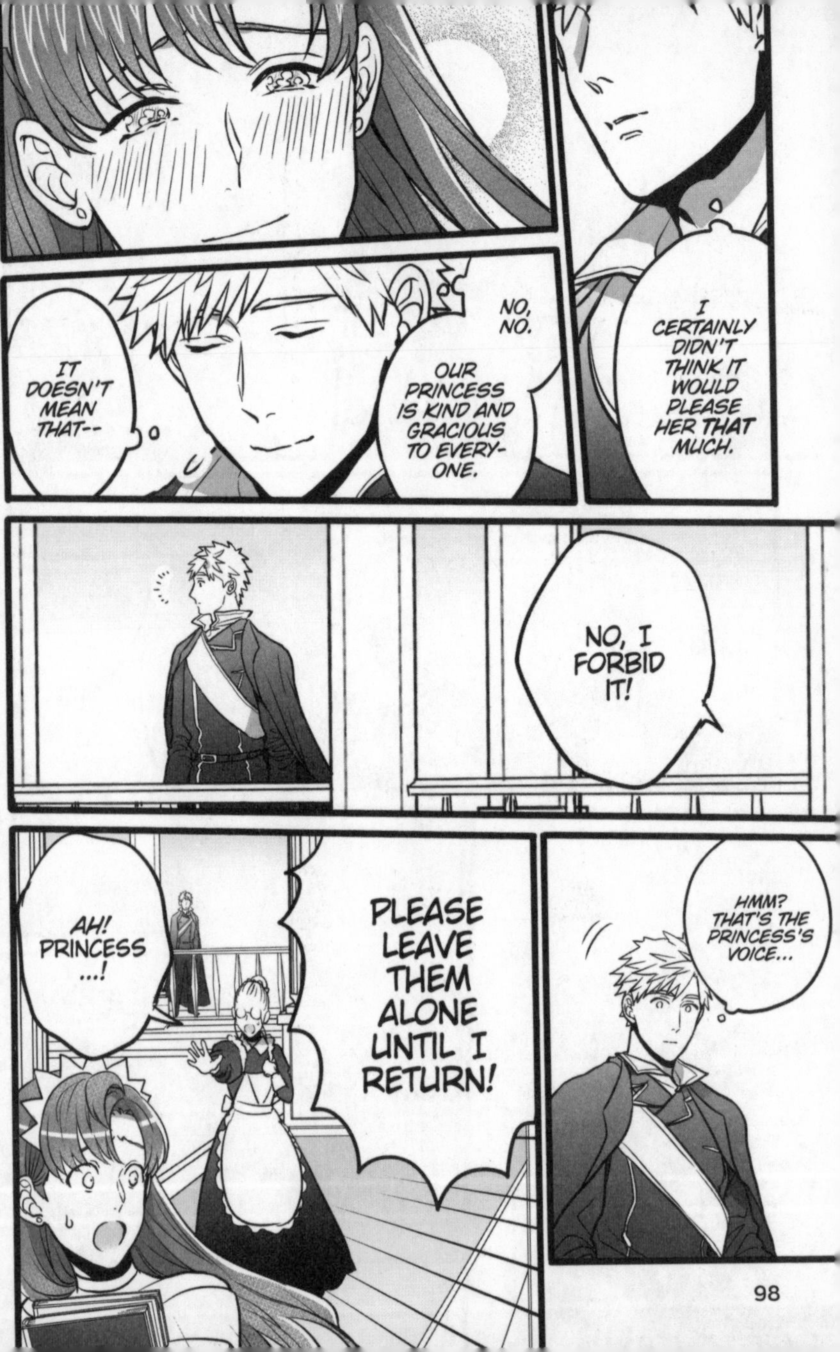
I CERTAINLY DIDN'T THINK IT WOULD PLEASE HER THAT MUCH.
NO, NO.
OUR PRINCESS IS KIND AND GRACIOUS TO EVERY-ONE.
IT DOESN'T MEAN THAT--
NO, I FORBID IT!
HMM? THAT'S THE PRINCESS'S VOICE...
PLEASE LEAVE THEM ALONE UNTIL I RETURN!
AH! PRINCESS ...!

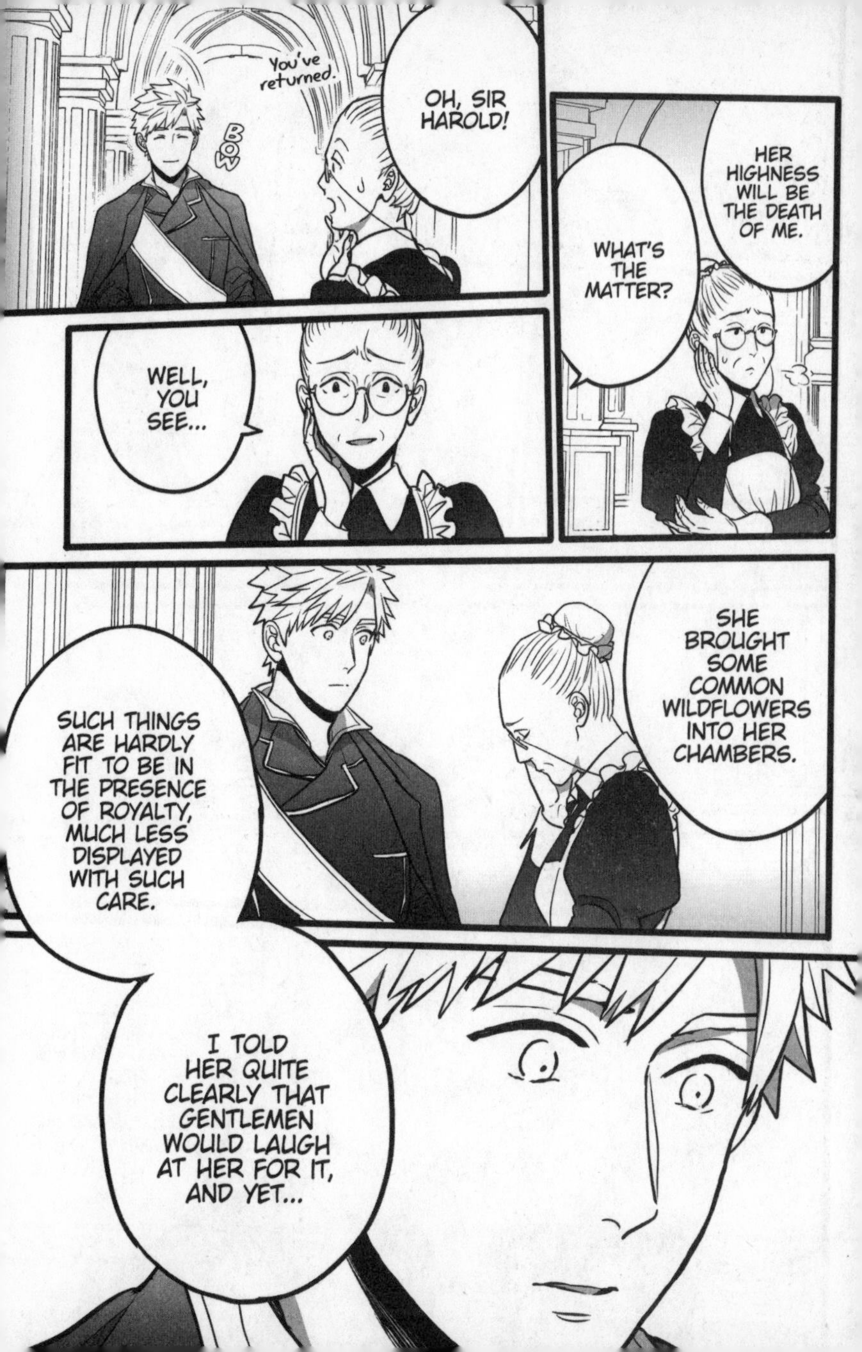
You've returned.
BOW
OH, SIR HAROLD!
HER HIGHNESS WILL BE THE DEATH OF ME.
WHAT'S THE MATTER?
WELL, YOU SEE...
SHE BROUGHT SOME COMMON WILDFLOWERS INTO HER CHAMBERS.
SUCH THINGS ARE HARDLY FIT TO BE IN THE PRESENCE OF ROYALTY, MUCH LESS DISPLAYED WITH SUCH CARE.
I TOLD HER QUITE CLEARLY THAT GENTLEMEN WOULD LAUGH AT HER FOR IT, AND YET...

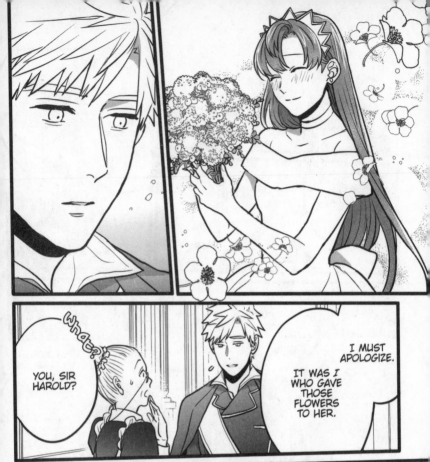

I MUST APOLOGIZE.
IT WAS *I* WHO GAVE THOSE FLOWERS TO HER.
WHAT?!
YOU, SIR HAROLD?
I'LL HAVE THE GARDENERS REPLACE THEM WITH MORE SUITABLE ONES.
BUT HER HIGHNESS ORDERED US TO LET THEM BE!

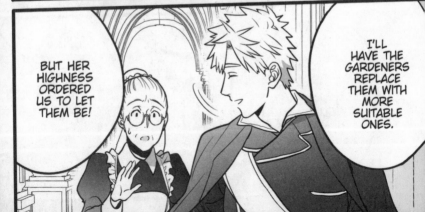

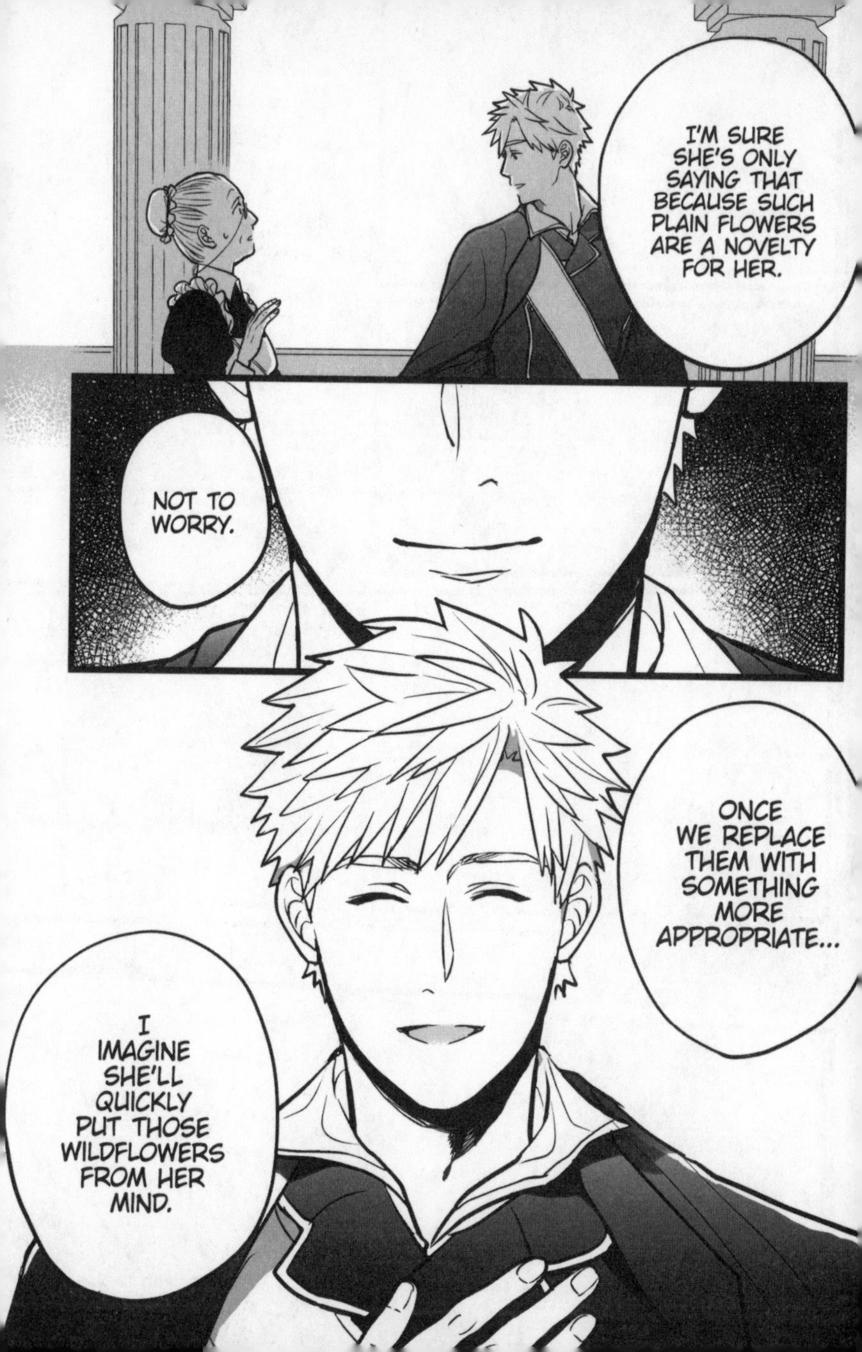
I'M SURE SHE'S ONLY SAYING THAT BECAUSE SUCH PLAIN FLOWERS ARE A NOVELTY FOR HER.
NOT TO WORRY.
ONCE WE REPLACE THEM WITH SOMETHING MORE APPROPRIATE...
I IMAGINE SHE'LL QUICKLY PUT THOSE WILDFLOWERS FROM HER MIND.

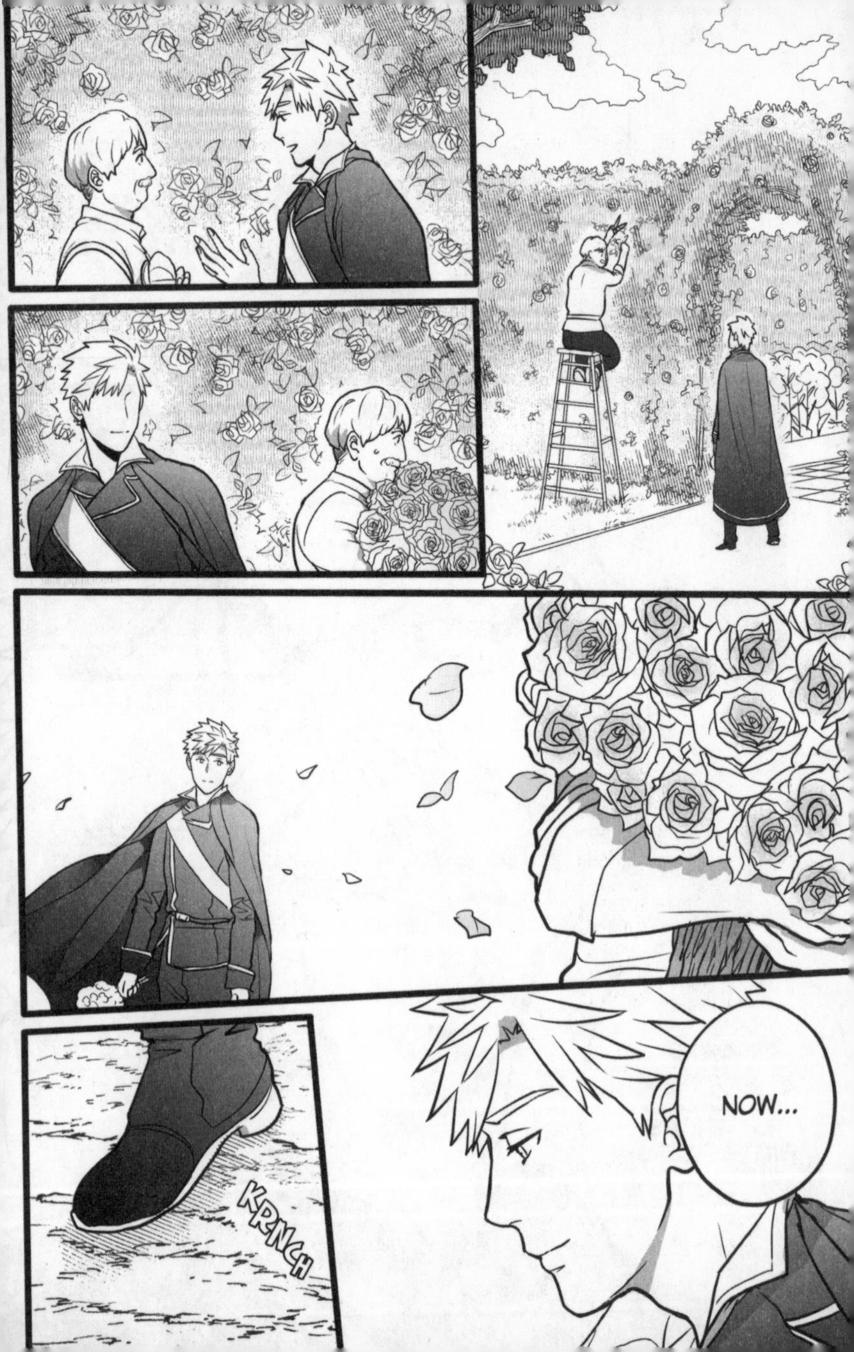
KRNCH
NOW...

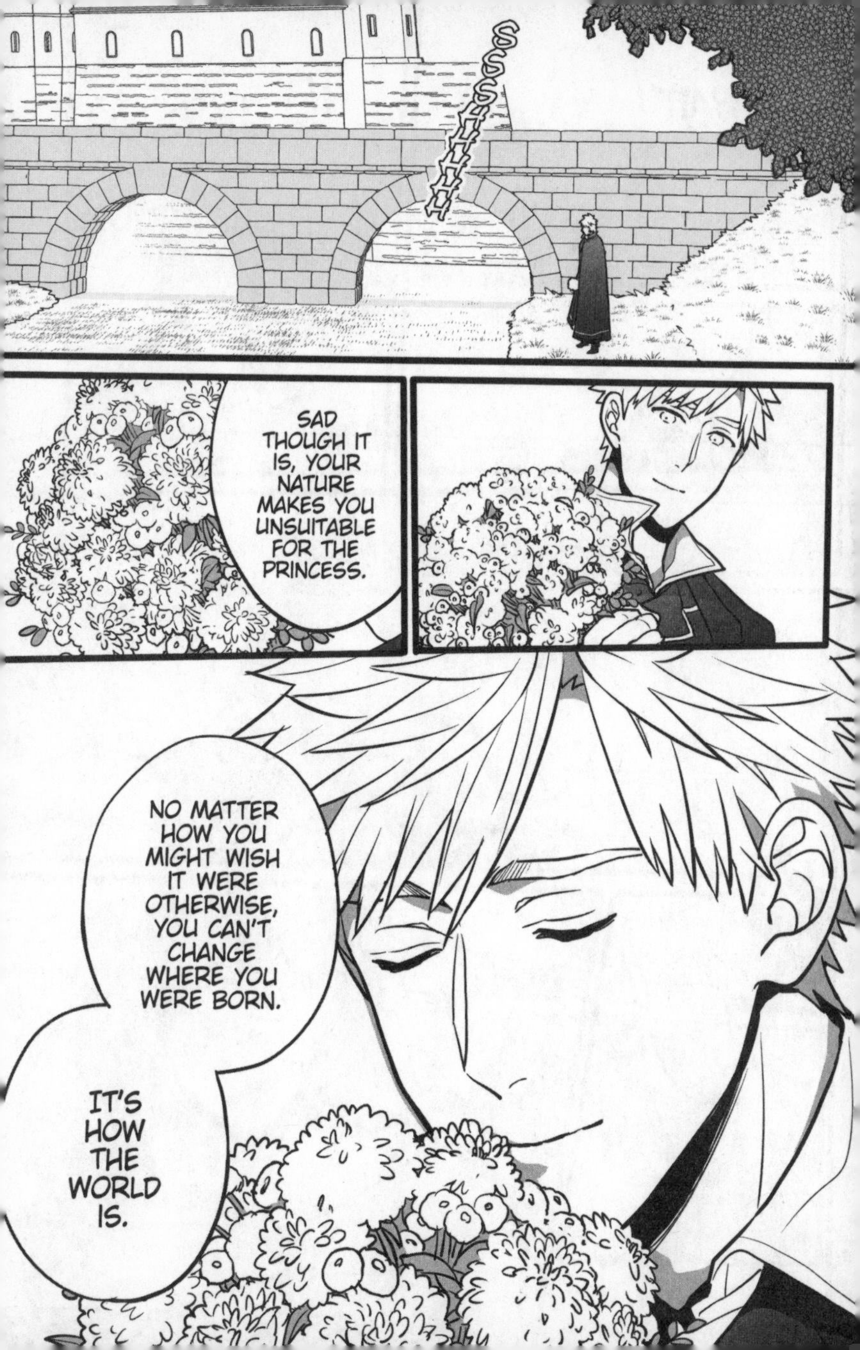
SSSHHHHH
SAD THOUGH IT IS, YOUR NATURE MAKES YOU UNSUITABLE FOR THE PRINCESS.
NO MATTER HOW YOU MIGHT WISH IT WERE OTHERWISE, YOU CAN'T CHANGE WHERE YOU WERE BORN.
IT'S HOW THE WORLD IS.

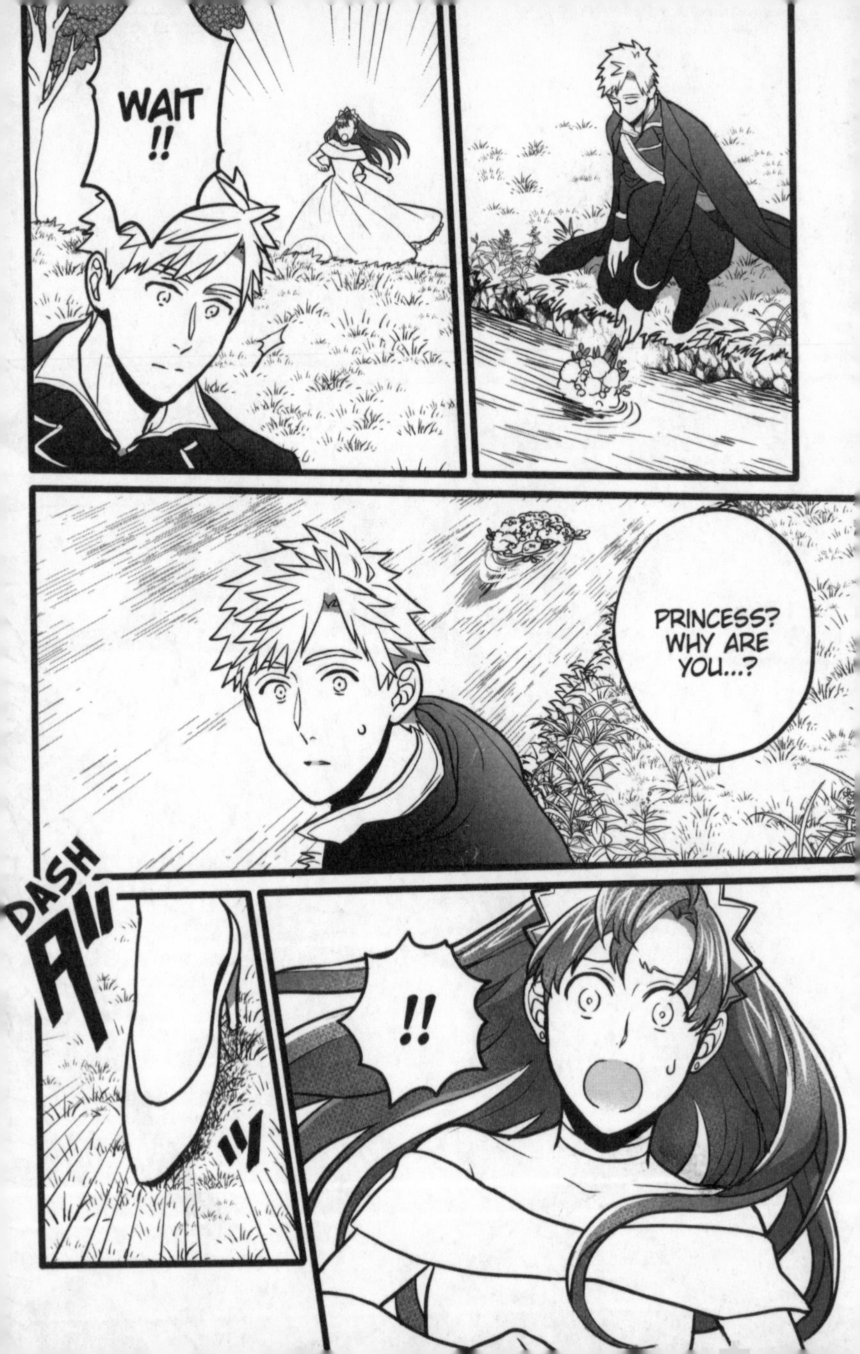
WAIT !!
PRINCESS? WHY ARE YOU...?
!!
DASH

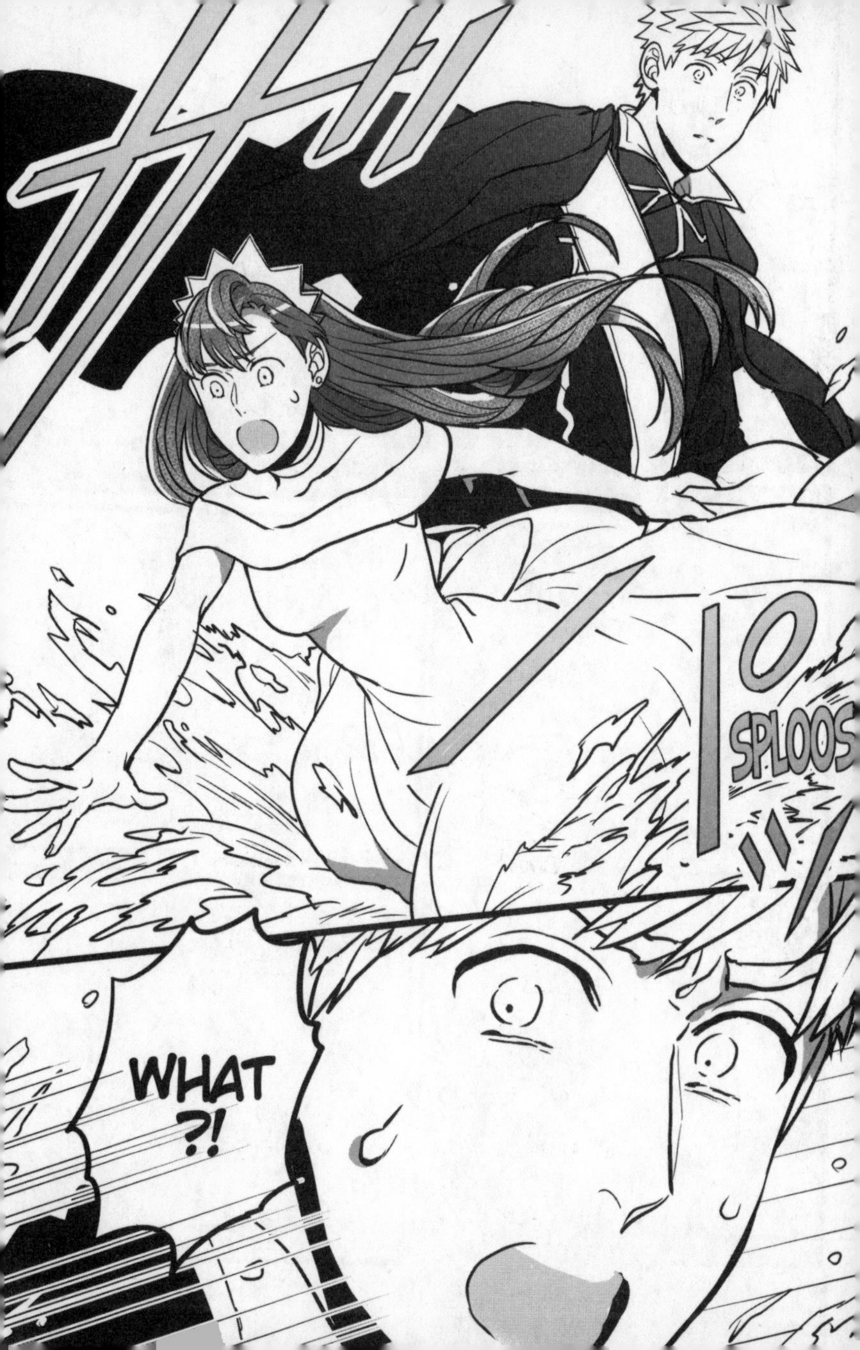
SPLOOS
WHAT ?!

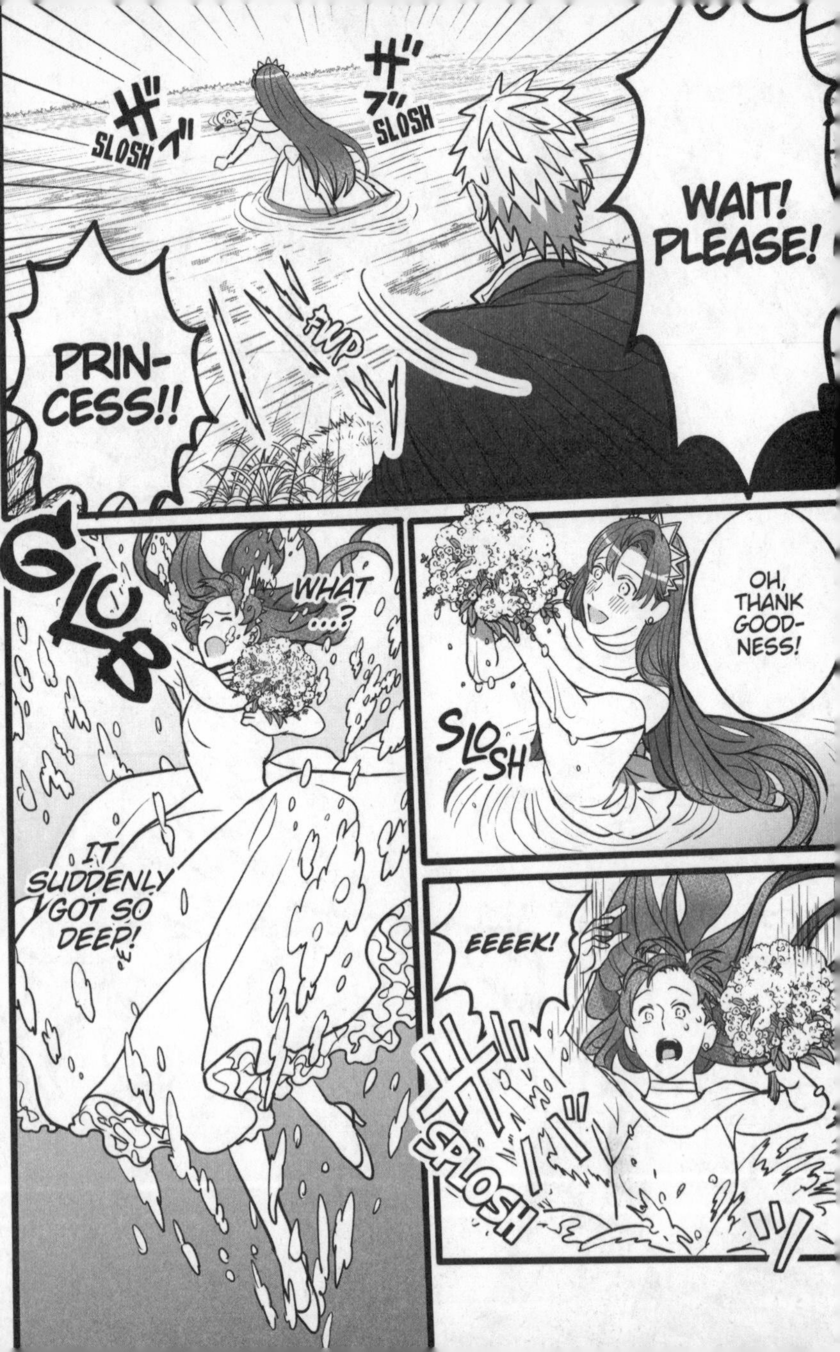
WAIT! PLEASE!
SLOSH
SLOSH
FWUP
PRIN-CESS!!
OH, THANK GOOD-NESS!
SLOSH
EEEEK!
SPLOSH
GLUB
WHAT ...?
IT SUDDENLY GOT SO DEEP!

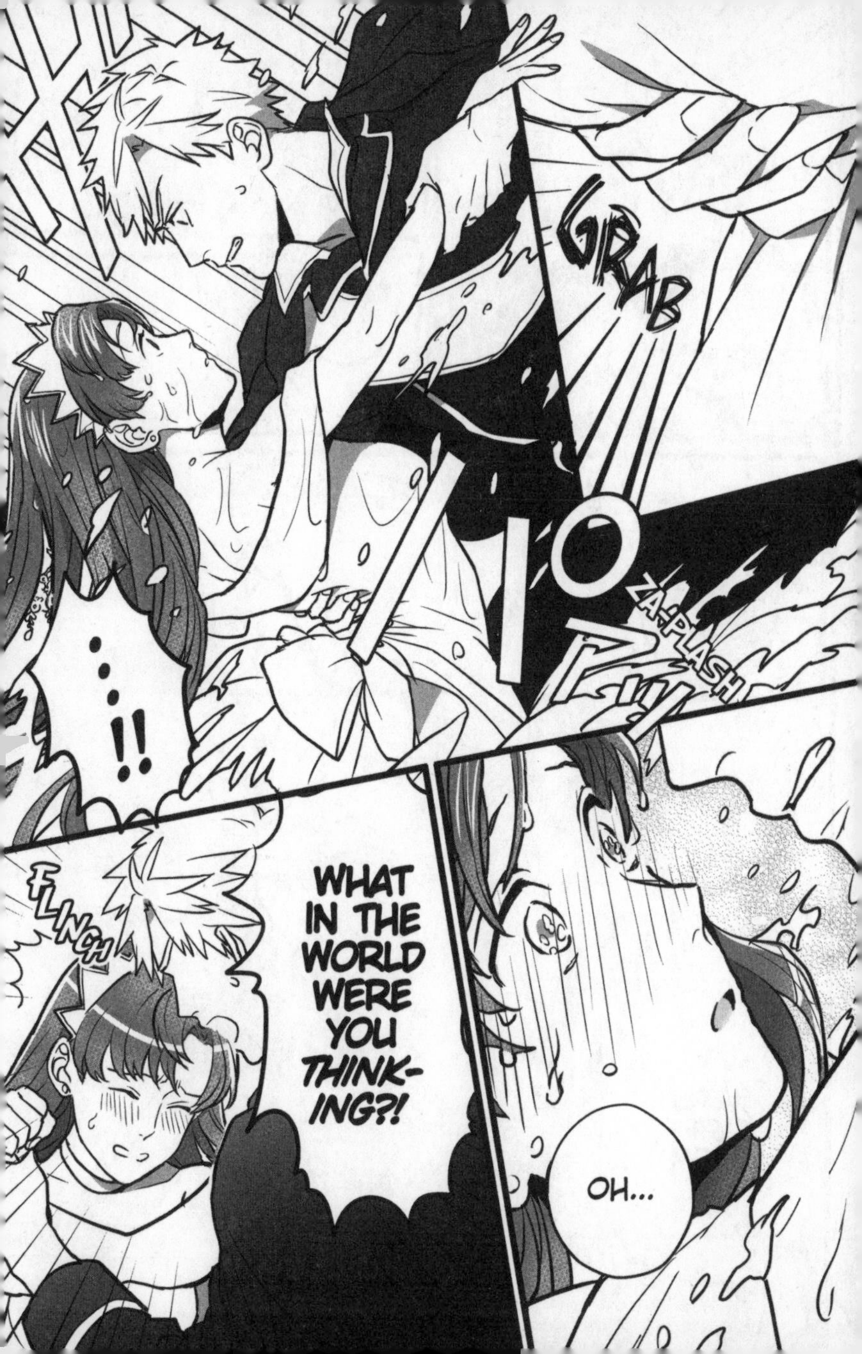
GRAB
ZA-PLASH
...!!
OH...
WHAT IN THE WORLD WERE YOU THINKING?!
FLINCH

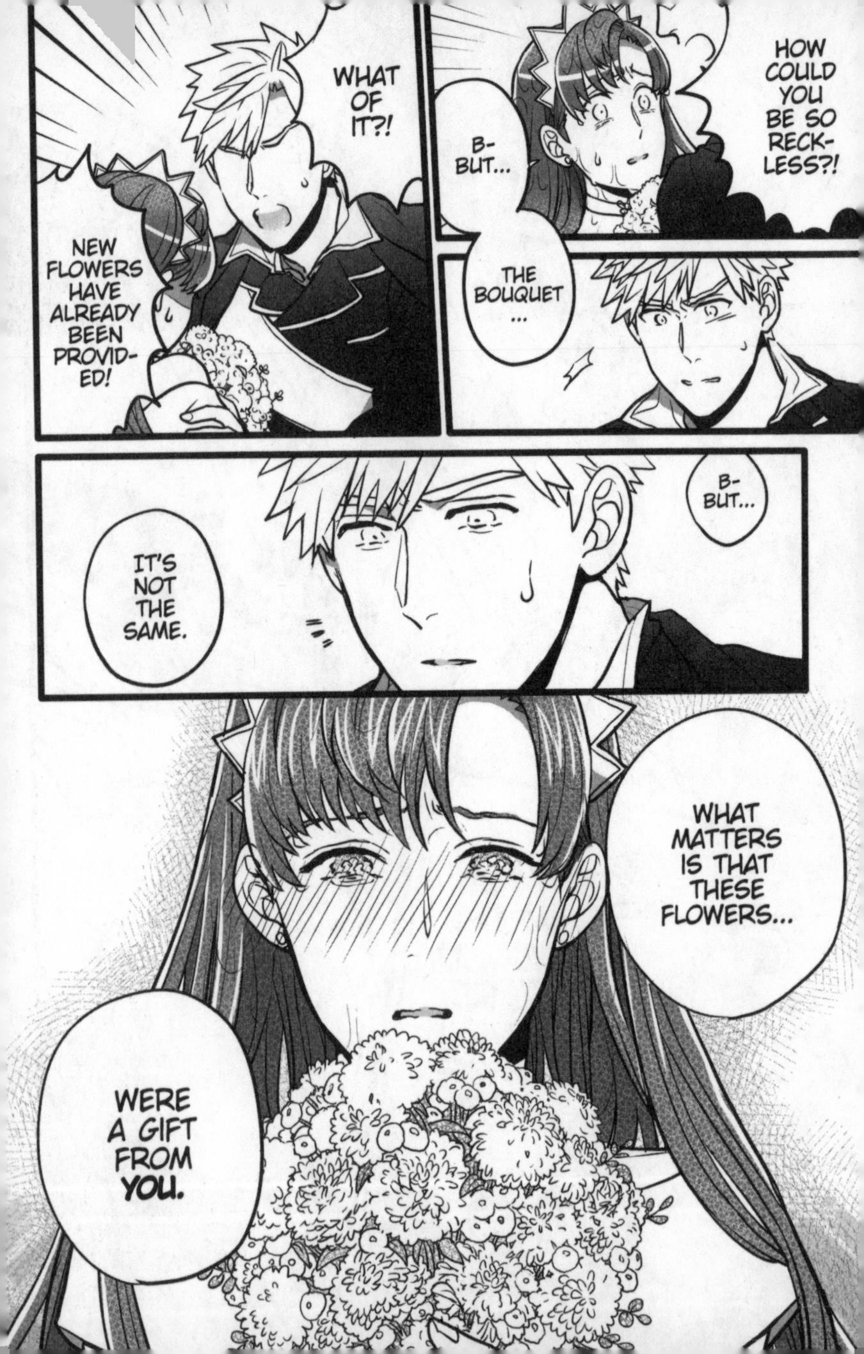

HOW COULD YOU BE SO RECKLESS?!
B-BUT...
THE BOUQUET...
WHAT OF IT?!
NEW FLOWERS HAVE ALREADY BEEN PROVIDED!
B-BUT...
IT'S NOT THE SAME.
WHAT MATTERS IS THAT THESE FLOWERS...
WERE A GIFT FROM **YOU.**

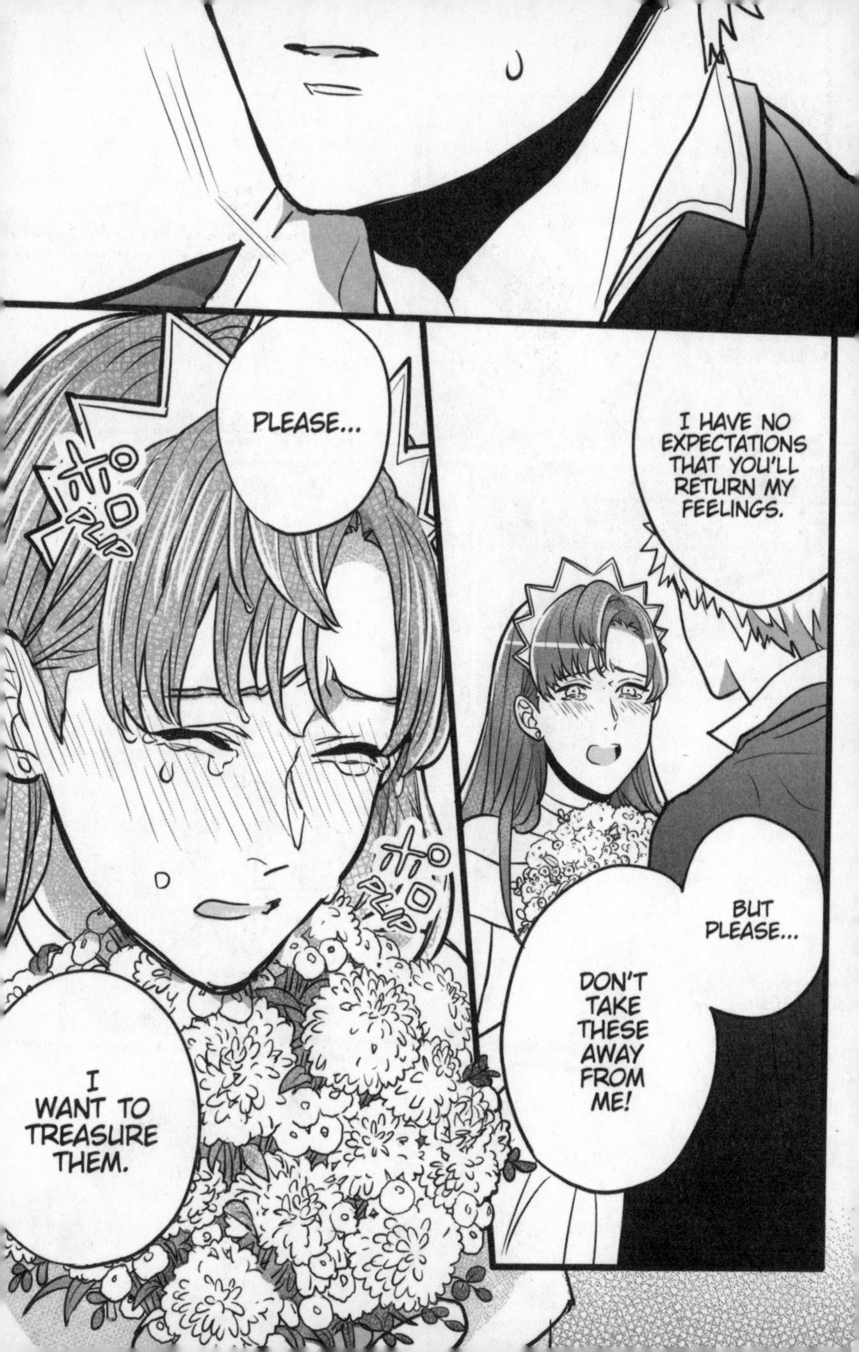
I HAVE NO EXPECTATIONS THAT YOU'LL RETURN MY FEELINGS.
BUT PLEASE...
DON'T TAKE THESE AWAY FROM ME!
PLEASE...
PLIP
PLIP
I WANT TO TREASURE THEM.

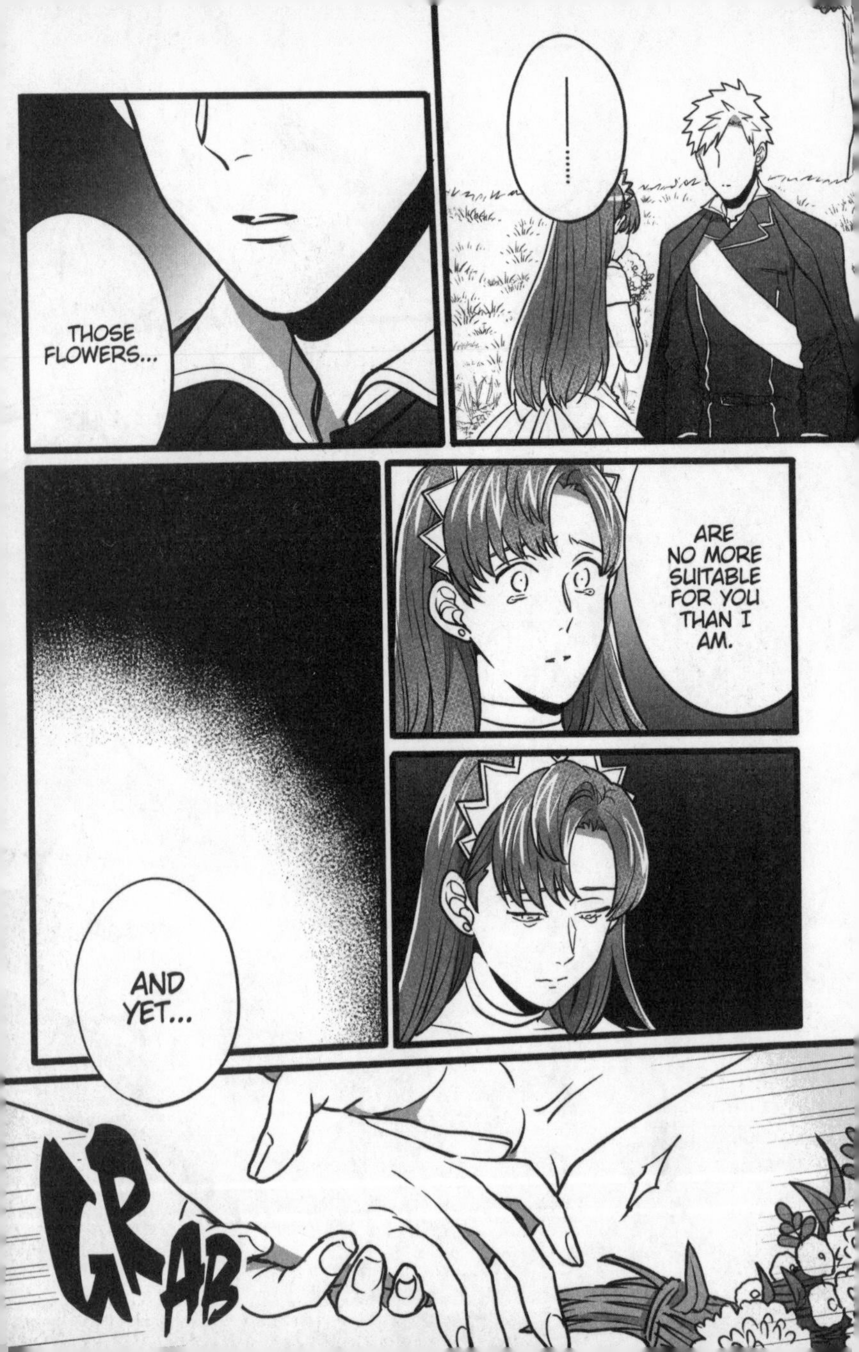
THOSE FLOWERS...
ARE NO MORE SUITABLE FOR YOU THAN I AM.
AND YET...
GRAB

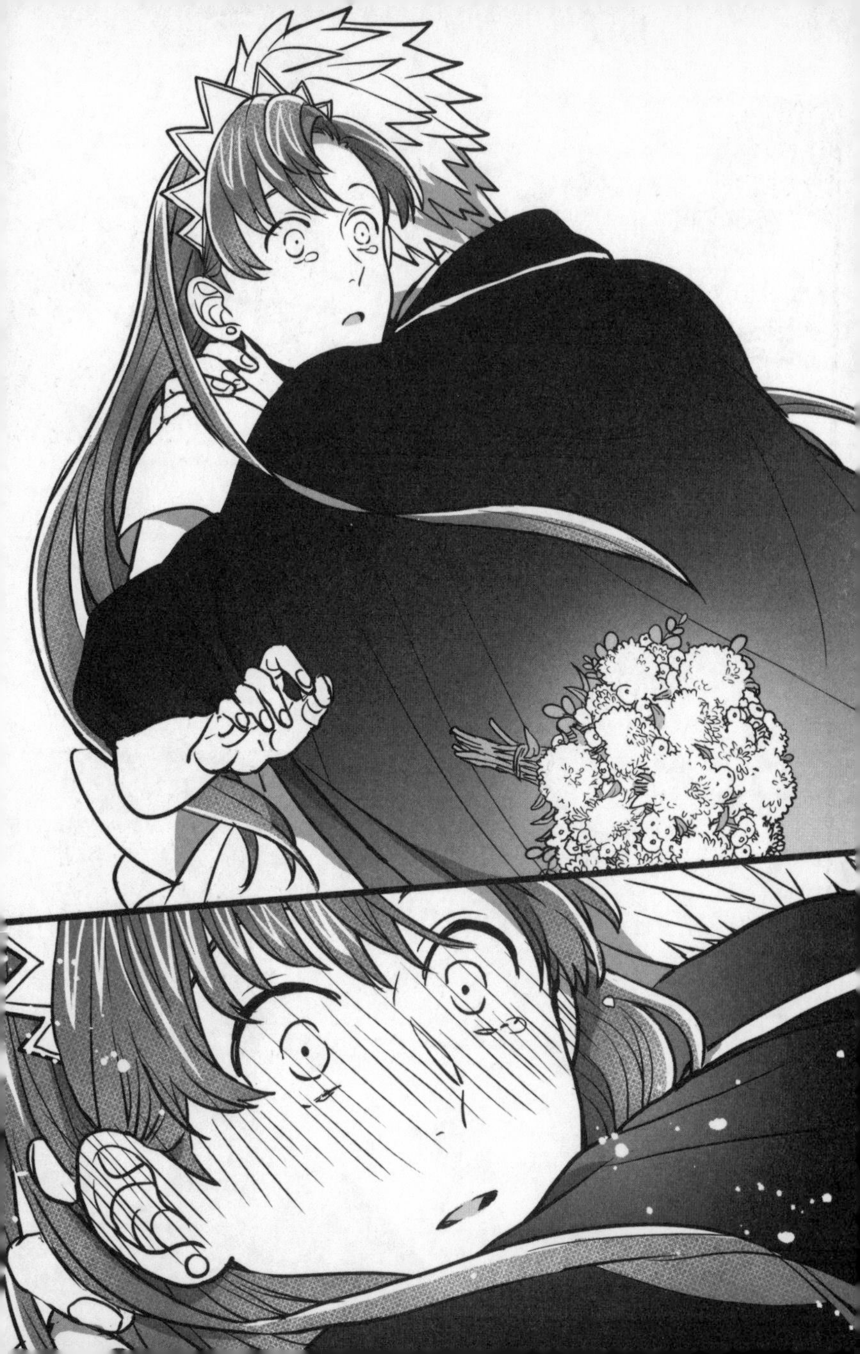

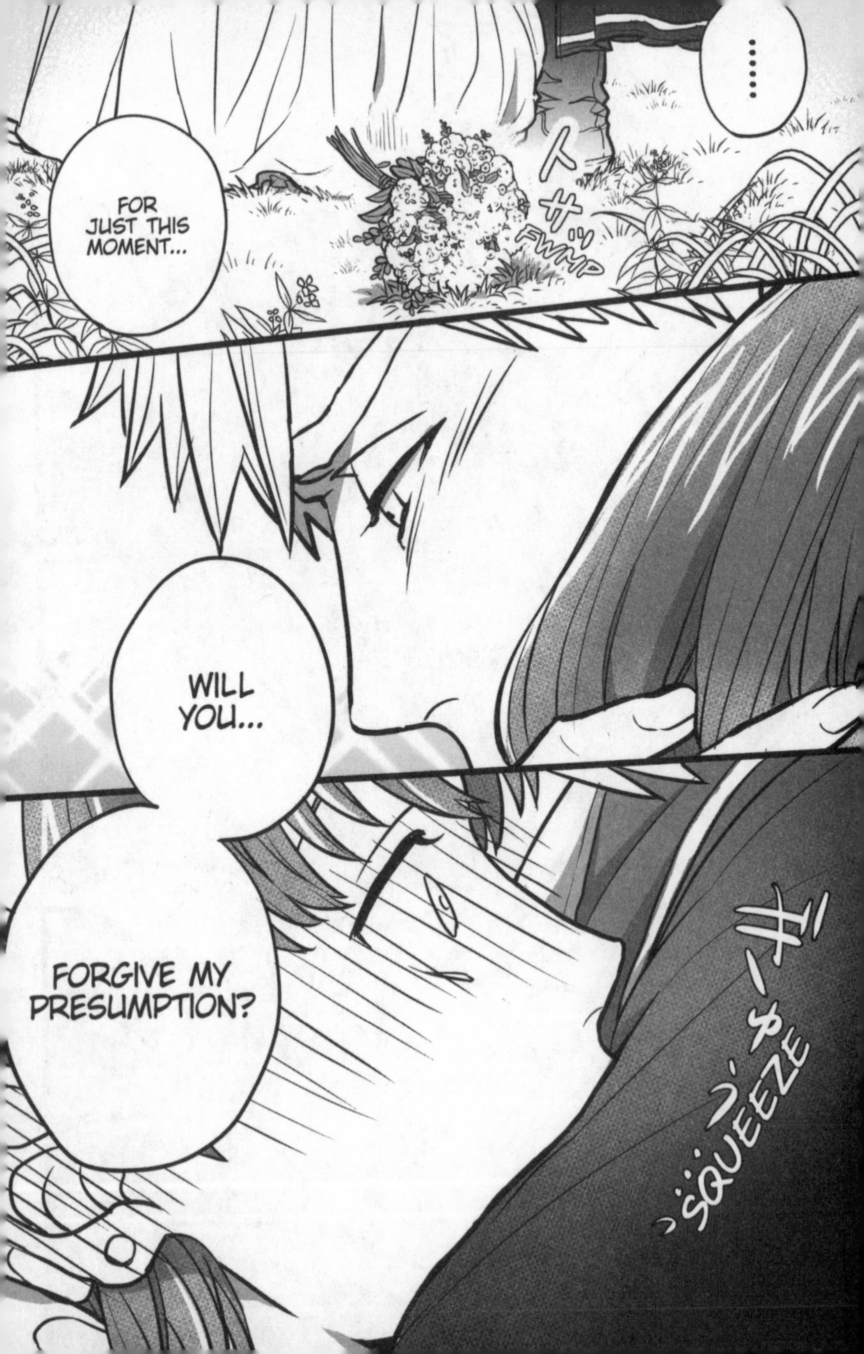
……
FOR JUST THIS MOMENT...
トサッ
FWMP
WILL YOU...
FORGIVE MY PRESUMPTION?
SQUEEZE

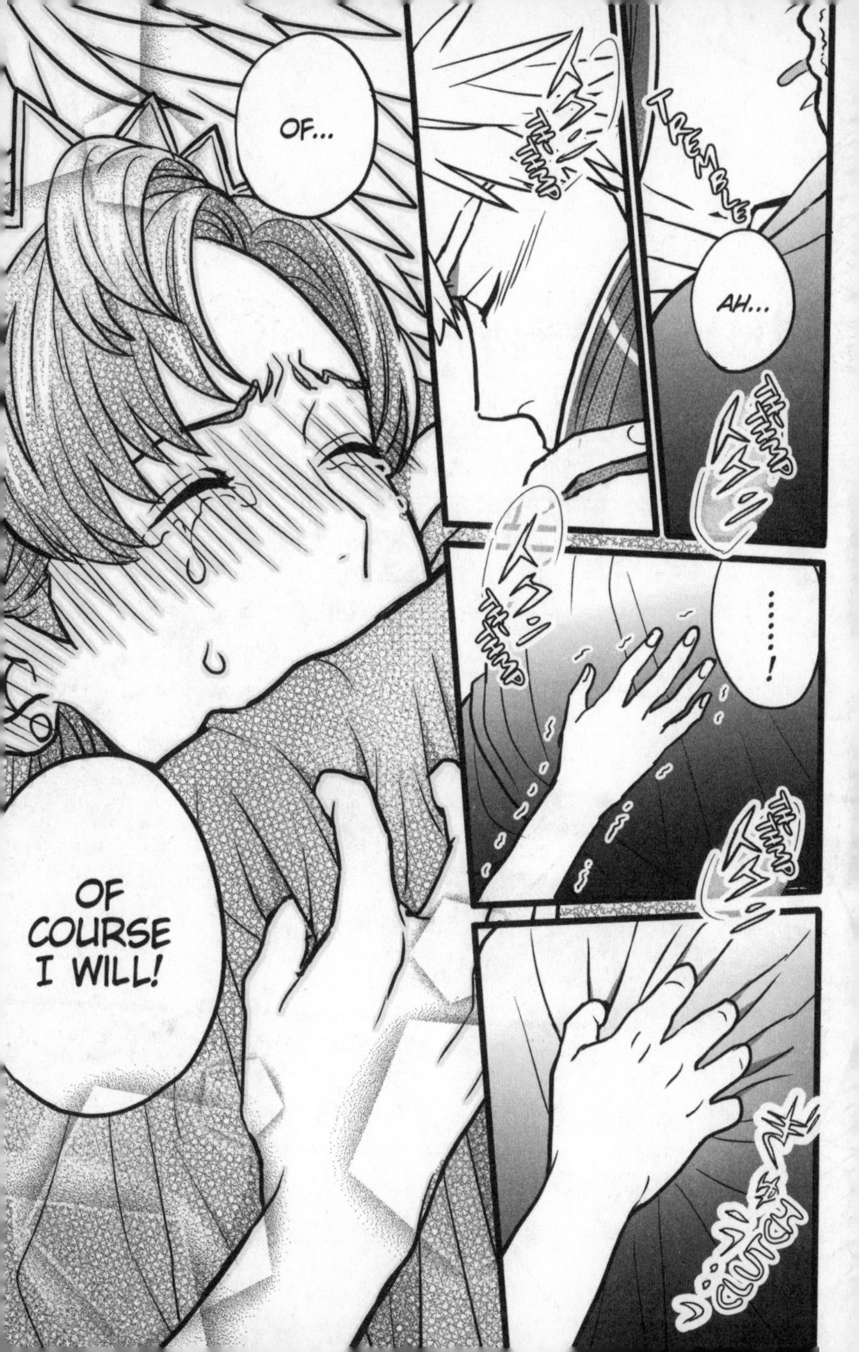
TREMBLE
AH...
TH-THMP
TH-THMP
.....!
TH-THMP
TH-THMP
CLUTCH
OF...
OF COURSE I WILL!

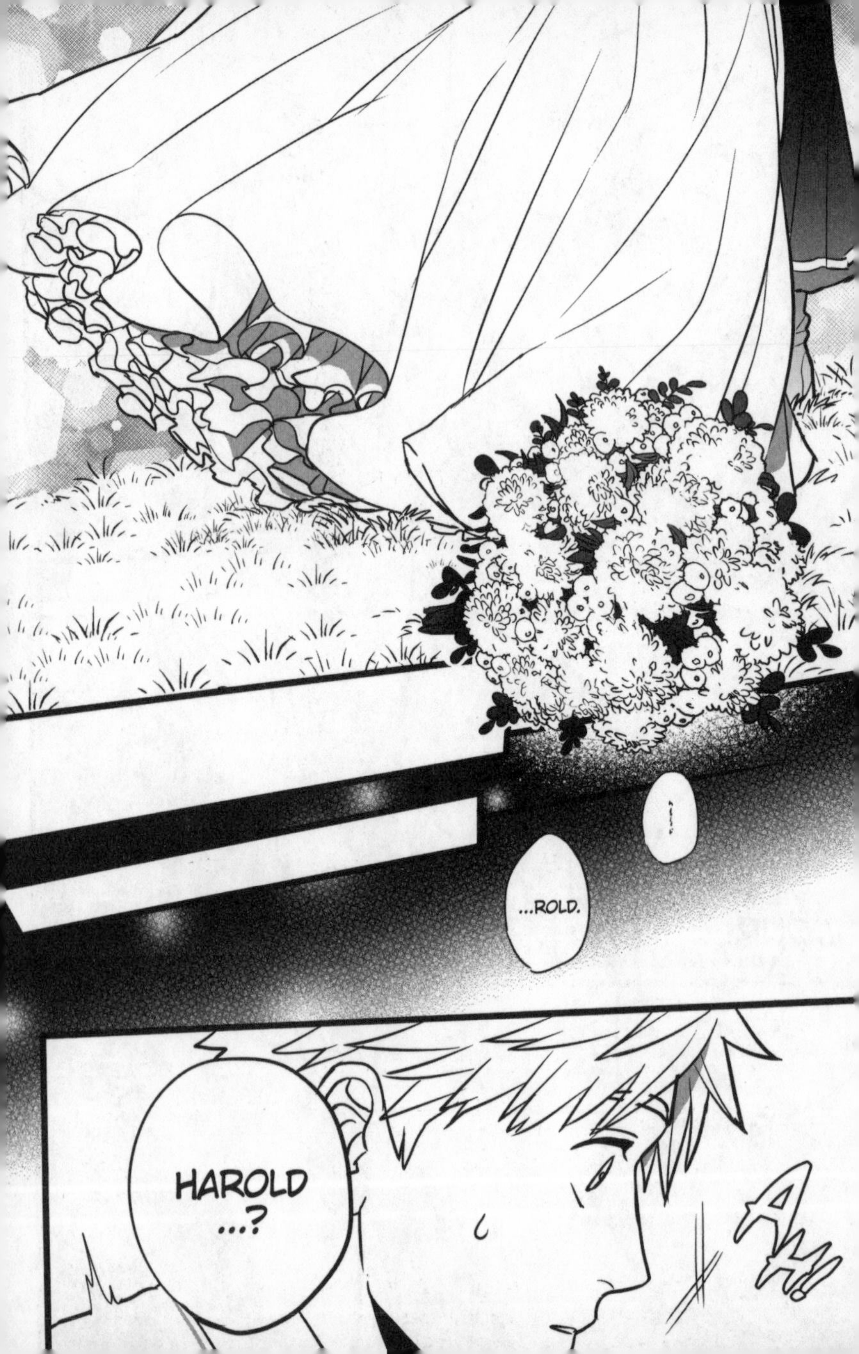
...
...ROLD.
AH!!
HAROLD ...?

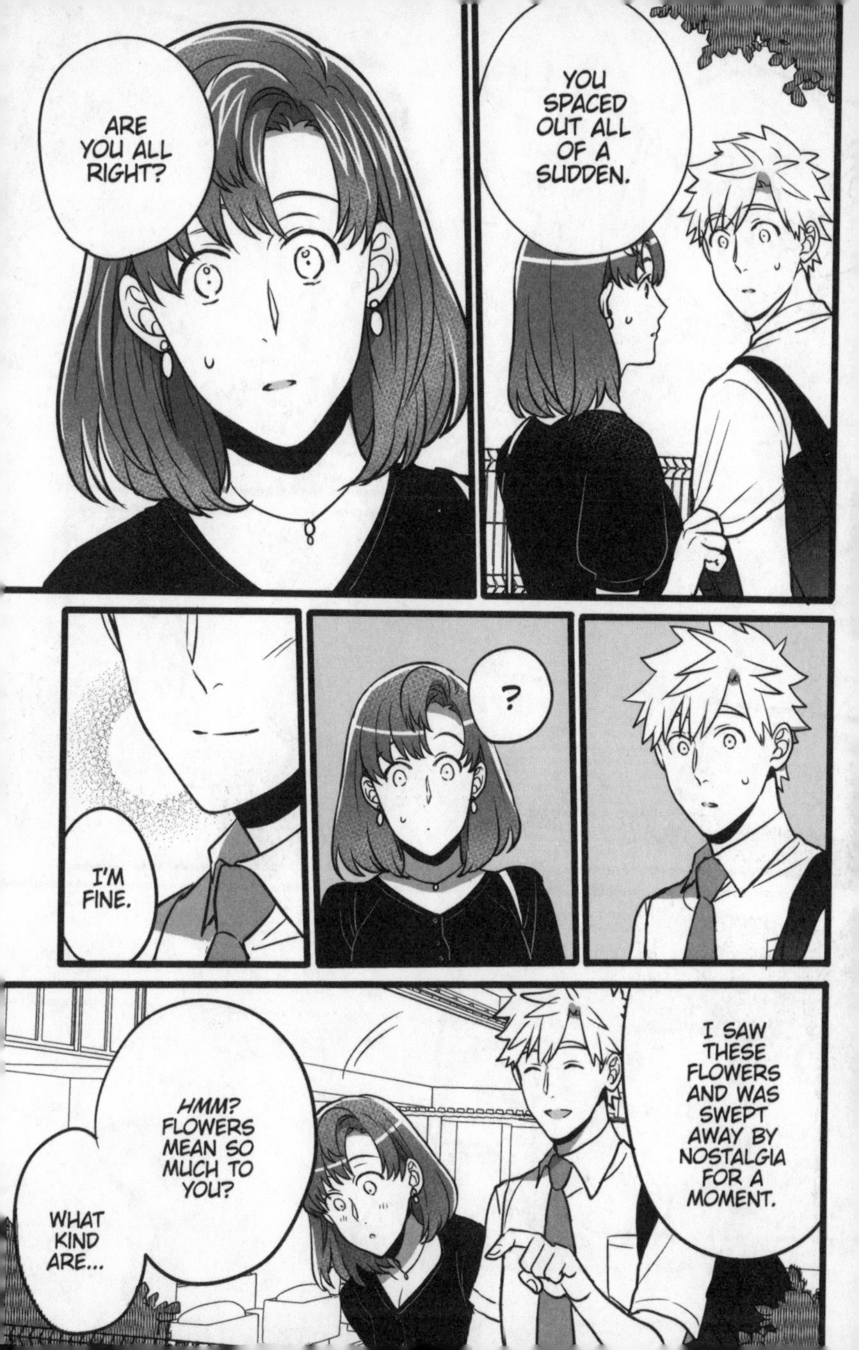
YOU SPACED OUT ALL OF A SUDDEN.
ARE YOU ALL RIGHT?
?
I'M FINE.
I SAW THESE FLOWERS AND WAS SWEPT AWAY BY NOSTALGIA FOR A MOMENT.
HMM? FLOWERS MEAN SO MUCH TO YOU?
WHAT KIND ARE...

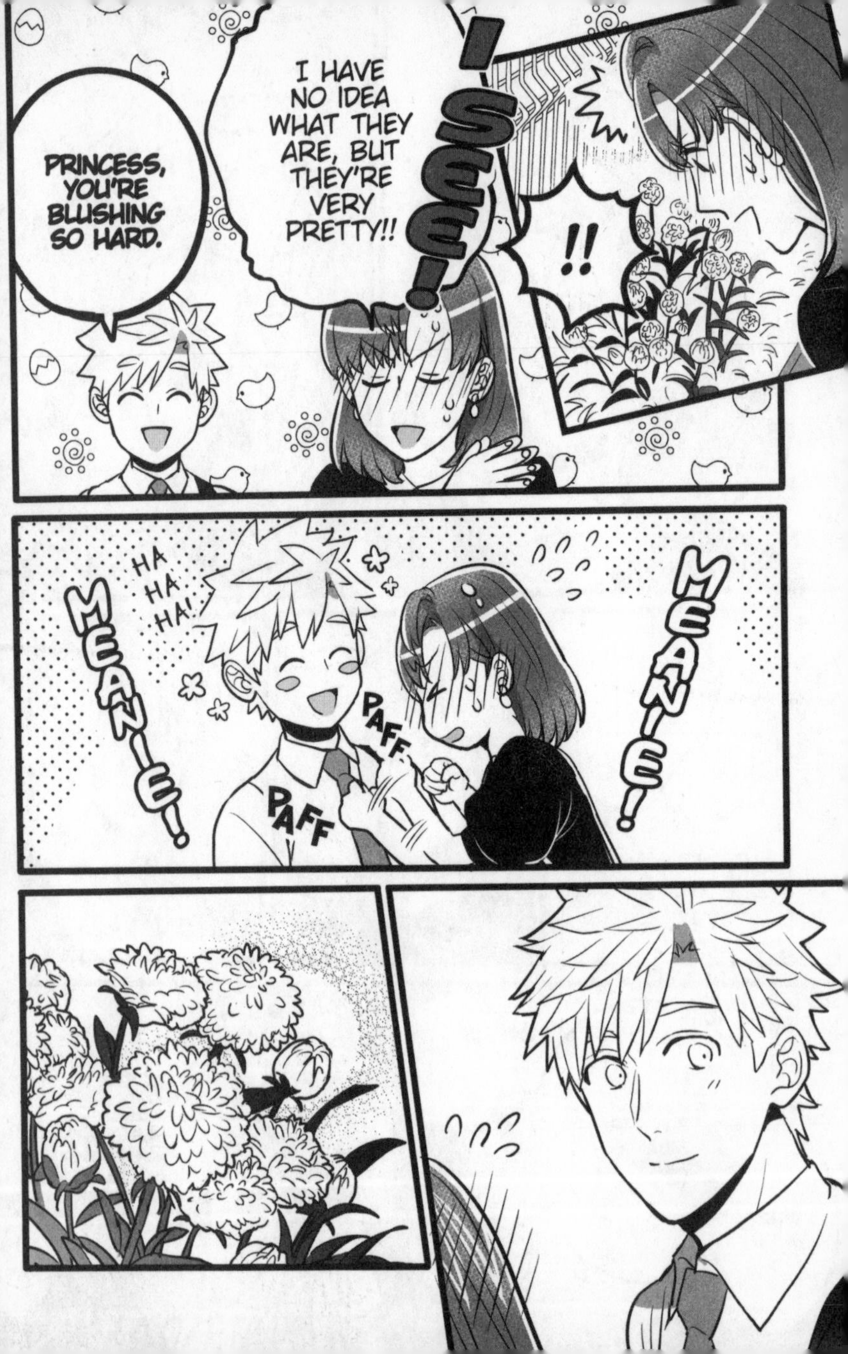
!!
SEE!
I HAVE NO IDEA WHAT THEY ARE, BUT THEY'RE VERY PRETTY!!
PRINCESS, YOU'RE BLUSHING SO HARD.
MEANIE!
PAFF
PAFF
HA HA HA!
MEANIE!

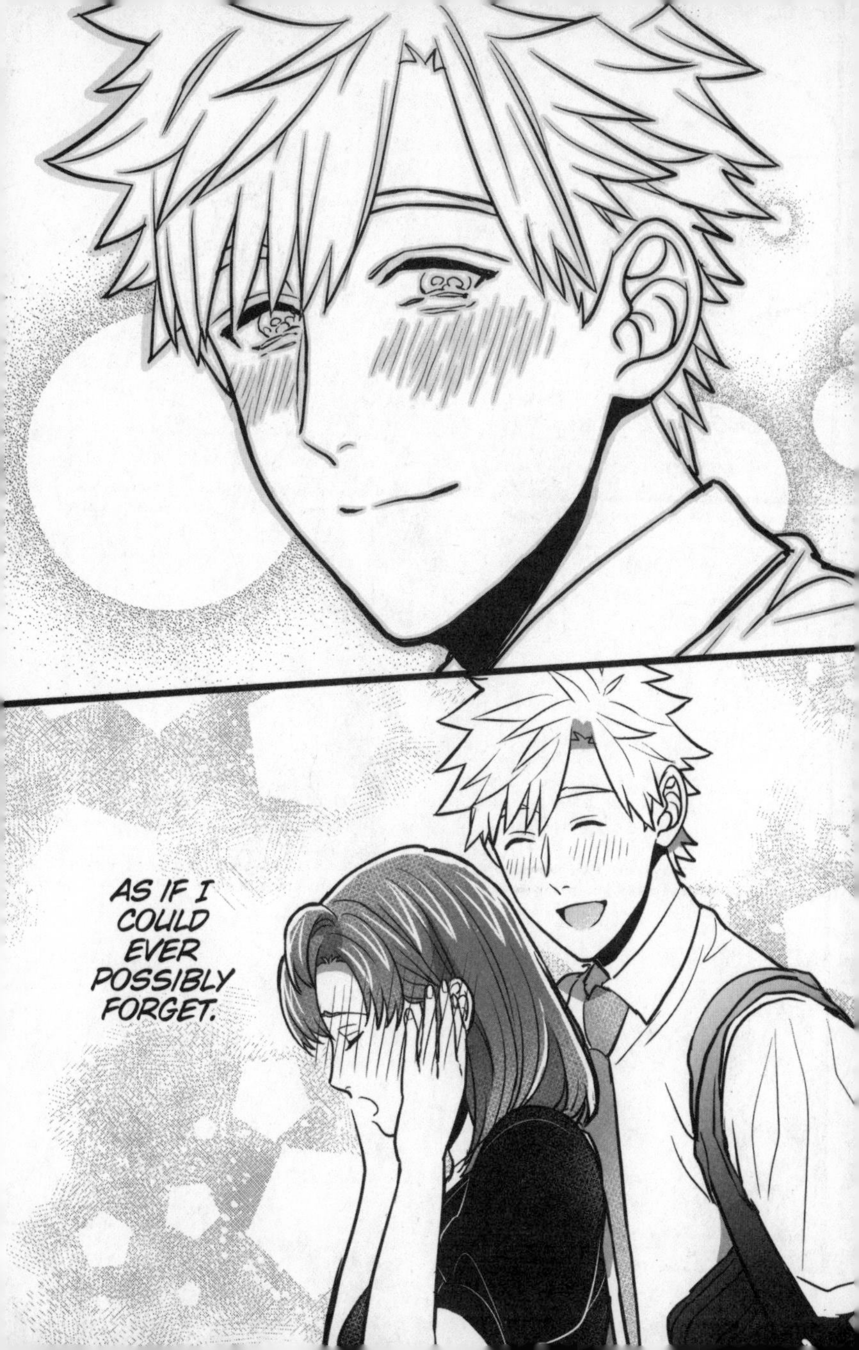
AS IF I COULD EVER POSSIBLY FORGET.

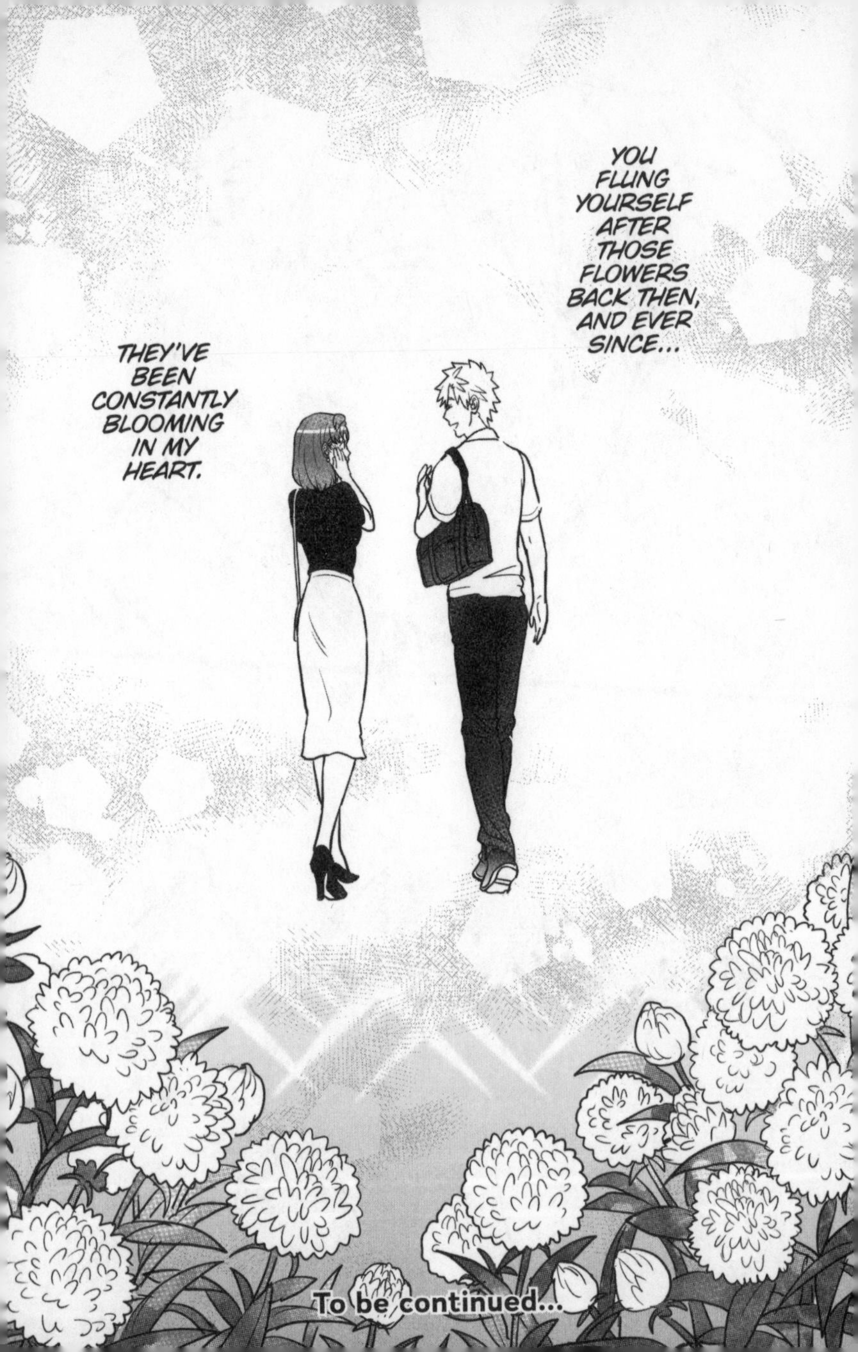
YOU FLUNG YOURSELF AFTER THOSE FLOWERS BACK THEN, AND EVER SINCE...
THEY'VE BEEN CONSTANTLY BLOOMING IN MY HEART.
To be continued...

We Swore to Meet in the Next Life and That's When Things Got Weird!

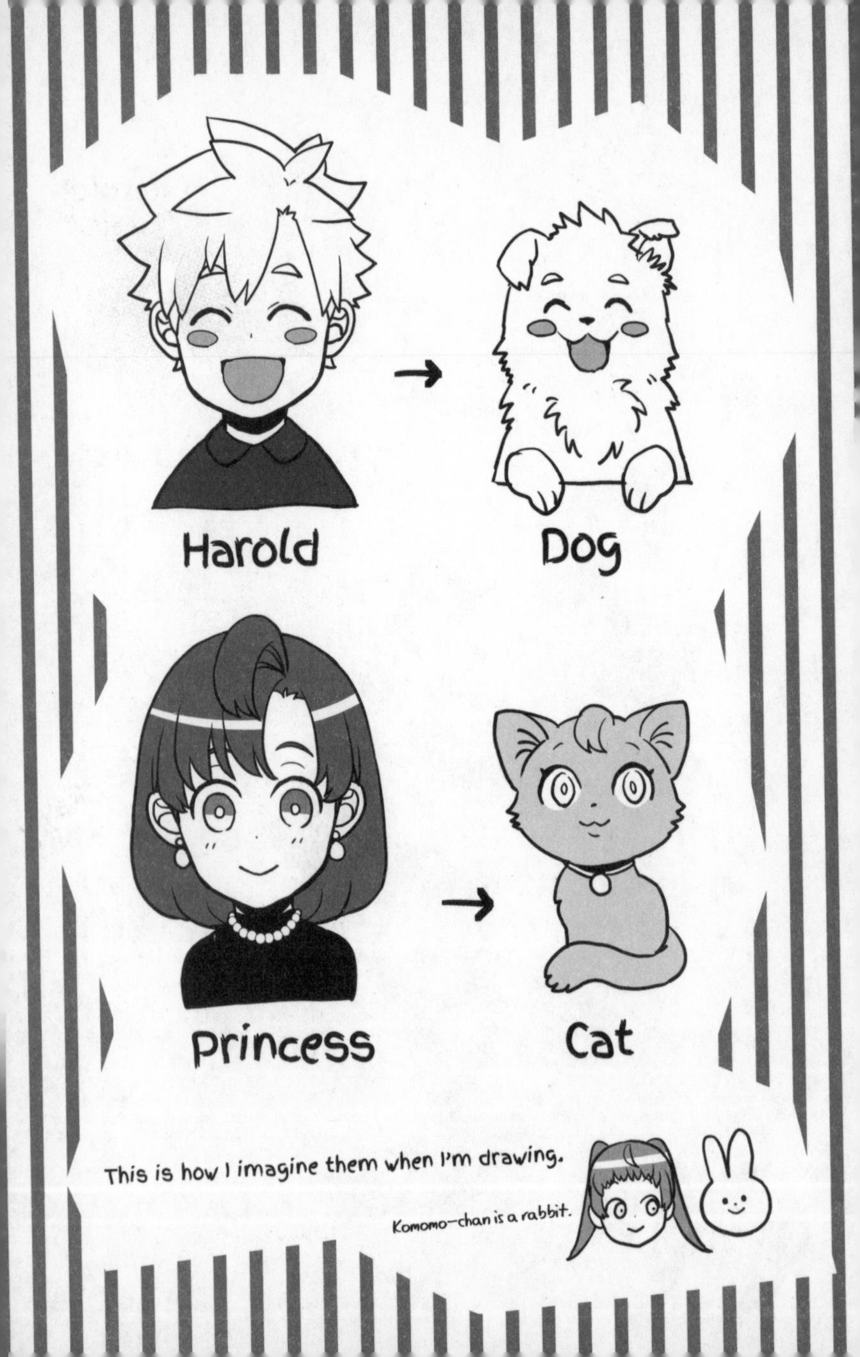

Harold
Dog
Princess
Cat
This is how I imagine them when I'm drawing.
Komomo-chan is a rabbit.

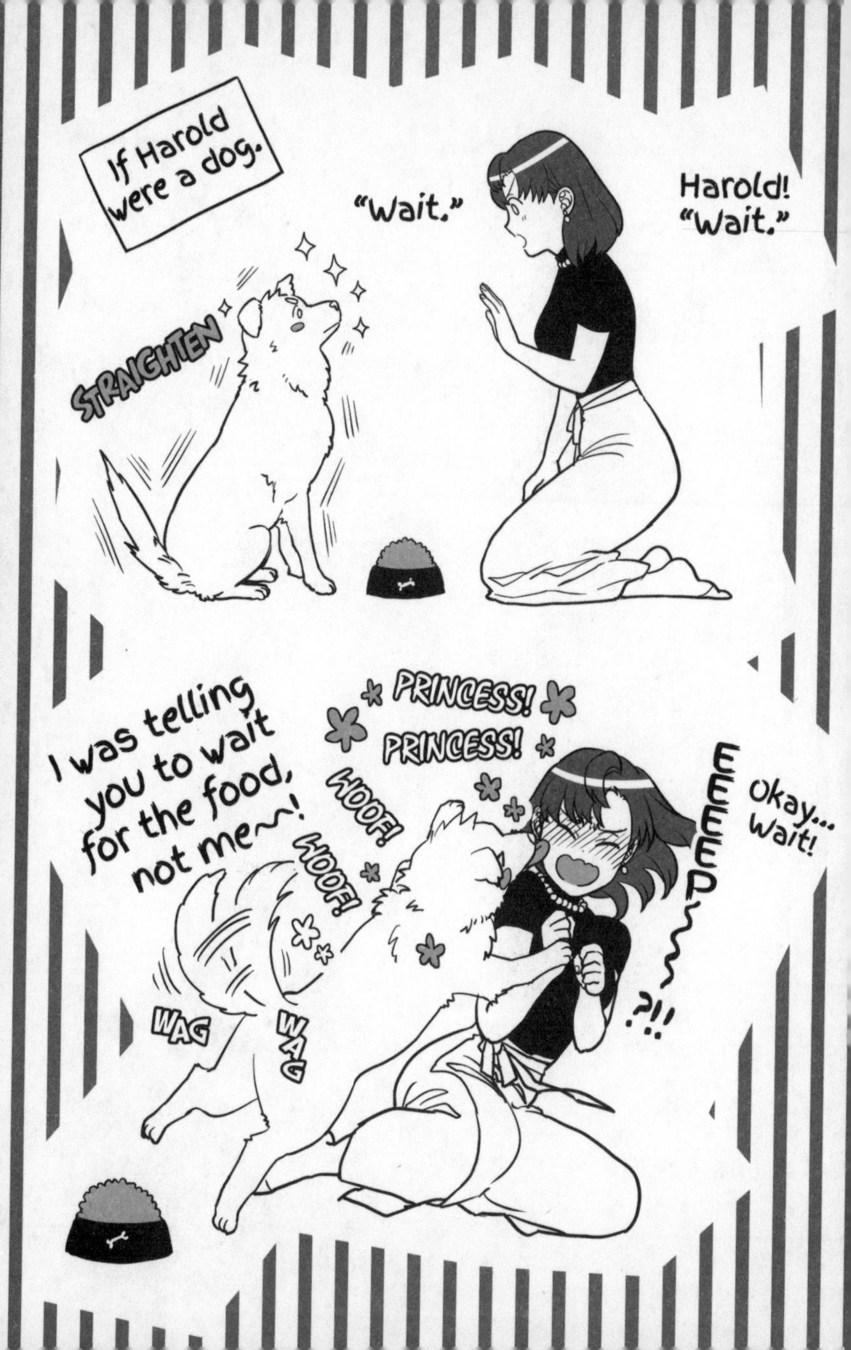
If Harold were a dog.
Harold! "Wait."
"Wait."
STRAIGHTEN
Okay... wait!
EEEEEP~
?!!
PRINCESS!
PRINCESS!
I was telling you to wait for the food, not me~!
WOOF!
WOOF!
WAG
WAG

We Swore to Meet in the Next Life **and That's When** Things Got **Weird!**

We Swore to Meet in the Next Life **and That's When** Things Got **Weird!**

SEVEN SEAS ENTERTAINMENT PRESENTS

We Swore to Meet in the Next Life and That's When Things Got Weird!

story and art by HATO HACHIYA VOLUME 1

TRANSLATION
Angela Liu

ADAPTATION
Ysabet Reinhardt MacFarlane

LETTERING AND RETOUCH
Annaliese Christman

COVER DESIGN
Nicky Lim

PROOFREADER
Kurestin Armada

EDITOR
Peter Adrian Behravesh

PREPRESS TECHNICIAN
Rhiannon Rasmussen-Silverstein

MANAGING EDITOR
Julie Davis

ASSOCIATE PUBLISHER
Adam Arnold

PUBLISHER
Jason DeAngelis

WE SWORE TO MEET IN THE NEXT LIFE AND THAT'S WHEN THINGS GOT WEIRD! VOL. 1
RAISE WO CHIKATTE TENSEISHITARA TAIHENNAKOTONINATTA VOL. 1

First published in Japan in 2019 by Ichijinsha Inc., Tokyo.
Publication rights for this English edition arranged through Kodansha Ltd., Tokyo.

Seven Seas press and purchase enquiries can be sent to Marketing Manager Lianne Sentar at press@gomanga.com. Information regarding the distribution and purchase of digital editions is available from Digital Manager CK Russell at digital@gomanga.com.

ISBN: 978-1-64505-841-0

Printed in Canada

First Printing: September 2020

10 9 8 7 6 5 4 3 2 1

FOLLOW US ONLINE: www.sevenseasentertainment.com

READING DIRECTIONS

This book reads from ***right to left***, Japanese style. If this is your first time reading manga, you start reading from the top right panel on each page and take it from there. If you get lost, just follow the numbered diagram here. It may seem backwards at first, but you'll get the hang of it! Have fun!!

1
2
3
4
5
6
7
8
9

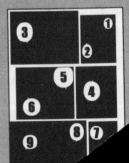